THE BEDFORD SERIES IN HISTORY AND CULTURE

Incidents in the Life of a Slave Girl
Written by Herself
by Harriet Jacobs

with Related Documents

SECOND EDITION

Edited with an Introduction by

Jennifer Fleischner

Adelphi University

bedford/st.martin's
Macmillan Learning
Boston | New York

For Bedford/St. Martin's

Vice President, Editorial, Macmillan Learning Humanities: Leasa Burton
Senior Program Director for History: Michael Rosenberg
Senior Executive Program Manager for History: William J. Lombardo
History Marketing Manager: Melissa Rodriguez
Developmental Editor: Mollie Chandler
Senior Content Project Manager: Lidia MacDonald-Carr
Senior Workflow Project Manager: Jennifer Wetzel
Production Coordinator: Brianna Lester
Executive Media Project Manager: Michelle Camisa
Senior Manager of Publishing Services: Andrea Cava
Project Management: Lumina Datamatics, Inc.
Composition: Lumina Datamatics, Inc.
Director of Rights and Permissions: Hilary Newman
Permissions Associate: Michael McCarty
Text Researcher: Elaine Kosta, Lumina Datamatics, Inc.
Director of Design, Content Management: Diana Blume
Cover Design: William Boardman
Cover Image: GRANGER/GRANGER—All rights reserved.
Printing and Binding: LSC Communications

Manufactured in the United States of America.

1 2 3 4 5 6 24 23 22 21 20 19

For information, write: Bedford/St. Martin's, 75 Arlington Street, Boston, MA 02116

ISBN 978-1-319-16925-1

Acknowledgments

Acknowledgments and copyrights appear on the same page as the text and art selections they cover; these acknowledgments and copyrights constitute an extension of the copyright page.

Document 2: The Will of Margaret Horniblow. From THE HARRIET JACOBS FAMILY PAPERS. Copyright © 2008 by Jean Fagan Yellin. Used by permission of the University of North Carolina Press. www.uncpress.org.

Foreword

The Bedford Series in History and Culture is designed so that readers can study the past as historians do.

The historian's first task is finding the evidence. Documents, letters, memoirs, interviews, pictures, movies, novels, or poems can provide facts and clues. Then the historian questions and compares the sources. There is more to do than in a courtroom, for hearsay evidence is welcome, and the historian is usually looking for answers beyond act and motive. Different views of an event may be as important as a single verdict. How a story is told may yield as much information as what it says.

Along the way the historian seeks help from other historians and perhaps from specialists in other disciplines. Finally, it is time to write, to decide on an interpretation and how to arrange the evidence for readers.

Each book in this series contains an important historical document or group of documents, each document a witness from the past and open to interpretation in different ways. The documents are combined with some element of historical narrative—an introduction or a biographical essay, for example—that provides students with an analysis of the primary source material and important background information about the world in which it was produced.

Each book in the series focuses on a specific topic within a specific historical period. Each provides a basis for lively thought and discussion about several aspects of the topic and the historian's role. Each is short enough (and inexpensive enough) to be a reasonable one-week assignment in a college course. Whether as classroom or personal reading, each book in the series provides firsthand experience of the challenge—and fun—of discovering, recreating, and interpreting the past.

Lynn Hunt
David W. Blight
Bonnie G. Smith

Preface

Harriet Jacobs's *Incidents in the Life of a Slave Girl* is the most important antebellum slave woman's narrative available today. It stands alongside *Narrative of the Life of Frederick Douglass*—the most widely read male narrative—as the classic women's slave narrative and remains a powerful historical testimony about what it was like to be a female slave. Never before had anyone written such a sustained eyewitness indictment of the sexual exploitation of slave girls and women under slavery in the American South. And never before had a woman written with such candor about her own humiliation and suffering at the hands of her master. *Incidents* offers students of history a critical view into the world of abuse, resistance, and struggle for identity and integrity of slave women and their families. Similarly, it provides a window into the ideological and political debates that shaped abolitionism and from which this narrative emerged.

Jacobs's narrative also demonstrates the power of language and the written word as a means to overcome the crushing legacy of enslavement. Therefore, this narrative can be used to study literary history as well and must be treated as a literary text. Jacobs agonized about the story she had to tell because she knew that its sexual content would shock and offend her readers. She drew upon everything she had read to find the words to tell her story in a way that would engage readers' sympathies for, as she put it, the "two millions of women at the South, still in bondage." She warned her contemporary readers that her story of abuse was no fiction. Twenty-first-century readers might need the same warning. The story Jacobs tells of sexual harassment, brutal violence, and American hypocrisy remains difficult to comprehend and accept.

The introductory essay in Part One introduces readers to the world in which Jacobs lived, thus enabling students to read the narrative in its historical context. The updated introduction analyzes Jacobs's complex engagement with the cultural beliefs of her day—especially the cult of domesticity—and emphasizes the significance of her struggle with religion. This new edition examines Jacobs's ambivalence toward the two strands in the African American Christian tradition: the pious embrace of forbearance in suffering and the view that violent resistance—even murderous rebellion—is a "holy cause" that is sanctioned by faith. The updated introduction also explains her take on the American legal system in light of the use proslavery ideologues made of religion and law to support slavery. Jacobs's bitter criticism of American hypocrisy and the ways in which her narrative was explicitly linked to abolitionism—another example of how slaves and former slaves were central to the abolitionist movement—are explored in the introduction as well. Finally, the introduction highlights some of the problems of interpretation that previous scholars have noted, including the question of whether Jacobs's master actually raped her, walking students through the different ways of addressing such difficult questions.

Part Two of the book provides Jacobs's complete account of her life under and escape from slavery. The annotations to this edition of her narrative are extensive. They identify historical events, people, and places; provide definitions; and clarify Jacobs's wide-ranging allusions to the Bible, literary texts, and other written sources.

The related documents in Part Three bring Jacobs's story into sharper relief and engage students in the analysis of some difficult questions posed by the narrative itself. New to this edition is a transcript of the will of Margaret Horniblow, Jacobs's first mistress, and the codicil that was added on the day she died, in which students may see firsthand the commodification of Jacobs as a slave. Also included are new image sources, including a scan of the title page of the first edition of *Incidents in the Life of a Slave Girl* and a medallion showing the kneeling black slave, one of the most iconic symbols in Anglo-American abolitionism. These new image sources will give students a chance to interpret visual artifacts of the period. This section also contains the full text of Jacobs's brother John S. Jacobs's *A True Tale of Slavery*, which students may read in comparison with *Incidents*. Also included are several letters Jacobs wrote to her confidante, Amy Post, which will help students understand the conditions under which Jacobs wrote her narrative; editor Lydia Maria Child's letter to Jacobs recommending specific changes to her narrative; and "Life among the Contrabands," Jacobs's important article published in the abolitionist newspaper the *Liberator* in 1862, which details her experiences helping slaves who fled to Washington, D.C., during the Civil War. These and other documents make this edition particularly useful for developing students' understanding of the interest and importance of primary source material.

To aid students further, a list of pseudonyms used for the real people mentioned in Jacobs's narrative precedes the texts. The extensive chronology at the end of the book lists key points in her life both during and after slavery. The appendix also includes new and updated questions for consideration to enrich classroom learning, as well as an enhanced selected bibliography for those interested in expanding their knowledge of Jacobs and this crucial time in American history.

Harriet Jacobs's narrative is a painful reminder of the radical system of abuse that slavery entailed and America tolerated. Yet the other side of the story Jacobs tells, one equally important to the student of American history, is a tale of ingenuity, courage, dignity, and truth telling in the face of pressure to be silent. It is also, finally, a story of great hope, of a faith in the possibility of change. Indeed, Jacobs's capacity for hope was the key to her magnificent survival.

A NOTE ABOUT THE TEXT

In Part Two, the version of *Incidents in the Life of a Slave Girl, Written by Herself* is a reproduction of the original 1861 Boston edition written by Harriet Jacobs. It was obtained via the University of Michigan Library on Google Books. It is reproduced here as it was written, with variations in spelling of certain words and the use of pseudonyms intact. This was done to maintain the historical integrity and texture of the document.

Jacobs took for herself the name Linda Brent in recounting her life under slavery and her escape to freedom. This pseudonym, which was set in all capital letters in her edition, enabled her to write more freely about the sexual exploitation she experienced in ways that would be acceptable to, and inspire sympathy among, her white female audience. Using pseudonyms throughout her narrative also enabled her to protect family and friends still in slavery.

In the related documents in Part Three, Jacobs's letters are reproduced exactly as she wrote them—including the absence of punctuation and the capitalization of words not normally capitalized. This was done, as above, to maintain their historical integrity but, more importantly, to demonstrate that the quest for literacy, which Jacobs and other former slaves endured, was a lifelong struggle. To "correct" the punctuation and spelling would have erased the marks of her enslavement in the writing, something I did not want to do. Reproducing the letters just as Jacobs wrote them also enables students to see how she developed as a writer over time. Significantly, the letters she wrote after the manuscript was published include punctuation.

ACKNOWLEDGMENTS

Many thanks to my colleague and Bedford Series in History and Culture editor David W. Blight for inviting me to produce the first edition of this volume for the series and for allowing me to join his National Endowment for the Humanities summer seminar, one of the liveliest discussions of Harriet Jacobs I have experienced. For their help with this new edition, I am indebted to the editorial team at Bedford/St. Martin's, especially Senior Program Director Michael Rosenberg, Senior Executive Program Manager William Lombardo, Senior Editor Heidi Hood, History Marketing Manager Melissa Rodriguez, Senior Content Project Manager Lidia MacDonald-Carr, Cover Designer William Boardman; and to Development Editor Mollie Chandler for her help on this second edition. The reviewers for the first edition of this book—Eleanor Alexander, Georgia Tech; Michael Bottoms, George Mason University; Tracey Deutsch, University of Minnesota; Carolyn Dupont, Eastern Kentucky University; James Fell, University of Colorado, Denver; Brett Mizelle, California State University, Long Beach; Patrick Reagan, Tennessee Tech University; Michael Sherfy, Western Illinois University; and Manisha Sinha, University of Massachusetts Amherst—made invaluable suggestions for revision. I am particularly grateful to my development editor for the first edition, Debra Michals, whose wisdom, patience, and good humor guided me to create a much better book than I could have done on my own.

I also wish to acknowledge the help of the librarians and archivists at the University of Rochester Library; the Sophia Smith Collection, Smith College; and the University of North Carolina Special Collections. I am especially grateful to Mary Manning of the University Archives and Special Collections at Adelphi University for her help with the documents in Part Three.

A faculty development grant from Adelphi University helped support my research for the first edition. I am also thankful for the support of many of my colleagues at Adelphi University, but especially the late Laura Reitano, whom I love and miss, and Gayle Insler, who, when she was dean of the College of Arts and Sciences, unfailingly backed all my projects. As always, I wish to thank Alex, Annie, and Irwin Schwartz, whose presence in my life makes it all possible.

Jennifer Fleischner

Contents

Illustrations

PART ONE

Introduction: A New Voice for Freedom

> *I have My dear friend—Striven faithfully to give a true and just account of my own life in Slavery—God knows I have tried to do it in a Christian spirit—there are somethings that I might have made plainer I know—Woman can whisper—her cruel wrongs into the ear of a very dear friend—much easier than she can record them for the world to read.* —Harriet Jacobs to Amy Post, June 21, 1857

Harriet Jacobs wrote one of the most important and enduring autobiographical narratives to emerge from the crucible of slavery. *LINDA: Incidents in the Life of a Slave Girl, Seven Years Concealed in Slavery, Written by Herself* (the original title) is the first known full-length narrative by a former slave woman published in the United States. In its focused, extended indictment of the sexual exploitation of slave girls and women and of the impact of this sexual abuse on slave families, this account undermined several core beliefs of Southern slave society, including those concerning racial differences, the sanctity of the family, and biblical justifications for slavery. With bitterness and insight, Jacobs exposed the hypocrisy of the South's various justifications for slavery by describing the brutal treatment of black slaves.

This is a remarkable narrative, written by a woman who, instead of being felled by early suffering, was able to turn her own experiences into a life of activism on behalf of others. Harriet Jacobs's life, which spanned nearly the entire nineteenth century, was shaped by the political and social upheavals of her time. She was born a slave in 1813—ten years after the Louisiana Purchase had more than doubled the size of the country, opening new territories to slavery or freedom, and during a war with Britain over unsettled land and rights. She escaped to the North twenty-nine years later, during another critical period of westward expansion, when the central question facing the nation was whether these new territories were going to be slave or free. Engaging the debate over slavery in the 1850s, she joined the interracial circle of New York and Massachusetts abolitionists, then wrote and finally published her slave narrative in 1861, just three months before the first shots in the Civil War were fired. During the hopeful postwar years, Jacobs gained recognition as a writer, teacher, reformer, and civil rights activist. Yet by the time she died in 1897, the United States was on the brink of a new age of imperial expansion (this time overseas, in Cuba and the Philippines), with colonialist implications; she had witnessed the dismantling of the civil rights gains of Reconstruction; and, in the Supreme Court ruling in *Plessy v. Ferguson*, she had seen the establishment of Jim Crow segregation—the antithesis of her egalitarian beliefs—as the law of the land.[1]

Jacobs's experiences as a slave were central to her worldview. Yet her experiences as a female slave were what framed her understanding of her condition both under and after slavery. Slavery, Jacobs famously wrote, was bad for men, but it was "far more terrible for women."[2] The sexual exploitation of female slaves by white masters made the lives of slave girls and women incomparably horrible. This is the central theme of Jacobs's narrative, and nothing in the narratives of men or women before her approached the candor and complexity of her account of her sexual history as a female slave.

Jacobs's most important contribution to American history and literature, therefore, is her account of her personal experiences as an enslaved woman. This story could not have been told by any man, including her brother, John S. Jacobs, in whose brief narrative her history is summarized (Document 11).[3] Indeed, in his narrative, John Jacobs elides the story of his sister's prolonged sexual harassment by their master, Dr. James Norcom, despite its being central to both of their plights. (Norcom imprisoned John to pressure Harriet into complying with his advances, and John was eventually bought by Samuel Tredwell Sawyer, the father of Harriet's two children.) Even the eloquent Frederick Douglass, who wrote devastatingly about slavery's impact on family life in three versions of his autobiography and was himself the child of a master and his slave, did not explore the inner life of the sexually exploited female slave.[4] Harriet Jacobs knew that the sensational content of her story would sound to her readers like fiction—or at least that they would wish it to be so, given the gap it exposed between white Victorian visions of the idealized woman in the era's "cult of domesticity" and the debasement of actual, particularly nonwhite, women. To dispel any doubts, she admonished in the opening line of her preface, "Reader, be assured this narrative is no fiction."[5]

Significantly, given the "reader" Jacobs addressed—the middle-class Northern woman whose sympathies she sought to arouse—she knew that she could not write explicitly about her sexual past. For one thing, white middle-class women embraced a prudery about such topics that would have made them turn away from a sexually explicit narrative. For another, what she could not write was a black woman's version of the popular sentimental novel, which followed the heroine from childhood through courtship to marriage, because a black woman's life did not follow that sentimental track. ("Reader, my story ends with freedom; not in the usual way, with marriage," she wrote.)[6] Instead, she argued forcefully that slave women should not be judged by the moral standards of white society because they were not free to act according to that society's—or their own—moral values. This was a key point in her attack on the supporters of slavery, who maintained that white people were intellectually and morally superior to blacks and therefore justifiably their masters.

It is important to remember that Jacobs shared her audience's moral code governing the sexual lives of women. Indeed, Jacobs battled her own feelings of guilt about her consensual sexual relationship with a (white) man who was not her husband and by whom she had two children. She may also have shared her audience's qualms about interracial sex. As she told her friend, the white Quaker reformer Amy Post, she could not speak openly about all that had happened to her because revealing her true sexual history—"how they had driven me into a great sin"[7]—would place her outside the cultural norms she shared with her audience. In her narrative, as in her life, Jacobs strove for respectability—the supreme benefit that comes with freedom—and this striving shaped the story she allowed herself to tell. Even so, it is her struggle against acquiescing to culturally reinforced silence that electrifies that story.

Writing about sex in nineteenth-century America wasn't easy for anyone, but it was especially difficult for a woman like Jacobs, given the complex circumstances in which she wrote. Because of this, she had to use rhetorical strategies, such as the use of pseudonyms, to tell her unsettling story without betraying her readers' values. Her narrative could not do the political work of arousing sympathy for the antislavery cause if it violated the beliefs of an audience steeped in the cult of true womanhood, which the nineteenth century associated with female chastity, monogamy, and piety. And so although she was not able to follow the idealized white woman's path from innocence to its apotheosis in a happy marriage and motherhood, she could show that this path might have been the natural one for black women if not for the sin of slavery, which was a degradation of their God-given nature. By portraying her grandmother Molly as an upholder of "true womanhood," despite the stain of slavery on Molly's own sexual history as the mother of mixed-race children, Jacobs created a symbol of goodness and moral strength. To further her argument about the moral integrity of the slave family, she also simplified and streamlined her family's sexual history by leaving out that her father remarried and had another son after her mother's death. These authorial choices make her narrative no less "true," because the truth of her narrative lies in its being an accurate reflection of her thoughts, feelings, wishes, and needs as she wrote about her past. Autobiography, like all history writing, is shaped as much by the times in which it is written as by the past about which it is written.

Jacobs understood slavery to be a fundamental betrayal of human relations and a violation of the individual's identity. She saw her struggle against her master as a battle of wills, hers against his. Her master, Dr. Norcom (Dr. Flint in the narrative), wanted to control her very identity—her memories, her beliefs, her desires, her body—in order to render her his absolute slave. She knew that at the core of his mastery over her was his control of her memories and self-expression. Indeed, in his efforts to subdue her, he told her that he "wish[ed] the past"—that is, when his efforts to overpower her sexually had become violent—"could be forgotten, and that we might never think of it."[8] But by refusing to forget or to remain silent—by ultimately writing this narrative—Jacobs offered the most powerful counter to that abuse at her command. The "written by herself" tag in the title, a convention of slave narratives that was meant to assert the literacy and authority of the slave narrator against the doubts of a skeptical audience, underlines the significance that Jacobs and other former slaves attached to speaking out for themselves. Literacy not only literally saved some slaves from discovery and recapture—note how Jacobs duped Norcom into thinking she was in the North by writing fake letters home while she was in fact hiding nearby—it also enabled fugitives such as Jacobs to write for the abolitionist movement. Being able to write one's own story, to author and authorize one's own life, was a tool of both physical and psychological liberation.

JACOBS'S EARLY LIFE

Harriet Jacobs was born in Edenton, North Carolina, in 1813, the first of Delilah Horniblow and Elijah Jacobs's two children. Their second child, John, was born in 1815. Delilah, one of six children of Molly Horniblow (the daughter of a slave woman and her master), was owned by Margaret Horniblow, the invalid daughter of a tavern owner. Elijah's slave master was Dr. Andrew Knox, who owned a plantation near Edenton. We do not know who Delilah's father was, but Elijah's father was Henry Jacobs, an illiterate white farmer who owned no slaves. Therefore, Harriet's ancestors on both sides were interracial.

Though illiterate, Elijah became a skilled carpenter and seems to have been hired out by his master to work on houses in town and the surrounding countryside. In this way, he developed the proud bearing of a free and independent man, which his children would later recall in their narratives. Reflecting this sense of autonomy, the Jacobs family, though enslaved, lived together in one of the outbuildings behind Horniblow's Tavern, with grandmother Molly and aunts and uncles nearby. Living as an intact family was an unusual "privilege," and it had a striking effect on Harriet's sense of herself. As she insists in her narrative, she did not know that she was a slave until she was six, when her mother died and she overheard others talking about the fact that she was a slave. Margaret had promised Delilah that her children "should never suffer for anything" (Harriet's words). Yet when Harriet was just twelve, Margaret died, leaving Harriet to the three-year-old daughter of her brother-in-law and physician, Dr. James Norcom, along with "my bureau & work table & their contents" (Document 2). Ten-year-old John became the property of Margaret's mother but was loaned to Norcom, and soon both children were moved into the Norcom household in Edenton.[9]

Harriet never forgot her mistress's betrayal of her mother's dying wish, and this bitter memory, along with what she remembered of her gentle, dignified mother and her intelligent, independent-minded father (who died when she was thirteen, leaving her with the formative memory of his outrage at his enslavement), inspired her hatred of and resistance to slavery. Important, too, in her long battle against Norcom, was the support network of her grandmother Molly, who ran her own bakery business; her aunts and uncles; and neighbors and friends (black and white).[10] Although Harriet's story is an example of the power of an individual to struggle against persecution, it is also an example of the importance of a strong family network and a supportive community in battling oppression.[11]

For Harriet, the battle began in earnest when she was fifteen and Norcom, thirty-five years her senior, began harassing her for sex. Tormented by his unrelenting and crude abuse, and mistreated by his jealous and angry wife, Harriet took the daring step of becoming sexually involved with Samuel Tredwell Sawyer, an Edenton lawyer who presented himself to her in the guise of protector and friend. Significantly, Harriet called this involvement "a perilous passage in the slave girl's life."[12] For her, choosing to submit to this seemingly attentive white man was preferable to being forced into sexual enslavement by her master. She may also have thought that Norcom would back off if she became the mistress of a white man of higher status. When she bore two children, Joseph and Louisa, she was hopeful that Sawyer would eventually purchase and free them.

At this point, Harriet's life was dominated by Norcom's obsession with subduing her, his vindictiveness toward her and her family when he failed, and the strategies she used to elude him. When she refused to become his concubine, Norcom banished Harriet to Auburn, his country plantation. Realizing that he was separating her from her family in order to render her more vulnerable to his abuse, Harriet ran away from the plantation in 1835. For seven years, she lived in a damp, cramped crawl space above her grandmother's kitchen, just one block from Norcom's home. (Molly had been freed in 1828.) Harriet knew that fleeing north with two small children would be treacherous and would likely lead to recapture. Yet until she had done what she could to secure her children's freedom (which she believed her disappearance would effect), she would not leave them behind. (Family bonds prevented many slaves from running away, particularly slave mothers. This was one reason for the larger number of fugitive men than women. In this case, Harriet believed that Norcom would not want to be saddled with the children and that someone sympathetic to her would buy them.)

In 1837, Samuel Sawyer bought Harriet's brother, John, and her children from Norcom. The following year, John escaped while in New York City with Sawyer, and soon Sawyer sent Louisa to Brooklyn to work for his relatives there. With one child in the North and her hiding place increasingly vulnerable to discovery, Harriet made preparations to leave North Carolina. In 1842, with the help of one of her uncles, she secretly boarded a schooner headed north. She arrived first in Philadelphia, where she was aided by members of the local Vigilance Committee, one of many such committees formed by free blacks in the North to help escaped slaves.[13] With a train ticket purchased for her by the Vigilance Committee, she went to New York City, where she located her daughter.

Eventually, she would have Joseph brought to Boston, where he would join her brother, who had returned from a whaling voyage he had sailed on after his escape.

Harriet found work in New York as the nurse of the infant daughter of an Englishwoman named Mary Stace Willis and her American husband, Nathaniel Parker Willis, a journalist and author. Yet even there, she was not beyond Norcom's reach, and he made numerous trips to New York to attempt to recapture her. In October 1844, forewarned that Norcom was coming to New York once again, Mrs. Willis helped Harriet and Louisa flee to Boston. The following March, Mrs. Willis died, and Harriet went with Mr. Willis and his daughter to visit his wife's parents in England. Louisa and Joseph stayed in Boston. By the time she returned to Boston in 1846, Joseph had shipped out to sea, but she remained there with Louisa.

In the meantime, John had become deeply involved in antislavery work as a lecturer and writer. In 1849, at his urging, Harriet moved to Rochester, New York, where John was then living. She joined his antislavery circle, which included Isaac and Amy Post and Frederick Douglass, who published his abolitionist newspaper, the North Star, there. Harriet began working at the Anti-Slavery Office and Reading Room, the center of Rochester's abolitionist activities. There Harriet read, talked, and sewed with abolitionists, becoming part of the community of activists engaged in the urgent mission to see slavery abolished. She lived in the Posts' home, a much-used stop on the Underground Railroad, for nine months. In Amy Post she found a sympathetic spirit and friend, to whom she could confide the trials of her life and, eventually, her ambition to write her life's story.

WHAT REALLY HAPPENED?

Many have found parts of Jacobs's story difficult to believe. Did she really hide undetected for seven years in the crawl space above her grandmother's kitchen, practically next door to Norcom? Did he really never rape her when he obviously had the chance in a culture that tacitly accepted the rape of enslaved black women? Although the question of what really happened is one that can be asked of any autobiography (or any nonfiction work, for that matter), that question seems particularly pertinent when the autobiography derives its force from telling the truth about slavery and the concomitant sexual abuse of women.

The first question seems answerable through a variety of documents external to the narrative that confirm Jacobs's account: Norcom's advertisement for her capture, printed in a local newspaper (Document 3); correspondence concerning his business dealings and trips to the North; a letter the Philadelphia black abolitionist Robert Purvis wrote describing her ordeal; John S. Jacobs's narrative (Document 11); and weather reports and ship schedules and passages that correspond to her narrative version. Even the severe rheumatism that plagued Jacobs the rest of her life, which she mentions often in her letters to her friend Amy Post, supports her account of how her body broke down during her long confinement.[14] These and other documents, which verify Jacobs's story, were brought to light by the diligent archival work of Dorothy Sterling and Jean Fagan Yellin, Jacobs's biographer.[15]

The second question—did Norcom never rape or try to rape her—is more difficult to answer with the external evidence afforded by historical documents. Not surprisingly, given the secrecy typically surrounding sexual abuse (even today), the best evidence for the rape of slave women by white men lay in the mixed-race faces of their children and, beyond that, in their own or their children's testimony after the fact.[16] Jacobs mentions no children by Norcom, and far from stating explicitly that he took her by force, she seems to suggest that she escaped actual sexual assault. She also suggests that Norcom restrained himself because of her grandmother Molly's stature in Edenton, the respect accorded the Jacobs family in general, and Norcom's need to preserve his reputation.

Yet it seems unbelievable that a man of Norcom's violent temper and brutal nature would not at least have tried to physically overpower her. As Jacobs's own narrative demonstrates, white masters typically saw adolescent slave girls as sexual property to be treated as they wished, and it was culturally acceptable for a master to rape his slave, though not someone else's. The language and symbols of the narrative support the contention that Norcom did rape the teenage Jacobs. In the words of one critic, P. Gabrielle Foreman, Jacobs "undertells both slave's abuse and white guilt," at the same time she points toward abuse and guilt by using "sexualized language" to describe owner-slave encounters. This includes the grotesque scene in which Mrs. Norcom leans over her bed and, pretending to be Dr. Norcom, whispers suggestively into young Harriet's ear.[17] In various passages, Jacobs also emphasizes the secrecy surrounding Norcom's sexual victims and his punishment of those who revealed his abuse.[18] She herself knew of the "terrible consequences" Norcom inflicted on his victims who spoke.[19] She would never forget the sounds of Norcom savagely whipping a slave whose wife had been one of his slave mistresses. The wife had given birth to a "fair child," causing her husband to quarrel with her. When Norcom sold them both, the lesson Jacobs drew from this was the danger of naming the abuser: This woman "had forgotten that it was a crime for a slave to tell who was the father of her child."[20] In another passage, she writes that what Norcom demanded of her was not merely silence but amnesia: He "wished the past could be forgotten, and that we might never think of it."[21] Finally, she admitted to her confidante, Amy Post, that she could not state clearly certain "cruel wrongs" in her narrative, "wrongs" that she found easier to "whisper" to a woman friend than to "record . . . for the world to read" (Document 7). These details all seem to point to the likelihood that if Norcom did rape Jacobs, she would not have felt free to write about it explicitly in her narrative. In this way, Jacobs struggled against the legacy of slavery as she wrote, even after she was no longer physically or legally enslaved.

Jean Fagan Yellin argues that the death of Jacobs's grandmother in 1853 freed her to write about her sexual history—albeit in veiled language—something she would not have done as long as her grandmother was alive. Even so, the narrative conveys the internal conflict that telling her story created for Jacobs. It is both a confession, with its feelings of guilt and shame—a story of "how my early sufferings in slavery . . . nearly crushed me . . . [and] how they had driven me into a great sin" (sex with Sawyer)—and, in her refusal of secrecy, an angry, urgent exposé of the real sinners—the white slaveholders, men and women, who wrapped their crimes in the mantles of law and faith.[22]

OTHER DOMINANT THEMES

Jacobs's narrative offers a profound critique of American law and religion, both of which were used to support the institution of slavery. Written over the course of four years, between 1853 and 1857, *Incidents* is framed by two matters of law—the Fugitive Slave Act and the *Dred Scott* decision. Both vividly reminded Jacobs, if she needed to be reminded, of how U.S. law devalued African Americans. The Fugitive Slave Act of 1850 required Northerners to recapture and return slaves to their masters in the South. This meant it was illegal for a Northerner to refuse to be, in effect, a slave catcher. It also meant that there was no safe place for fugitive slaves to live in the United States. Seven years later, the Supreme Court essentially barred free African Americans from the rights of citizenship when it ruled against the slaves Dred and Harriet Scott, who filed a lawsuit claiming that because they had resided in free territory with their master, they were free.[23] Not only were the Scotts still slaves according to the Supreme Court ruling, but no black person could be a U.S. citizen with rights that anyone was required to respect. This meant that Scott had no right to bring his lawsuit in the first place. These legal actions effectively denied to African Americans the very personhood Jacobs spent a lifetime struggling to attain. As bookends to her narrative, they shaped her skeptical attitude toward the law.

Jacobs devotes a chapter to the Fugitive Slave Act. In it, she shows the ways in which the law not only affected her personally but also became a turning point in the national battle over the legitimacy of slavery. For antislavery Northerners, disobeying this law, with violence if necessary, became a critical part of the abolitionist agenda, and Jacobs's advocacy of such disobedience was in line with this thinking. At the same time, the new law encouraged Southern slaveholders to go north to reclaim their slaves. It was under the auspices of this law that first Dr. Norcom and then his daughter and son-in-law went to New York City to find Jacobs, and passage of the law was the reason Jacobs scanned the newspapers for the names of Southerners staying in New York hotels. This strategy ultimately allowed her to elude her pursuers.

Jacobs's view that abiding by laws legitimizing slavery was immoral explains her distress and even disgust when she learned that the second Mrs. Willis had bought her freedom. "So I was sold at last!" she writes, scorning the exchange of cash for a human being as revolting and wrong.[24] Indeed, as Jacobs asserts, to be truly free, she had to be "free from the operation of the law" of the land—the whole land, both North and South.[25] Thus Jacobs mentions how the Fugitive Slave Act drove many runaway slaves to Canada or England, where slavery was illegal. For these fugitives, as Jacobs notes, living outside the reach of American racism and slavery came as a blessed relief. Indeed, she herself experienced this relief when she visited England for the first time in 1845–1846.

Similarly, according to Jacobs, to be religious as religion was practiced in the South was to be enmeshed in an immoral institution. True Christianity, Jacobs suggests, could be found only among people untainted by American slavery. "There is a great difference between Christianity and religion at the south," Jacobs writes in a chapter called "The Church and Slavery."[26] The hypocrisy of the Southern church, an institution called upon to justify the enslavement and ownership of human beings, appalled Jacobs. With bitter irony, she often pointed out the contradiction between slaveholders' behavior and the Christian precepts masters and mistresses taught their slaves. "Do unto others as you would have them do unto you" read the Golden Rule. Treat your neighbors as you would want them to treat you. But, as Jacobs wryly observes, she supposed slaveholders did not see slaves as neighbors. For her, such unabashed hypocrisy made swallowing whole the faith of the master class impossible. When Jacobs wrote to Amy Post that she had "tried to [write about her life in slavery] in a Christian spirit" (Document 7), she was above all alluding to the difficulty she had forgiving her mistresses and master. But the "Christian spirit" that she meant was not the one she experienced in the South, or even in the North. It was the spirit of Christianity that she found only after she left the slaveholding United States, during her tenmonth stay in England beginning in 1845. It was then, as Jacobs writes, that "grace entered my heart, and I knelt at the communion table, I trust, in true humility of soul."[27]

Jacobs's personal struggle with faith is a central theme of the narrative, beginning after her father died when she was a child and her "heart rebelled against God, who had taken from me mother, father, mistress, and friend." Molly tries to soothe Harriet's rebellious spirit by advising her granddaughter to put her faith in God because God's "ways" are impossible for humans to fathom.[28] Similarly, Jacobs finds it hard to attain a state of Christian forgiveness toward anyone who treated her as property. She admits that she has to force herself to "think with less bitterness" about her mistress, who had "bequeathed me to her sister's daughter," breaking the promise she'd made to Jacobs's dying mother that "her children should never suffer for anything." Jacobs, who had loved her mistress, could not forgive her for this betrayal.[29] If faith meant piously resigning oneself to suffering—becoming a model of forgiveness and forbearance—Jacobs would find it hard to acquiesce.

Yet an alternative strand in the tradition of African American Christianity also emerges in the narrative, in Jacobs's eyewitness account of the impact on Edenton of the news of Nat Turner's rebellion. Nat Turner was a slave preacher who believed "the Spirit" had sent him a series of signs to lead a revolution against slavery. In August 1831, in Southampton County, Virginia, just over sixty miles from Edenton, Turner led nearly sixty slaves as they rode through eleven farms, killing fifty-seven to sixty white men, women, and children. A local militia captured or killed all of the rebels by the next day, except for Turner, who hid for two months in the vicinity before being caught.[30]

The view that violence against slavery was "a holy cause" was already a formidable line of argument within abolitionism, articulated by black activists like David Walker, who warned Americans in 1829 that unless they repented and ended slavery, America would be destroyed.[31] The white abolitionist and editor William Lloyd Garrison wrote that Nat Turner's rebellion was truly the fulfillment of a prophecy that "the hour of vengeance" was near, even while he condemned the rebels' violence.[32]

Nat Turner's rebellion was one of the largest slave rebellions in the history of the United States, one that shattered white Southerners' illusions of control, and in the chapter called "Fear of Insurrection," Jacobs describes in detail how in the aftermath of the revolt, panicked white mobs terrorized enslaved and free black people in waves of brutal violence. She also describes the repressive "black codes" local slaveholders designed to prevent their own slaves from conspiring against them, including how slaves were forbidden to visit between plantations or to congregate at their own church, which was demolished. Instead, as Jacobs writes, they were told to attend the white churches and sit in blacks-only sections in the balconies. Not until the initial panic subsided, Jacobs ironically observes, did white slaveholders decide "that it would be well to give the slaves enough religious instruction to keep them from murdering their masters."[33] As Jacobs makes clear, this was the kind of religious instruction meant to instill obedience in the hearts and minds of slaves.

Interestingly, Jacobs says nothing about Nat Turner's rebellion itself. She gives no indication of whether she supported Turner's use of radical violence or not. Yet we do know that Jacobs supported another violent uprising—the one led by white abolitionist John Brown. In fact, Jacobs decided she wanted to end her narrative with a tribute to Brown, who had led a raid on the federal arsenal at Harpers Ferry, Virginia, in 1859. Lydia Maria Child advised Jacobs to retain her original ending, a tribute to her grandmother, and Jacobs deleted the addendum on Brown, ending instead with the "solace" of "tender memories of my good old grandmother,"[34] meant to lighten dark thoughts of the past. Instead of memorializing revolutionary fervor, she ends by remembering devotion, forbearance, and hope.

THE POWER OF THE PEN

Interestingly, the themes, language, and structure of *Incidents* reflect a number of influences, suggesting the range of Jacobs's reading before and during the writing of her narrative. Based on the many allusions in her narrative, the Bible, contemporary fiction and poetry, and Shakespeare seem to have been the most important literary influences.

The literature of the abolitionist movement, which developed in the United States during the 1820s and 1830s, gave Jacobs crucial models for her narrative. Chapters such as "The Slaves' New Year's Day," "Sketches of Neighboring Slaveholders," and "The Church and Slavery" seem drawn at least as much from abolitionist literature—sermons, speeches, editorials, antislavery pamphlets, and slave narratives—as from her own experience.[35] Jean Fagan Yellin points out that Jacobs read through the most important of these works sitting in the Antislavery Office and Reading Room above the office of the *North Star*, where she went to work in 1849.

Many of her themes reflect what she was reading in contemporary antislavery writings. Of these, the most influential was the weekly Boston abolitionist newspaper, the *Liberator*, founded in 1831 by William Lloyd Garrison, whose printing office had issued *Narrative of the Life of Frederick Douglass, an American Slave* in June 1845.[36] For thirty-five years, the *Liberator* provided a forum for abolitionist thinking, publishing African American and white writers without distinction, a remarkable occurrence in itself in antebellum America. The earliest stirrings of an American abolitionist movement were in evidence during the Revolutionary War, but these early activists were mostly content to believe that slavery, left alone, would die a natural death. By 1830, however, a boom in Southern cotton production, the expansion of slavery into the Southwest, and the growing commitment to slavery in the South made it clear that the "peculiar institution" would not simply fade away. Influenced by a powerful British antislavery movement, Northern reformers became increasingly radicalized and founded antislavery societies across the North, organizing themselves into a formidable movement. Former slaves such as Harriet and John Jacobs, Frederick Douglass, Sojourner Truth, Henry Bibb, and William Wells Brown were central to the antislavery movement. Not only could they could give chilling, forceful eyewitness accounts of what it was like to be enslaved, but their criticisms of slavery helped shape the arguments and goals of the abolitionist movement. As fugitive slaves, they embodied the justification for a revolutionary resistance to slavery. Free black activists such as Martin Delany, Alexander Crummel, Henry Highland Garnet (who was a boy when his father led his family in a daring escape from enslavement in Maryland), Robert Purvis, Benjamin Lundy, William C. Nell, Sarah M. Douglass, and Sarah Forten also devoted their lives to ending slavery and advancing the interests of African Americans. By the time Jacobs published her autobiography, she had come into contact with many of these abolitionists and other prominent members of the antislavery movement.[37]

From enslavement to authorship was an extraordinary journey. That is, to move from the world into which Jacobs was born—in which she was taught that she and her kind had no public existence and were not entitled to an education—to one of her own invention, in which she not only spoke and wrote but also published her story for all the world to read, was to assert her humanity against the inhumanity of slavery in an astonishing way. Millions of slaves died in silence, disappearing as if into a mass grave. Indeed, the very idea of the slave narrator who wrote his or her own narrative was virtually inconceivable to scholars well into the twentieth century, when a revolution in scholarship, coinciding with the civil rights movement in the 1950s and 1960s, began to see slave narratives as authentic, reliable sources.[38] Until then, slave narratives that were read in their own time, including *Incidents*, remained mostly undervalued, unavailable, and unread.

Yet *Incidents* had to wait another two decades after the civil rights movement for its recovery from obscurity. Women's slave narratives were not reprinted until the 1980s, two decades after the flowering of an effort to reprint men's slave narratives, when feminist scholars working on slavery came into their own. By then, historian John Blassingame, a forceful advocate for using slave testimony to write about slavery, had made the classic case *against* taking Jacobs's narrative seriously as a historical document. In *The Slave Community* (1972), Blassingame dismissed *Incidents* as "not credible" because it was "too orderly . . . too melodramatic."[39] For Blassingame, evidence of a self-conscious literary hand shaping the narrative pointed away from Jacobs's authorship and toward Lydia Maria Child, Jacobs's white editor. Beyond that, however, Blassingame's dismissal of Jacobs's narrative as "orderly" and "melodramatic" suggests his devaluation of the values, themes, and forms of the feminine genre—the sentimental narrative—that guided Jacobs's writing. This blinkered view of women's modes of writing had to be revised before women's writing could be treated on a par with men's. Yet in 1981, the year Jean Fagan Yellin first demonstrated that Harriet Jacobs had indeed written the narrative, Blassingame was one of the first scholars to acknowledge the success of her work. By then, feminist scholars in history and literature had begun arguing persuasively that the literary qualities that Blassingame deemed inauthentic were historically, psychologically, and linguistically authentic for a woman in Harriet Jacobs's position, time, and place.

Literate from an early age, Jacobs (like Frederick Douglass) understood not only the power of the written word in general but the specific power it gave her, as distinct from so many others, to master her situation. Her mistress Margaret Horniblow taught her to read and write, a privilege, she notes, "which so rarely falls to the lot of a slave."[40] Moreover, the kind early treatment she received from her mistress reinforced the lessons of selfhood she learned from her strong, independent-minded family, lessons that enabled her psychologically not only to survive enslavement but also to escape it and, ultimately, to write about it. Being a slave of "privilege" from a large, stable, proud family, nurtured and strengthened her spirited resistance to enslavement, just as her grandmother's cakes nurtured and strengthened her body.

In addition, Jacobs's impulse for activism, also part of her inheritance, motivated her to consider writing her story. When she and John were in Rochester, John tried to persuade her to tell her story for the cause of abolition, and reading abolitionist literature showed her how this could be done. Her friend Amy Post made the same suggestion. Still, she struggled with her feelings that telling the truth of her life would be mortifying: "My stubborn pride would not yeild [*sic*]," she wrote to Post (Document 4). Yet she had devised a sort of compromise: She asked Post to write to Harriet Beecher Stowe, author of the best-selling *Uncle Tom's Cabin*, to ask if Stowe would be willing to write Jacobs's story for her. Instead of answering Post directly, Stowe responded to Cornelia Grinnell Willis, who also had written to Stowe, asking that she take her daughter Louisa with her to England (Document 5). Stowe enclosed Post's letter, asked if what Post had said about Jacobs's story was true, and stated that if it was, she would be willing to include some of it in her follow-up to *Uncle Tom's Cabin*, a book called *A Key to Uncle Tom's Cabin*, which she was hurrying to finish before leaving for England. Jacobs was so insulted by this dismissive and opportunistic treatment that she determined to write her story herself. "I wished it to be a history of my life entirely by itsslf [*sic*]," not bits and pieces of it in someone else's story, she wrote to Post in April 1853 (Document 5). "It needed no romance," she added.

Spurred by what she called "a spirit of rivalry" (Document 5), Jacobs began to write, and by October, she confided to Post, she had made headway in writing about her own life. In fact, by then Jacobs was already a published writer, practicing her craft in letters to newspapers responding to articles about slavery. Her first two public letters had appeared in the *New York Tribune* in June and July 1853 and were signed "A Fugitive Slave." Significantly, they reveal an author ready to enter into the public debate, drawing her authority from her own experiences. This self-assured voice comes through on the pages of her autobiography as well, as she denounces slavery and those who would support it, wittingly or unwittingly. In this way, Jacobs became part of a literary movement of African American writers who were writing not only autobiographies but also biographies and essays: Frederick Douglass (who was writing his second narrative), William C. Nell, William J. Anderson, William Green, William Allen, William Wells Brown, Josephine Brown (who was writing a biography of her father, William Wells Brown), Daniel Peterson, Austin Steward, Samuel Ringgold Ward, and others.

Jacobs worked on her manuscript for four years, from 1853 to 1857, while she sewed, cleaned, and took care of the Willis children in Cornwall-on-Hudson, New York. She took occasional restorative breaks in Boston and New York City, where she was energized by antislavery meetings and the company of other black and white abolitionists. After the *Dred Scott* decision of March 1857, the urgency of the plight of African Americans, enslaved and free, prompted her to finish a draft. Eager to see her manuscript in print, Jacobs eventually approached the Boston publishers Thayer and Eldridge, whom she knew from their antislavery publications. They said they would publish her manuscript if she could supply an introduction by Lydia Maria Child. A fervent abolitionist, Child had made her reputation as a fiction writer before publishing her sweeping indictment of slavery, *An Appeal in Favor of That Class of Americans Called Africans*, in 1833. A former editor of the *National Anti-Slavery Standard* and author of numerous other antislavery pamphlets, Child was hailed by Garrison as "the first woman in the republic."[41] The publishers' request was in keeping with the conventions of other existing slave narratives, which were printed surrounded by testimonials from white abolitionists willing to testify to the slave writers' authenticity and integrity. Child undertook not only to write an introduction but to edit the manuscript as well, shortening it and rearranging sentences and pages so that it flowed more smoothly (typical editorial interventions).

Scholars today accept that the narrative was, as Jacobs says, "written by herself" (Document 1); in editing Jacobs's manuscript, as Child told a friend, she "abridged and struck out superfluous words sometimes, but I don't think I altered fifty words in the whole volume."[42] Child wrote to Jacobs that she was primarily reordering sentences so as "to bring the story into continuous *order*, and the remarks into *appropriate* places." This would make "the story much more clear and entertaining."[43] For example, Child asked Jacobs to add specific details to her descriptions of the violence inflicted against Edenton after Turner's uprising. "What *were* those inflictions? Were any tortured to make them confess? Were any killed?"[44] (Document 8). Child's advice that Jacobs render the violence more vivid in this section further complicates how readers might understand Child's contrasting advice that Jacobs delete the tribute to John Brown at the end of the narrative. When Child told Jacobs that ending with Brown didn't fit as well as ending with her grandmother, she was recognizing how the addendum changed the final effect of the work. It seems probable that Child also knew the risk of alienating the "reader" whose sympathies Jacobs wished to awaken by ending with support for a violent attack against a federal arsenal. Ending with the more benign image of her dead, devout grandmother surely encourages those sympathies.

Yet another way to view Jacobs's ending is through an understanding of the ways in which her narrative reflects upon the interconnection between the personal and the political. Much of the power of the narrative lies in Jacobs's painful realization that those connections she felt as most personal—her sexual, romantic, familial, and domestic relationships—could not be separated from the political (power) relationships structured by racism, sexism, and slavery. Her personal life was simply not hers to will, and ending with a vision of her grandmother—a personal vision—might be read as an assertion of a life-giving memory over the soul-murdering memories structured by slavery. Indeed, the traumatic content of her tale makes all the more remarkable the integrity with which Jacobs examines her motives and accepts responsibility for the decisions she makes that run against cultural norms—for instance, to have sex with Samuel Sawyer or to leave her children to escape Norcom by hiding in her grandmother's house.

Jacobs's narrative was published in January 1861 in Boston, where it sold for $1 (just over $24 by today's standards), and in 1862 in London, with the new title *The Deeper Wrong; or, Incidents in the Life of a Slave Girl, Written by Herself.* Reviews of the work in antislavery and sympathetic newspapers were serious and positive. They predicted that the book would have a powerful moral impact on readers, who would be moved to horror by the realistic, straightforward depictions of slavery presented by the author they knew only as "Linda." Although the book was published anonymously, Jacobs made no attempt to hide her identity, and she did what she could to promote it. However, the outbreak of the Civil War in April swamped whatever attention the book might have received, and it virtually disappeared.

Nonetheless, *Incidents* had turned Jacobs into a recognized spokeswoman for the movement against slavery and oppression. It had liberated her in a way that Cornelia Willis's purchase of her freedom had not. When Jacobs went to Washington, D.C., and Alexandria, Virginia, in 1862 to help the "contraband slaves"—men, women, and children who had run away from their owners after the war started and whom Northerners were not legally bound to return because they were declared "contrabands of war"—Garrison asked her to write a long piece for the *Liberator* about them. Having found her voice, Jacobs never lost it again. During the war, she raised money and did relief work for the contrabands, helping them find work, clothing, food, and shelter. After the war, as a representative of the New England Freedmen's Aid Society, she worked on behalf of newly freed slaves in Georgia, where she helped Louisa open a school. All the while, she continued to write articles for Northern newspapers about the plight of the freedmen. She earned her living not from her writing, however, but in one of the only ways open to a respectable black woman at the time, by running a boardinghouse, first in Cambridge, Massachusetts, and later in Washington, D.C. In March 1897, she died in Washington of breast cancer. She was buried in Cambridge's famous Mount Auburn Cemetery, where, twenty years later, Louisa was buried alongside her.

Although Jacobs was well known for her writings during her lifetime, attention to her vanished after her death, and it would take several generations of readers to rediscover the book, articles, and letters she wrote. The 1973 Teller edition of *Incidents* brought attention back, but it was not until 1987, when Jean Fagan Yellin edited a scholarly edition during a decade of significant feminist revisionist writing in history, that the book began to attract the intense literary and historical interest that it still commands today.[45] Significantly, although the manuscript for *Incidents* has disappeared, Jacobs is the only female slave whose papers are known to have survived.[46] In this way, her ultimate triumph over her vicious master, who wished to subdue her not only physically but psychologically and spiritually as well, stands virtually alone and remains a memorial to all those female voices irretrievably lost.

NOTES

[1]For the definitive biography of Jacobs, see Jean Fagan Yellin, *Harriet Jacobs: A Life* (New York: Basic Civitas Books, 2004). Yellin is the leading scholar on Harriet Jacobs and the editor of the two-volume edition of the Harriet Jacobs papers, *The Harriet Jacobs Family Papers: Volumes I and II* (Chapel Hill: University of North Carolina Press, 2008). These volumes include writings by Jacobs, her brother, John S. Jacobs, and her daughter, Louisa Matilda Jacobs; writings to and about them, and other private and public documents about the Jacobs family. Many of the documents cited in this book are published in *The Jacobs Family Papers*.

[2]Harriet Jacobs, *Incidents in the Life of a Slave Girl, Written by Herself,* page 98 in this volume. All subsequent references are to this volume. For a good short history on female slavery in the South, see Deborah Gray White, *Ar'n't I a Woman? Female Slaves in the Plantation South* (New York: W. W. Norton, 1985). See also Catherine Clinton, ed., *Half Sisters of History: Southern Women and the American Past* (Durham, N.C.: Duke University Press, 1994); David Barry Gaspar and Darlene Clark Hine, eds., *More Than Chattel: Black Women and Slavery in the Americas* (Bloomington: Indiana University Press, 1996); Jennifer L. Morgan, *Laboring Women: Reproduction and Gender in New World Slavery* (Philadelphia: University of Philadelphia Press, 2004); Dorothy Sterling, ed., *We Are Your Sisters: Black Women in the Nineteenth Century* (New York: W. W. Norton, 1984).

[3]John S. Jacobs, *A True Tale of Slavery* (Document 11), was published in installments in the *Leisure Hour: A Family Journal of Instruction and Recreation* (London) on February 7, 14, 21, and 28, 1861. British abolitionists welcomed African American fugitives from slavery in a way that many, including Harriet Jacobs, felt was free from the taint of American racism. In fact, Jacobs first hoped to publish her narrative in England.

[4]Frederick Douglass, *Narrative of the Life of Frederick Douglass, an American Slave, Written by Himself* (1845); *My Bondage and My Freedom* (1855); *Life and Times of Frederick Douglass* (1893). These books were reprinted together in a single volume, edited and with notes by Henry Louis Gates Jr. (New York: Library of America, 1994).

[5]Jacobs, *Incidents,* 25.

[6]Ibid., 207.

[7]Ibid., 193.

[8]Ibid., 157.

[9]For a searing account of the ways in which enslaved African American bodies were treated as commodities from birth through death—to be bought, sold, loaned, hired out, willed, bartered, mutilated, and studied—see Daina Ramey Berry, *The Price for Their Pound of Flesh: The Value of the Enslaved from Womb to Grave, in the Building of a Nation* (Boston: Beacon Press, 2017).

[10]This support network existed in the Edenton neighborhood that both enslaved and free blacks transformed for themselves. Historian Anthony Kaye has written about the profound effects of slave neighborhoods on enslaved people's personal and political lives. See Anthony Kaye, *Joining Places: Slave Neighborhoods in the Old South* (Chapel Hill: University of North Carolina Press, 2007).

[11]Scholars who have written on the relationships between Jacobs and her white mistresses and benefactresses include William L. Andrews, *To Tell a Free Story: The First Century of Afro-American Autobiography, 1760–1865* (Urbana: University of Illinois Press, 1986); Hazel V. Carby, *Reconstructing Womanhood: The Emergence of the Afro-American Woman Novelist* (New York: Oxford University Press, 1987); Frances Smith Foster, *Witnessing Slavery: The Development of the Ante-bellum Slave Narratives,* 2nd ed. (Madison: University of Wisconsin Press, 1994), and *Written by Herself: Literary Production by African American Women, 1746–1892* (Bloomington: Indiana University Press, 1993); Deborah M. Garfield, "Vexed Alliances: Race and Female Collaboration in the Life of Harriet Jacobs," in *Harriet Jacobs and "Incidents in the Life of a Slave Girl": New Critical Essays,* ed. Deborah M. Garfield and Rafia Zafar (New York: Cambridge University Press, 1996), 275–91; Elizabeth Fox-Genovese, *Within the Plantation Household: Black and White Women in the Old South* (Chapel Hill: University of North Carolina Press, 1988); Minrose C. Gwin, *Black and White Women of the Old South: The Peculiar Sisterhood in American Literature* (Knoxville: University of Tennessee Press, 1985); Dana D. Nelson, *The Word in Black and White: Reading "Race" in American Literature, 1638–1867* (New York: Oxford University Press, 1992); Jean Fagan Yellin,

Women and Sisters: The Antislavery Feminists in American Culture (New Haven, Conn.: Yale University Press, 1989).

[12]Jacobs, *Incidents*, 75.

[13]For Northern free black activism, see Leon Litwack and August Meier, eds., *Black Leaders of the Nineteenth Century* (Urbana: University of Illinois Press, 1991); Jane H. Pease and William H. Pease, *They Who Would Be Free: Blacks' Search for Freedom, 1830–1861* (New York: Atheneum, 1974); Yellin, *Harriet Jacobs*; Benjamin Quarles, *Black Abolitionists* (1969; repr., New York: Oxford University Press, 1991).

[14]The lifelong toll that being enslaved took on the body and mind is a common theme in slave narratives, especially women's. For twenty-first-century African American women writers, the impact of everyday racism on their own—and other African Americans'—bodies and minds is a necessary subject. See Claudia Rankine, *Citizen: An American Lyric* (Minneapolis: Graywolf Press, 2014).

[15]Sterling, *We Are Your Sisters*; Yellin, *Harriet Jacobs*.

[16]One of the most famous comments on the presence of mulatto children in slavery households is by the Southern diarist Mary Boykin Chesnut: "Like the patriarchs of old our men live in one house with their wives and concubines, and the mulattoes one sees in every family exactly resemble the white children—and every lady tells you who is the father of all of the mulatto children in everybody's household, but those in her own she seems to think drop from the clouds, or pretends to think so." C. Vann Woodward, ed., *Mary Chesnut's Civil War* (New Haven, Conn.: Yale University Press, 1981), 29.

[17]P. Gabrielle Foreman, "Earwitness: Female Abolitionism, Sexuality, and *Incidents in the Life of a Slave Girl*," in *Harriet Jacobs and "Incidents in the Life of a Slave Girl,"* 79.

[18]Ibid.; Jacobs, *Incidents*, 52.

[19]Jacobs, *Incidents*, 58.

[20]Ibid., 38.

[21]Ibid., 157.

[22]Ibid., 193.

[23]Jacobs did not write about the *Dred Scott* case directly in her narrative, although she did mention its consequences for African Americans in a letter written to Amy Post in March 1857, the month of the *Dred Scott* decision (Isaac and Amy Post Family Papers, Department of Rare Books and Special Collections, University of Rochester Library, Rochester, N.Y.).

[24]Jacobs, *Incidents*, 205.

[25]Ibid., 196.

[26]Ibid., 96.

[27]Ibid., 190. Although Jacobs's spiritual journey is a theme in the narrative, *Incidents* is essentially meant to reflect reality as it is—that is, to be realistic. However, there is also an important tradition of black spiritual autobiographies, in which the slave's life and experiences are meant to be read symbolically, in terms of particular biblical stories. The book of Exodus was an especially popular story through which enslaved African Americans could read their lives, for it carried the promise of deliverance from Egypt (the South) to the Promised Land (the North). Two good examples of narrators who used scriptural language as a way to understand the meaning of their lives are the female evangelist Jarena Lee (*Religious Experience and Journal of Mrs. Jarena Lee*, 1849) and the insurrectionist Nat Turner (*The Confessions of Nat Turner*, 1831). For more on the spiritual autobiography and different modes of autobiography, see Andrews, *To Tell a Free Story*.

[28]Jacobs, *Incidents*, 34.

[29]Ibid., 32.

[30]*The Confessions of Nat Turner, the Leader of the Late Insurrection in Southampton, Va. As fully and voluntarily made to Thomas R. Gray* (1831). For a good introduction to the narrative, see *The Confessions of Nat Turner, and Related Documents,* edited with an introduction by Kenneth S. Greenberg (Boston: Bedford/St. Martin's, 1996).

[31]*David Walker's Appeal to the Coloured Citizens of the World, but in Particular, and Very Expressly, to those of the United States* (1829).

[32]William Lloyd Garrison, *The Liberator,* 1831.

[33]Jacobs, *Incidents,* 89.

[34]Ibid., 207.

[35]In their form, these chapters resemble Theodore Dwight Weld's *American Slavery as It Is: Testimony of a Thousand Witnesses* (New York: American Anti-Slavery Society, 1839), a best-selling compendium of atrocities of slavery drawn entirely from Southern newspapers. Weld, a lecturer and secretary of the American Anti-Slavery Society, understood that Northerners would not believe what abolitionists said about slavery without eyewitness testimony.

[36]For a life of Garrison, see Henry Mayer, *All On Fire: William Garrison and the Abolition of Slavery* (New York: St. Martin's Press, 1998).

[37]For a comprehensive history of the role of black activists in the abolitionist movement, see Manisha Sinha, *The Slave's Cause: A History of Abolition* (New Haven, Conn.: Yale University Press, 2016). Describing American abolition as a "radical, interracial movement," Sinha argues that "slave resistance, not bourgeois liberalism, lay at the heart of the abolition movement" (1). For more on nineteenth-century interracial antislavery and civil rights activism, see also Stephen Kantrowitz, *More Than Freedom: Fighting for Black Citizenship in a White Republic, 1829–1889* (New York: Penguin, 2012), and John Stauffer, *The Black Hearts of Men: Radical Abolitionists and the Transformation of Race* (Cambridge, Mass.: Harvard University Press, 2002).

[38]For the revival of interest in slave narratives as authentic testimony, see John W. Blassingame, ed., *Slave Testimony: Two Centuries of Letters, Speeches, Interviews, and Autobiographies* (Baton Rouge: Louisiana State University Press, 1977). See also the collection of primary documents in Ira Berlin, Barbara Fields, Steven F. Miller, Joseph P. Reidy, and Leslie S. Rowland, eds., *Free At Last: A Documentary History of Slavery, Freedom, and the Civil War* (New York: New Press, 1992). For the histories of slavery that grew out of the shift in attitude toward slave testimony, see John W. Blassingame, *The Slave Community: Plantation Life in the Antebellum South* (New York: Oxford University Press, 1972); Eugene D. Genovese, *Roll, Jordan, Roll: The World the Slaves Made* (New York: Random House, 1974); Herbert G. Gutman, *The Black Family in Slavery and Freedom, 1750–1925* (New York: Random House, 1976); Lawrence W. Levine, *Black Culture and Black Consciousness* (New York: Oxford University Press, 1977). For a useful, short historiography of slavery, see Peter J. Parish, *Slavery: History and the Historians* (New York: Harper & Row, 1989).

[39]Blassingame, *The Slave Community,* 373. Many have taken up the question of authenticity in autobiography in general and in slave narratives in particular, but for a sense of the debates about the narratives, see Andrews, *To Tell a Free Story;* Jennifer Fleischner, *Mastering Slavery: Memory, Family, and Identity in Women's Slave Narratives* (New York: New York University Press, 1996); Charles T. Davis and Henry L. Gates Jr., eds., *The Slave's Narrative* (New York: Oxford University Press, 1985); Robert Stepto, *From Behind the Veil: A Study of Afro-American Narrative* (Urbana: University of Illinois Press, 1979).

[40]Jacobs, *Incidents,* 32.

[41]See Carolyn L. Karcher, *The First Woman in the Republic: A Cultural Biography of Lydia Maria Child* (Durham, N.C.: Duke University Press, 1994).

[42]Lydia Maria Child to Lucy Osgood, August 8, 1860, quoted in Yellin, *Harriet Jacobs: A Life*, 141.

[43]Lydia Maria Child to Harriet Jacobs, August 13, 1860, quoted in ibid.,

[44]Ibid.

[45]Harriet Jacobs, *Incidents in the Life of a Slave Girl, Written by Herself*, ed. Lydia Maria Child, new introduction and notes by Walter Teller (New York: Harcourt Brace Jovanovich, 1973); *Incidents*, ed. Yellin.

[46]Yellin, ed., *The Harriet Jacobs Family Papers*.

Pseudonyms of Key Figures in *Incidents in the Life of a Slave Girl, Written by Herself*

Linda Brent Harriet Jacobs

Aunt Martha Molly Horniblow, Harriet's grandmother

Uncle Phillip Mark Ramsey, Molly Horniblow's oldest son

Aunt Nancy Betty, Molly Horniblow's daughter

Uncle Benjamin Joseph, Molly Horniblow's youngest son

William John S. Jacobs, Harriet's brother

Benny Joseph Jacobs, Harriet's son

Ellen Louisa Jacobs, Harriet's daughter

Miss Fanny Hannah Pritchard

Dr. Flint Dr. James Norcom

Mrs. Flint Mary Matilda Horniblow Norcom, Dr. Norcom's wife

Young Mr. Flint James Norcom Jr.

Miss Emily Flint (later Mrs. Dodge) Mary Matilda Norcom, Dr. Norcom's daughter (later Mrs. Daniel) Messmore

Mr. Sands Samuel Tredwell Sawyer

Mr. and Mrs. Hobbs James Iredell Tredwell and Mary Bonner Blount Tredwell, Samuel Sawyer's cousins

Mr. Thorne Joseph Blount, Mary Tredwell's brother

Mr. Bruce Nathaniel Parker Willis

Mrs. Bruce Mary Stace Willis, Nathaniel Willis's first wife

Mary [Bruce] Imogen Willis, Mary and Nathaniel Willis's baby daughter

Second Mrs. Bruce Cornelia Grinnell Willis, Nathaniel Willis's second wife

PART TWO

Incidents in the Life of a Slave Girl

Written by Herself

Edited by L. Maria Child

PREFACE BY THE AUTHOR

Reader, be assured this narrative is no fiction. I am aware that some of my adventures may seem incredible; but they are, nevertheless, strictly true. I have not exaggerated the wrongs inflicted by Slavery; on the contrary, my descriptions fall far short of the facts. I have concealed the names of places, and given persons fictitious names. I had no motive for secrecy on my own account, but I deemed it kind and considerate towards others to pursue this course.

I wish I were more competent to the task I have undertaken. But I trust my readers will excuse deficiencies in consideration of circumstances. I was born and reared in Slavery; and I remained in a Slave State twenty-seven years. Since I have been at the North, it has been necessary for me to work diligently for my own support, and the education of my children. This has not left me much leisure to make up for the loss of early opportunities to improve myself; and it has compelled me to write these pages at irregular intervals, whenever I could snatch an hour from household duties.[1]

[1]Jacobs offers a common apology of slave narrators, who were aware of addressing better-educated white readers. Her remark about having to "snatch an hour" ironically recalls the condition of slaves who found time to attend to their own household needs only after laboring all day for their masters and mistresses.

When I first arrived in Philadelphia, Bishop Paine[2] advised me to publish a sketch of my life, but I told him I was altogether incompetent to such an undertaking. Though I have improved my mind somewhat since that time, I still remain of the same opinion; but I trust my motives will excuse what might otherwise seem presumptuous. I have not written my experiences in order to attract attention to myself; on the contrary, it would have been more pleasant to me to have been silent about my own history. Neither do I care to excite sympathy for my own sufferings. But I do earnestly desire to arouse the women of the North to a realizing sense of the condition of two millions of women at the South, still in bondage, suffering what I suffered, and most of them far worse.[3] I want to add my testimony to that of abler pens to convince the people of the Free States what Slavery really is. Only by experience can any one realize how deep, and dark, and foul is that pit of abominations. May the blessing of God rest on this imperfect effort in behalf of my persecuted people![4]

Linda Brent.

INTRODUCTION BY THE EDITOR

The author of the following autobiography is personally known to me, and her conversation and manners inspire me with confidence. During the last seventeen years, she has lived the greater part of the time with a distinguished family in New York, and has so deported herself as to be highly esteemed by them. This fact is sufficient, without further credentials of her character. I believe those who know her will not be disposed to doubt her veracity, though some incidents in her story are more romantic than fiction.[5]

[2]Daniel A. Payne (1811–1893), born a free black in Charleston, South Carolina, attended the Lutheran theological seminary in Gettysburg, Pennsylvania, was a successful itinerant minister, and became the sixth bishop of the African Methodist Episcopal Church in 1852. He was later president of Wilberforce University, a black university in Ohio founded in 1856 by white members of the Methodist Church and taken over in 1863, with Payne's help, by the African Methodist Episcopal Church. He wrote *Recollections of Seventy Years* (Nashville, Tenn.: A.M.E. Sunday School Union, 1888).

[3]In 1860, there were 3.9 million slaves in the South, 262,000 free black people, and 5 million white people.

[4]Reference to Psalm 3.

[5]Writer, editor, and activist Lydia Maria Child (1802–1880) authenticates Jacobs's narrative and identity and guarantees her social acceptability, all conventions of editors' introductions in slave narratives. Child, who was white, was required by the conventions of the genre to vouch for the authenticity, integrity, and literacy of the black author. (For a biography of Child, see Carolyn L. Karcher, *The First Woman in the Republic: A Cultural Biography of Lydia Maria Child* [Durham, N.C.: Duke University Press, 1994].) In the nineteenth century, the "romance" genre was understood to contain supernatural elements, whereas "fiction" (or the novel) was realistic.

At her request, I have revised her manuscript; but such changes as I have made have been mainly for purposes of condensation and orderly arrangement. I have not added any thing to the incidents, or changed the import of her very pertinent remarks. With trifling exceptions, both the ideas and the language are her own. I pruned excrescences a little, but otherwise I had no reason for changing her lively and dramatic way of telling her own story. The names of both persons and places are known to me; but for good reasons I suppress them.

It will naturally excite surprise that a woman reared in Slavery should be able to write so well. But circumstances will explain this. In the first place, nature endowed her with quick perceptions. Secondly, the mistress, with whom she lived till she was twelve years old, was a kind, considerate friend, who taught her to read and spell. Thirdly, she was placed in favorable circumstances after she came to the North; having frequent intercourse with intelligent persons, who felt a friendly interest in her welfare, and were disposed to give her opportunities for self-improvement.[6]

I am well aware that many will accuse me of indecorum for presenting these pages to the public; for the experiences of this intelligent and much-injured woman belong to a class which some call delicate subjects, and others indelicate. This peculiar phase of Slavery has generally been kept veiled; but the public ought to be made acquainted with its monstrous features, and I willingly take the responsibility of presenting them with the veil withdrawn. I do this for the sake of my sisters in bondage, who are suffering wrongs so foul, that our ears are too delicate to listen to them. I do it with the hope of arousing conscientious and reflecting women at the North to a sense of their duty in the exertion of moral influence on the question of Slavery, on all possible occasions. I do it with the hope that every man who reads this narrative will swear solemnly before God that, so far as he has power to prevent it, no fugitive from Slavery shall ever be sent back to suffer in that loathsome den of corruption and cruelty.[7]

L. Maria Child.

[6]Contemporary white readers typically charged that a slave could not possibly be literate enough to write a narrative. Here Child anticipates this attack. Such charges against the authenticity of slave narratives extended well into the twentieth century.

[7]Child ends her introduction by alluding to the sexual abuse and exploitation that Jacobs describes in her narrative. Her euphemism for the abuse—"This peculiar phase of Slavery"—plays off the abolitionists' term for slavery as the "peculiar institution." The sexual degradation of slave women was a central theme in antislavery writing, particularly by women. However, Victorian notions of propriety made it difficult to discuss sexual abuse openly, and the idealization of women (i.e., white women) alongside the denigration of black women's sexuality made black women who were abused understandably reluctant to reveal their stories. Child's language in her final sentence evokes images of sin and hell, typical of abolitionist literature, drawing upon Protestant beliefs.

I. CHILDHOOD

I was born a slave; but I never knew it till six years of happy childhood had passed away.[8] My father was a carpenter, and considered so intelligent and skilful in his trade, that, when buildings out of the common line were to be erected, he was sent for from long distances, to be head workman. On condition of paying his mistress two hundred dollars a year, and supporting himself, he was allowed to work at his trade, and manage his own affairs. His strongest wish was to purchase his children; but, though he several times offered his hard earnings for that purpose, he never succeeded. In complexion my parents were a light shade of brownish yellow, and were termed mulattoes.[9] They lived together in a comfortable home; and, though we were all slaves, I was so fondly shielded that I never dreamed I was a piece of merchandise, trusted to them for safe keeping, and liable to be demanded of them at any moment. I had one brother, William, who was two years younger

[8]Evidence suggests that Jacobs was born in 1813. This opening sentence encapsulates the experience of her early childhood in slavery, with its emphasis on what the young Harriet did not know about herself, including the exact date of her birth and what it meant to be enslaved. The denial of basic self-knowledge is a conventional theme in slave narratives, illustrating the dehumanization of enslaved people. Jacobs scholar Jean Fagan Yellin discusses how her discovery of Jacobs's letters led her to establish the biographical facts of Jacobs's life and the authenticity of her narrative in "Written by Herself: Harriet Jacobs's Slave Narrative," *American Literature* 53 (November 1981): 479–86. Yellin published many of her findings in her notes to her edition of *Incidents in the Life of a Slave Girl, Written by Herself* (Cambridge, Mass.: Harvard University Press, 1987). She has also written the most authoritative biography to date, *Harriet Jacobs: A Life* (New York: Basic Civitas Books, 2004).

[9]Jacobs's father was Elijah (17?–1826), the son of a slave woman, Athena, and Henry Jacobs, an illiterate white farmer who owned no slaves and lived with his family near the plantation of Dr. Andrew Knox in Pasquotank County, North Carolina, where Athena was a slave. Though illiterate, Elijah became a skilled carpenter and worked on houses in nearby Edenton, where he met Jacobs's mother, Delilah Horniblow. Knox permitted Elijah to remain in Edenton with Delilah and their two children. After Elijah became the property of Knox's daughter, her husband, James Coffield, ordered Elijah to move out to his plantation, Green Hall. By then, Elijah, a widower, was remarried to a free woman and had an infant son, Elijah Jr. (b. 1824), a fact that neither Harriet nor John mentions in their narratives. Harriet and John remembered their father as proud and independent, and although they attribute his death to a depression triggered by the separation from his family, they suggest that years of suppressed rage about being unable to act the part of father and husband to his family was a contributing factor. From Elijah, Harriet and John learned valuable lessons of self-respect and a thirst for liberty. For John's memoir, see John S. Jacobs, *A True Tale of Slavery* (1861), reprinted as Document 11. Less is known about Harriet's mother, Delilah (ca. 1797–1819), whom Jacobs idealizes throughout her narrative as a model of virtuous womanhood, against which she measures her own failures to remain chaste, a value of nineteenth-century domestic culture. Delilah's death when Jacobs was six removed a first layer of protection from the harsh realities of slavery.

than myself — a bright, affectionate child.[10] I had also a great treasure in my maternal grandmother, who was a remarkable woman in many respects. She was the daughter of a planter in South Carolina, who, at his death, left her mother and his three children free, with money to go to St. Augustine, where they had relatives. It was during the Revolutionary War; and they were captured on their passage, carried back, and sold to different purchasers. Such was the story my grandmother used to tell me; but I do not remember all the particulars. She was a little girl when she was captured and sold to the keeper of a large hotel.[11]

[10]"William" is John S. Jacobs (1815–1873), whose close bond with Harriet was a source of strength and inspiration to both throughout their lives. As John notes in the first sentence of his narrative, he had "four different owners in eighteen years" (*A True Tale of Slavery*, chap. I; see Document 11). Although John writes that his first mistress was Penelope Horniblow, it was actually Margaret Horniblow who owned Delilah and her children and who in 1825 willed John to his second mistress, her mother, Elizabeth Horniblow (his grandmother's mistress). Elizabeth Horniblow loaned John to Dr. James Norcom, her brother-in-law and neighbor, at the same time his sister became a slave in the Norcom household. At age twenty-three, he ran away from his fourth master, Samuel Tredwell Sawyer, the Edenton lawyer who fathered Harriet's children. By the late 1840s, he had become an antislavery activist in a circle that included Frederick Douglass and was lecturing in New England and New York. In 1850, John went to California, which had just been admitted to the Union as a free state, to escape the reach of the newly signed Fugitive Slave Act and also to search for gold. From there he went to Australia. By 1857, he was working as a sailor in Great Britain, where Harriet joined him while trying to find a publisher for her manuscript. Harriet returned to the States, having failed to get her book published in England. One month after her narrative was finally published in the United States, in 1861, John had his *A True Tale of Slavery* serialized in *Leisure Hour*, the journal of Britain's Religious Tract Society. He married an English widow with two children and had a son. In 1873, he returned to Cambridge, Massachusetts, to be near Harriet, but he died soon thereafter. Comparing *Incidents in the Life of a Slave Girl* with *A True Tale of Slavery* reveals interesting differences in perspective, tone, and voice, due partly to temperamental differences between the sister and brother, but also to differences in cultural expectations for feminine and masculine behavior. Throughout her narrative, Harriet describes her struggles against her angry and bitter feelings, as befit ideas about proper womanhood at the time. In contrast, John was culturally freer to express aggression in all forms (although as a black man, expressions of aggression could land him in jail or worse). Focusing on themes of masculine self-reliance, mastery, and Garrisonian abolitionism, John may have modeled his narrative on Douglass's influential *Narrative of the Life of Frederick Douglass, an American Slave, Written by Himself* (1845).

[11]Jacobs's grandmother, Molly Horniblow (d. 1853), was the most important maternal figure in Jacobs's life. Symbolically, Molly was associated with warmth, sustenance, protection, goodness, and faith. Literally, her watchful presence shamed Norcom into a modicum of self-restraint, while her supplements to Jacobs's meager diet and wardrobe kept Jacobs from starving and freezing. And, of course, it was the crawl space over her grandmother's kitchen where Jacobs hid from Norcom for almost seven years. Molly was not entirely benign, however; her rejection of Jacobs when she took a white lover was devastating to the adolescent mother-to-be. Molly was ultimately a conservative, devotional voice in Jacobs's life, and her advice to accept God's will acted as a brake on the more radical spirit of defiance that Jacobs and her brother inherited from their father.

I have often heard her tell how hard she fared during childhood. But as she grew older she evinced so much intelligence, and was so faithful, that her master and mistress could not help seeing it was for their interest to take care of such a valuable piece of property. She became an indispensable personage in the household, officiating in all capacities, from cook and wet nurse to seamstress. She was much praised for her cooking; and her nice crackers became so famous in the neighborhood that many people were desirous of obtaining them. In consequence of numerous requests of this kind, she asked permission of her mistress to bake crackers at night, after all the household work was done; and she obtained leave to do it, provided she would clothe herself and her children from the profits. Upon these terms, after working hard all day for her mistress, she began her midnight bakings, assisted by her two oldest children.[12] The business proved profitable; and each year she laid by a little, which was saved for a fund to purchase her children. Her master died, and the property was divided among his heirs.[13] The widow had her dower in the hotel, which she continued to keep open. My grandmother remained in her service as a slave; but her children were divided among her master's children. As she had five, Benjamin, the youngest one,[14] was sold, in order that each heir might have an equal portion of dollars and cents. There was so little difference in our ages that he seemed more like my brother than my uncle. He was a bright, handsome lad, nearly white; for he inherited the complexion my grandmother had derived from Anglo-Saxon ancestors. Though only ten years old, seven hundred and twenty dollars[15] were paid for him. His sale was a terrible blow to my grandmother; but she was naturally hopeful, and she went to work with renewed energy, trusting in time to be able to purchase some of her children. She had laid up three hundred dollars, which her mistress one day begged as a loan, promising to pay her soon. The reader probably knows that no promise or writing given to a slave is legally binding; for, according to Southern laws, a slave, being property, can hold no property. When my grandmother lent

[12]Two of Molly's three daughters probably helped her. Molly kept her baking business for the rest of her life.

[13]John Horniblow's widow was his third wife, Elizabeth Pritchard Horniblow (d. 1827). There were two divisions of the property, and under the second, effected in 1813, his slaves were grouped into four equal shares, except for Molly's youngest son, Joseph, whom Norcom four years later petitioned, on behalf of his wife, Mary Horniblow Norcom, to have sold (Jacobs, *Incidents*, ed. Yellin, 261n).

[14]Harriet's uncle Joseph (b. 1808).

[15]Approximately $14,000 in 2018, or about nineteen times the dollar amount in 1818. For historical currency conversion, see www.measuringworth.com/guide/html.

her hard earnings to her mistress, she trusted solely to her honor.[16] The honor of a slaveholder to a slave!

To this good grandmother I was indebted for many comforts. My brother Willie and I often received portions of the crackers, cakes, and preserves, she made to sell; and after we ceased to be children we were indebted to her for many more important services.

Such were the unusually fortunate circumstances of my early childhood. When I was six years old, my mother died; and then, for the first time, I learned, by the talk around me, that I was a slave. My mother's mistress was the daughter of my grandmother's mistress. She was the foster sister of my mother; they were both nourished at my grandmother's breast. In fact, my mother had been weaned at three months old, that the babe of the mistress might obtain sufficient food. They played together as children; and, when they became women, my mother was a most faithful servant to her whiter foster sister.[17] On her death-bed her mistress promised that her children should never suffer for any thing; and during her lifetime she kept her word. They all spoke kindly of my dead mother, who had been a slave merely in name, but in nature was noble and womanly. I grieved for her, and my young mind was troubled with the thought who would now take care of me and my little brother. I was told that my home was now to be with her mistress; and I found it a happy one. No toilsome or disagreeable duties were imposed upon me. My mistress was so kind to me that I was always glad to do her bidding, and proud to labor for her as much as my young years

[16]"Honor" was a quintessentially nineteenth-century Southern value upon which elaborate codes of behavior were based. Jacobs's sarcasm is therefore quite pointed.

[17]Using slave women as wet nurses was common, so it was not unusual that Molly weaned her own baby girl Delilah to nurse Margaret Horniblow, her mistress's infant. Jacobs's emphasis on "foster" sisters calls early attention to the sexual exploitation of slave women. The allusion to an interracial "sisterhood" would also have resonated with her Northern white audience, which would have been familiar with popular antislavery depictions of a kneeling slave woman, arms upraised, above the legend "Am I Not a Woman and a Sister?" For a discussion of this image and its significance, see Jean Fagan Yellin, *Women and Sisters: The Antislavery Feminists in American Culture* (New Haven, Conn.: Yale University Press, 1989). For the experiences of slave women, see Dorothy Sterling, ed., *We Are Your Sisters: Black Women in the Nineteenth Century* (New York: W. W. Norton, 1984), and Deborah Gray White, *Ar'n't I a Woman? Female Slaves in the Plantation South* (New York: W. W. Norton, 1985). Jennifer Fleischner, *Mrs. Lincoln and Mrs. Keckly: The Remarkable Story of the Friendship between a First Lady and a Former Slave* (New York: Broadway Books, 2003), draws an in-depth portrait of the contrasting childhoods of mistresses and slave girls in the antebellum South. Elizabeth Fox-Genovese discusses relationships between mistresses and slave women in *Within the Plantation Household: Black and White Women in the Old South* (Chapel Hill: University of North Carolina Press, 1988). For more on the plantation mistress, see Catherine Clinton, *The Plantation Mistress* (New York: Pantheon, 1984).

would permit. I would sit by her side for hours, sewing diligently, with a heart as free from care as that of any free-born white child. When she thought I was tired, she would send me out to run and jump; and away I bounded, to gather berries or flowers to decorate her room. Those were happy days — too happy to last. The slave child had no thought for the morrow; but there came that blight, which too surely waits on every human being born to be a chattel.

When I was nearly twelve years old, my kind mistress sickened and died. As I saw the cheek grow paler, and the eye more glassy, how earnestly I prayed in my heart that she might live! I loved her; for she had been almost like a mother to me. My prayers were not answered. She died, and they buried her in the little churchyard, where, day after day, my tears fell upon her grave.

I was sent to spend a week with my grandmother. I was now old enough to begin to think of the future; and again and again I asked myself what they would do with me. I felt sure I should never find another mistress so kind as the one who was gone. She had promised my dying mother that her children should never suffer for any thing; and when I remembered that, and recalled her many proofs of attachment to me, I could not help having some hopes that she had left me free. My friends were almost certain it would be so. They thought she would be sure to do it, on account of my mother's love and faithful service. But, alas! we all know that the memory of a faithful slave does not avail much to save her children from the auction block.

After a brief period of suspense, the will of my mistress was read, and we learned that she had bequeathed me to her sister's daughter, a child of five years old.[18] So vanished our hopes. My mistress had taught me the precepts of God's Word: "Thou shalt love thy neighbor as thyself." "Whatsoever ye would that men should do unto you, do ye even so unto them."[19] But I was her slave, and I suppose she did not recognize me as her neighbor. I would give much to blot out from my memory that one great wrong. As a child, I loved my mistress; and, looking back on the happy days I spent with her, I try to think with less bitterness of this act of injustice. While I was with her, she taught me to read and spell; and for this privilege, which so rarely falls to the lot of a slave, I bless her memory.

[18]An unsigned deathbed codicil to Margaret Horniblow's will, dated July 3, 1825, left "my negro girl Harriet" and "my bureau & work table & their contents" to her three-year-old niece, Mary Matilda Norcom. Mary's father, Dr. James Norcom, and a Henry Flury witnessed the writing of the codicil (Yellin, *Harriet Jacobs*, 14–15).

[19]The biblical quotations are from Mark 12:31 and Matthew 7:12.

She possessed but few slaves; and at her death those were all distributed among her relatives. Five of them were my grandmother's children, and had shared the same milk that nourished her mother's children. Notwithstanding my grandmother's long and faithful service to her owners, not one of her children escaped the auction block. These God-breathing machines are no more, in the sight of their masters, than the cotton they plant, or the horses they tend.[20]

II. THE NEW MASTER AND MISTRESS

Dr. Flint, a physician in the neighborhood,[21] had married the sister of my mistress, and I was now the property of their little daughter. It was not without murmuring that I prepared for my new home; and what added to my unhappiness, was the fact that my brother William was purchased by the same family. My father, by his nature, as well as by the habit of transacting business as a skilful mechanic, had more of the feelings of a freeman than is common among slaves. My brother was a spirited boy; and being brought up under such influences, he early detested the name of master and mistress. One day, when his father and his mistress both happened to call him at the same time, he hesitated between the two; being perplexed to know which had the strongest claim upon his obedience. He finally concluded to go to his mistress. When my father reproved him for it, he said, "You both called me, and I didn't know which I ought to go to first."

[20]Images comparing humans and machines were common among Victorian writers who feared the mechanizing tendency of new technology and rising industry. The invention of the cotton gin and the mechanical reaper led to an astonishing boom in cotton production, from two million pounds in 1791 to one billion pounds in 1860. This in turn stimulated the demand for slaves, who in the early nineteenth century were still being imported into the United States in large numbers, although increasing birthrates also added greatly to the slave supply. For a classic study of slavery, see John Hope Franklin Jr. and Alfred A. Moss Jr., *From Slavery to Freedom: A History of African Americans*, 8th ed. (New York: Knopf, 2000).

[21]Dr. James Norcom (1778–1850) was born in Chowan County, North Carolina, and graduated from the Medical School of the University of Pennsylvania in 1797. In 1810, he married Mary Matilda Horniblow (1794–1868), two years after divorcing his first wife, Mary Custis, whom he charged with opium addiction, alcoholism, domestic mismanagement, and bearing a stillborn child. He and Mary Matilda had a daughter, also named Mary Matilda (b. 1822). Some undated musings written by Norcom illuminate his character as Jacobs's sexual persecutor: "In the prime & vigour, & in the Zenith of my day, I never intently sought the favour of a woman that I did not obtain it. . . . But awful has been the reverse when the Scene has changed: when deceit dissim[ulation], & falsehood have taken the place of truth & Sincerity. . . . Then it is that you are made our most terrible tormentors & become demons incarnate" (Yellin, *Harriet Jacobs*, 16–17).

"You are *my* child," replied our father, "and when I call you, you should come immediately, if you have to pass through fire and water."

Poor Willie! He was now to learn his first lesson of obedience to a master. Grandmother tried to cheer us with hopeful words, and they found an echo in the credulous hearts of youth.

When we entered our new home we encountered cold looks, cold words, and cold treatment. We were glad when the night came. On my narrow bed I moaned and wept, I felt so desolate and alone.

I had been there nearly a year, when a dear little friend of mine was buried. I heard her mother sob, as the clods fell on the coffin of her only child, and I turned away from the grave, feeling thankful that I still had something left to love. I met my grandmother, who said, "Come with me, Linda"; and from her tone I knew that something sad had happened. She led me apart from the people, and then said, "My child, your father is dead."[22] Dead! How could I believe it? He had died so suddenly I had not even heard that he was sick. I went home with my grandmother. My heart rebelled against God, who had taken from me mother, father, mistress, and friend. The good grandmother tried to comfort me. "Who knows the ways of God?" said she. "Perhaps they have been kindly taken from the evil days to come." Years afterwards I often thought of this. She promised to be a mother to her grandchildren, so far as she might be permitted to do so; and strengthened by her love, I returned to my master's. I thought I should be allowed to go to my father's house the next morning; but I was ordered to go for flowers, that my mistress's house might be decorated for an evening party. I spent the day gathering flowers and weaving them into festoons, while the dead body of my father was lying within a mile of me. What cared my owners for that? he was merely a piece of property. Moreover, they thought he had spoiled his children, by teaching them to feel that they were human beings. This was blasphemous doctrine for a slave to teach; presumptuous in him, and dangerous to the masters.

The next day I followed his remains to a humble grave beside that of my dear mother. There were those who knew my father's worth, and respected his memory.

My home now seemed more dreary than ever. The laugh of the little slave-children sounded harsh and cruel. It was selfish to feel so about the joy of others. My brother moved about with a very grave face. I tried to comfort him, by saying, "Take courage, Willie; brighter days will come by and by."

[22]Elijah died in 1826.

"You don't know any thing about it, Linda," he replied. "We shall have to stay here all our days; we shall never be free."

I argued that we were growing older and stronger, and that perhaps we might, before long, be allowed to hire our own time, and then we could earn money to buy our freedom.[23] William declared this was much easier to say than to do; moreover, he did not intend to buy his freedom. We held daily controversies upon this subject.

Little attention was paid to the slaves' meals in Dr. Flint's house. If they could catch a bit of food while it was going, well and good. I gave myself no trouble on that score, for on my various errands I passed my grandmother's house, where there was always something to spare for me. I was frequently threatened with punishment if I stopped there; and my grandmother, to avoid detaining me, often stood at the gate with something for my breakfast or dinner. I was indebted to *her* for all my comforts, spiritual or temporal. It was *her* labor that supplied my scanty wardrobe. I have a vivid recollection of the linsey-woolsey dress[24] given me every winter by Mrs. Flint. How I hated it! It was one of the badges of slavery.

While my grandmother was thus helping to support me from her hard earnings, the three hundred dollars she had lent her mistress were never repaid. When her mistress died, her son-in-law, Dr. Flint, was appointed executor. When grandmother applied to him for payment, he said the estate was insolvent, and the law prohibited payment. It did not, however, prohibit him from retaining the silver candelabra, which had been purchased with that money. I presume they will be handed down in the family, from generation to generation.

My grandmother's mistress had always promised her that, at her death, she should be free; and it was said that in her will she made good the promise. But when the estate was settled, Dr. Flint told the faithful old servant that, under existing circumstances, it was necessary she should be sold.

On the appointed day, the customary advertisement was posted up, proclaiming that there would be a "public sale of negroes, horses, &c." Dr. Flint called to tell my grandmother that he was unwilling to wound her feelings by putting her up at auction, and that he would

[23]The practice of hiring out slaves whose wages went to their owners was a way to capitalize on the labor of skilled slaves, especially in cities or towns. Here Jacobs writes about hiring her own time, like her grandmother, whose earnings from her bakery business allowed her to buy her own and her oldest son Mark Ramsey's freedom (see note 25).

[24]Linsey-woolsey was a coarse, cheap fabric made of linen or cotton fibers mixed with wool. Slaveholders did not wear clothing made of this material.

prefer to dispose of her at private sale. My grandmother saw through his hypocrisy; she understood very well that he was ashamed of the job. She was a very spirited woman, and if he was base enough to sell her, when her mistress intended she should be free, she was determined the public should know it. She had for a long time supplied many families with crackers and preserves; consequently, "Aunt Marthy," as she was called, was generally known, and every body who knew her respected her intelligence and good character. Her long and faithful service in the family was also well known, and the intention of her mistress to leave her free. When the day of sale came, she took her place among the chattels, and at the first call she sprang upon the auction-block. Many voices called out, "Shame! Shame! Who is going to sell *you*, aunt Marthy? Don't stand there! That is no place for *you*." Without saying a word, she quietly awaited her fate. No one bid for her. At last, a feeble voice said, "Fifty dollars." It came from a maiden lady, seventy years old, the sister of my grandmother's deceased mistress.[25] She had lived forty years under the same roof with my grandmother; she knew how faithfully she had served her owners, and how cruelly she had been defrauded of her rights; and she resolved to protect her. The auctioneer waited for a higher bid; but her wishes were respected; no one bid above her. She could neither read nor write; and when the bill of sale was made out, she signed it with a cross. But what consequence was that, when she had a big heart overflowing with human kindness? She gave the old servant her freedom.

At that time, my grandmother was just fifty years old. Laborious years had passed since then; and now my brother and I were slaves to the man who had defrauded her of her money, and tried to defraud her of her freedom. One of my mother's sisters, called Aunt Nancy, was also a slave in his family.[26] She was a kind, good aunt to me; and supplied the place of both housekeeper and waiting-maid to her mistress. She was, in fact, at the beginning and end of every thing.

Mrs. Flint, like many southern women, was totally deficient in energy. She had not strength to superintend her household affairs; but her nerves were so strong, that she could sit in her easy chair and see

[25]Hannah Pritchard (d. 1838) bought Molly for $52.25 and Mark for $406, using Molly's money. According to Yellin, Molly had made arrangements before the auction with Pritchard and a local lawyer, Alfred M. Gatlin, for the sale. Later that spring, on April 10, 1828, Gatlin helped Pritchard successfully petition the superior court to emancipate Molly (Yellin, *Harriet Jacobs*, 21–22). Norcom bought John Jacobs at the same sale. Compare Harriet's account with John's in *A True Tale of Slavery*, chap. II (Document 11).

[26]Aunt Betty (ca. 1794–1841).

a woman whipped, till the blood trickled from every stroke of the lash. She was a member of the church; but partaking of the Lord's supper did not seem to put her in a Christian frame of mind. If dinner was not served at the exact time on that particular Sunday, she would station herself in the kitchen, and wait till it was dished, and then spit in all the kettles and pans that had been used for cooking. She did this to prevent the cook and her children from eking out their meagre fare with the remains of the gravy and other scrapings. The slaves could get nothing to eat except what she chose to give them. Provisions were weighed out by the pound and ounce, three times a day. I can assure you she gave them no chance to eat wheat bread from her flour barrel. She knew how many biscuits a quart of flour would make, and exactly what size they ought to be.

Dr. Flint was an epicure. The cook never sent a dinner to his table without fear and trembling; for if there happened to be a dish not to his liking, he would either order her to be whipped, or compel her to eat every mouthful of it in his presence. The poor, hungry creature might not have objected to eating it; but she did object to having her master cram it down her throat till she choked.

They had a pet dog, that was a nuisance in the house. The cook was ordered to make some Indian mush[27] for him. He refused to eat, and when his head was held over it, the froth flowed from his mouth into the basin. He died a few minutes after. When Dr. Flint came in, he said the mush had not been well cooked, and that was the reason the animal would not eat it. He sent for the cook, and compelled her to eat it. He thought that the woman's stomach was stronger than the dog's; but her sufferings afterwards proved that he was mistaken. This poor woman endured many cruelties from her master and mistress; sometimes she was locked up, away from her nursing baby, for a whole day and night.

When I had been in the family a few weeks, one of the plantation slaves was brought to town, by order of his master. It was near night when he arrived, and Dr. Flint ordered him to be taken to the work house, and tied up to the joist, so that his feet would just escape the ground. In that situation he was to wait till the doctor had taken his tea. I shall never forget that night. Never before, in my life, had I heard hundreds of blows fall, in succession, on a human being. His piteous groans, and his "O, pray don't, massa," rang in my ear for months afterwards. There were many conjectures as to the cause of this terrible punishment. Some said master accused him of stealing corn; others said

[27]Corn porridge.

the slave had quarrelled with his wife, in presence of the overseer, and had accused his master of being the father of her child. They were both black, and the child was very fair.

I went into the work house next morning, and saw the cowhide still wet with blood, and the boards all covered with gore. The poor man lived, and continued to quarrel with his wife. A few months afterwards Dr. Flint handed them both over to a slave-trader. The guilty man put their value into his pocket, and had the satisfaction of knowing that they were out of sight and hearing. When the mother was delivered into the trader's hands, she said, "You *promised* to treat me well." To which he replied, "You have let your tongue run too far; damn you!" She had forgotten that it was a crime for a slave to tell who was the father of her child.

From others than the master persecution also comes in such cases. I once saw a young slave girl dying soon after the birth of a child nearly white. In her agony she cried out, "O Lord, come and take me!" Her mistress stood by, and mocked at her like an incarnate fiend. "You suffer, do you?" she exclaimed. "I am glad of it. You deserve it all, and more too."

The girl's mother said, "The baby is dead, thank God; and I hope my poor child will soon be in heaven, too."

"Heaven!" retorted the mistress. "There is no such place for the like of her and her bastard."

The poor mother turned away, sobbing. Her dying daughter called her, feebly, and as she bent over her, I heard her say, "Don't grieve so, mother; God knows all about it; and he will have mercy upon me."

Her sufferings, afterwards, became so intense, that her mistress felt unable to stay; but when she left the room, the scornful smile was still on her lips. Seven children called her mother. The poor black woman had but the one child, whose eyes she saw closing in death, while she thanked God for taking her away from the greater bitterness of life.

III. THE SLAVES' NEW YEAR'S DAY

Dr. Flint owned a fine residence in town, several farms, and about fifty slaves, besides hiring a number by the year.[28]

[28]Edenton in the eighteenth and early nineteenth centuries was a thriving port town in northeastern North Carolina, sitting on the Chowan River where the river empties into Albemarle Sound. In 1820, 634 whites, 499 slaves, and 67 free blacks lived in Edenton. According to Norcom's 1827 tax statement, his property consisted of 1,770 acres in Chowan County, 7 town lots, and 19 black slaves (Jacobs, *Incidents*, ed. Yellin, 263n). He also owned a farm in Kentucky. In 1829, during the economic downturn throughout the South, he attempted to sell off his property, including his "Medical Establishment" (Yellin, *Harriet Jacobs*, 32).

Hiring-day at the south takes place on the 1st of January. On the 2d, the slaves are expected to go to their new masters. On a farm, they work until the corn and cotton are laid. They then have two holidays. Some masters give them a good dinner under the trees. This over, they work until Christmas eve. If no heavy charges are meantime brought against them, they are given four or five holidays, whichever the master or overseer may think proper. Then comes New Year's eve; and they gather together their little alls, or more properly speaking, their little nothings, and wait anxiously for the dawning of day. At the appointed hour the grounds are thronged with men, women, and children, waiting, like criminals, to hear their doom pronounced. The slave is sure to know who is the most humane, or cruel master, within forty miles of him.

It is easy to find out, on that day, who clothes and feeds his slaves well; for he is surrounded by a crowd, begging, "Please, massa, hire me this year. I will work *very* hard, massa."

If a slave is unwilling to go with his new master, he is whipped, or locked up in jail, until he consents to go, and promises not to run away during the year. Should he chance to change his mind, thinking it justifiable to violate an extorted promise, woe unto him if he is caught! The whip is used till the blood flows at his feet; and his stiffened limbs are put in chains, to be dragged in the field for days and days!

If he lives until the next year, perhaps the same man will hire him again, without even giving him an opportunity of going to the hiring-ground. After those for hire are disposed of, those for sale are called up.

O, you happy free women, contrast *your* New Year's day with that of the poor bond-woman! With you it is a pleasant season, and the light of the day is blessed. Friendly wishes meet you every where, and gifts are showered upon you. Even hearts that have been estranged from you soften at this season, and lips that have been silent echo back, "I wish you a happy New Year." Children bring their little offerings, and raise their rosy lips for a caress. They are your own, and no hand but that of death can take them from you.

But to the slave mother New Year's day comes laden with peculiar sorrows. She sits on her cold cabin floor, watching the children who may all be torn from her the next morning; and often does she wish that she and they might die before the day dawns. She may be an ignorant creature, degraded by the system that has brutalized her from childhood; but she has a mother's instincts, and is capable of feeling a mother's agonies.

On one of these sale days, I saw a mother lead seven children to the auction-block. She knew that *some* of them would be taken from her;

but they took *all*. The children were sold to a slave-trader, and their mother was bought by a man in her own town. Before night her children were all far away. She begged the trader to tell her where he intended to take them; this he refused to do: How *could* he, when he knew he would sell them, one by one, wherever he could command the highest price? I met that mother in the street, and her wild, haggard face lives to-day in my mind. She wrung her hands in anguish, and exclaimed, "Gone! All gone! Why *don't* God kill me?"[29] I had no words wherewith to comfort her. Instances of this kind are of daily, yea, of hourly occurrence.

Slaveholders have a method, peculiar to their institution, of getting rid of *old* slaves, whose lives have been worn out in their service. I knew an old woman, who for seventy years faithfully served her master. She had become almost helpless, from hard labor and disease. Her owners moved to Alabama, and the old black woman was left to be sold to any body who would give twenty dollars for her.

IV. THE SLAVE WHO DARED TO FEEL LIKE A MAN[30]

Two years had passed since I entered Dr. Flint's family, and those years had brought much of the knowledge that comes from experience, though they had afforded little opportunity for any other kinds of knowledge.[31]

My grandmother had, as much as possible, been a mother to her orphan grandchildren. By perseverance and unwearied industry, she was now mistress of a snug little home, surrounded with the necessaries of life.[32] She would have been happy could her children have shared them with her. There remained but three children and two grandchildren, all slaves. Most earnestly did she strive to make us feel that it was the will of God: that He had seen fit to place us under such circumstances; and though it seemed hard, we ought to pray for contentment.

[29]The mother's question echoes the biblical Job's lament. In her narrative, Jacobs alludes frequently to Job's basic problem of why God allows the righteous to suffer.

[30]The denial of manhood to male slaves is a central theme of slave narratives, including John S. Jacobs's *A True Tale of Slavery* (Document 11) and Douglass's *Narrative of the Life of Frederick Douglass, an American Slave, Written by Himself* (1845).

[31]In 1827, Jacobs was fourteen.

[32]Three years later, in 1830, Molly Horniblow bought her home on West King Street for one dollar from Alfred M. Gatlin, the lawyer who two years earlier had helped her buy herself and Mark (Jacobs, *Incidents*, ed. Yellin, 263n). Her home was one block away from Norcom's home in Eden Alley.

It was a beautiful faith, coming from a mother who could not call her children her own. But I, and Benjamin, her youngest boy, condemned it. We reasoned that it was much more the will of God that we should be situated as she was. We longed for a home like hers. There we always found sweet balsam for our troubles.[33] She was so loving, so sympathizing! She always met us with a smile, and listened with patience to all our sorrows. She spoke so hopefully, that unconsciously the clouds gave place to sunshine. There was a grand big oven there, too, that baked bread and nice things for the town, and we knew there was always a choice bit in store for us.

But, alas! even the charms of the old oven failed to reconcile us to our hard lot. Benjamin was now a tall, handsome lad, strongly and gracefully made, and with a spirit too bold and daring for a slave. My brother William, now twelve years old, had the same aversion to the word master that he had when he was an urchin of seven years. I was his confidant. He came to me with all his troubles. I remember one instance in particular. It was on a lovely spring morning, and when I marked the sunlight dancing here and there, its beauty seemed to mock my sadness. For my master, whose restless, craving, vicious nature roved about day and night, seeking whom to devour, had just left me, with stinging, scorching words; words that scathed ear and brain like fire. O, how I despised him! I thought how glad I should be, if some day when he walked the earth, it would open and swallow him up, and disencumber the world of a plague.

When he told me that I was made for his use, made to obey his command in *every* thing; that I was nothing but a slave, whose will must and should surrender to his, never before had my puny arm felt half so strong.

So deeply was I absorbed in painful reflections afterwards, that I neither saw nor heard the entrance of any one, till the voice of William sounded close beside me. "Linda," said he, "what makes you look so sad? I love you. O, Linda, isn't this a bad world? Every body seems so cross and unhappy. I wish I had died when poor father did."

I told him that every body was *not* cross, or unhappy; that those who had pleasant homes, and kind friends, and who were not afraid to love them, were happy. But we, who were slave-children, without father or mother, could not expect to be happy. We must be good; perhaps that would bring us contentment.

[33]"Sweet balsam" was a balm made of resin. The phrase may refer to the healing balm of Gilead mentioned in Jeremiah 8:22, made from an evergreen tree native to Africa and Asia. An African American spiritual opens with the lines "There is a balm in Gilead / to heal the sin sick soul."

"Yes," he said, "I try to be good; but what's the use? They are all the time troubling me." Then he proceeded to relate his afternoon's difficulty with young master Nicholas.[34] It seemed that the brother of master Nicholas had pleased himself with making up stories about William. Master Nicholas said he should be flogged, and he would do it. Whereupon he went to work; but William fought bravely, and the young master, finding he was getting the better of him, undertook to tie his hands behind him. He failed in that likewise. By dint of kicking and fisting, William came out of the skirmish none the worse for a few scratches.

He continued to discourse on his young master's *meanness*; how he whipped the *little* boys, but was a perfect coward when a tussle ensued between him and white boys of his own size. On such occasions he always took to his legs. William had other charges to make against him. One was his rubbing up pennies with quicksilver, and passing them off for quarters of a dollar on an old man who kept a fruit stall. William was often sent to buy fruit, and he earnestly inquired of me what he ought to do under such circumstances. I told him it was certainly wrong to deceive the old man, and that it was his duty to tell him of the impositions practised by his young master. I assured him the old man would not be slow to comprehend the whole, and there the matter would end. William thought it might with the old man, but not with *him*. He said he did not mind the smart of the whip, but he did not like the *idea* of being whipped.[35]

While I advised him to be good and forgiving I was not unconscious of the beam in my own eye.[36] It was the very knowledge of my own shortcomings that urged me to retain, if possible, some sparks of my brother's God-given nature. I had not lived fourteen years in slavery for nothing. I had felt, seen, and heard enough, to read the characters, and question the motives, of those around me. The war of my life had begun; and though one of God's most powerless creatures, I resolved never to be conquered. Alas, for me!

If there was one pure, sunny spot for me, I believed it to be in Benjamin's heart, and in another's, whom I loved with all the ardor of a girl's first love. My owner knew of it, and sought in every way to render me miserable. He did not resort to corporal punishment, but to all the petty, tyrannical ways that human ingenuity could devise.

[34]James Norcom Jr. (b. 1811). His brother was John Norcom.
[35]The idea of being whipped was, for John, a symbol of his powerlessness as a slave.
[36]Reference to Luke 6:42.

I remember the first time I was punished. It was in the month of February. My grandmother had taken my old shoes, and replaced them with a new pair. I needed them; for several inches of snow had fallen, and it still continued to fall. When I walked through Mrs. Flint's room, their creaking grated harshly on her refined nerves. She called me to her, and asked what I had about me that made such a horrid noise. I told her it was my new shoes. "Take them off," said she; "and if you put them on again, I'll throw them into the fire."

I took them off, and my stockings also. She then sent me a long distance, on an errand. As I went through the snow, my bare feet tingled. That night I was very hoarse; and I went to bed thinking the next day would find me sick, perhaps dead. What was my grief on waking to find myself quite well!

I had imagined if I died, or was laid up for some time, that my mistress would feel a twinge of remorse that she had so hated "the little imp," as she styled me. It was my ignorance of that mistress that gave rise to such extravagant imaginings.

Dr. Flint occasionally had high prices offered for me; but he always said, "She don't belong to me. She is my daughter's property, and I have no right to sell her." Good, honest man! My young mistress was still a child, and I could look for no protection from her. I loved her, and she returned my affection. I once heard her father allude to her attachment to me; and his wife promptly replied that it proceeded from fear. This put unpleasant doubts into my mind. Did the child feign what she did not feel? or was her mother jealous of the mite of love she bestowed on me? I concluded it must be the latter. I said to myself, "Surely, little children are true."

One afternoon I sat at my sewing, feeling unusual depression of spirits. My mistress had been accusing me of an offence, of which I assured her I was perfectly innocent; but I saw, by the contemptuous curl of her lip, that she believed I was telling a lie.

I wondered for what wise purpose God was leading me through such thorny paths, and whether still darker days were in store for me.[37] As I sat musing thus, the door opened softly, and William came in. "Well, brother," said I, "what is the matter this time?"

"O Linda, Ben and his master have had a dreadful time!" said he.

My first thought was that Benjamin was killed. "Don't be frightened, Linda," said William; "I will tell you all about it."

[37]Refers generally to the difficulties God lay before her, perhaps as a test, but also may refer to the first parable of Jesus in Mark 4:2–9, 13–20; Matthew 13:3–9, 18–23; and Luke 8:4–8, 11–14.

It appeared that Benjamin's master[38] had sent for him, and he did not immediately obey the summons. When he did, his master was angry, and began to whip him. He resisted. Master and slave fought, and finally the master was thrown. Benjamin had cause to tremble; for he had thrown to the ground his master—one of the richest men in town. I anxiously awaited the result.

That night I stole to my grandmother's house, and Benjamin also stole thither from his master's. My grandmother had gone to spend a day or two with an old friend living in the country.

"I have come," said Benjamin, "to tell you good by. I am going away."

I inquired where.

"To the north," he replied.

I looked at him to see whether he was in earnest. I saw it all in his firm, set mouth. I implored him not to go, but he paid no heed to my words. He said he was no longer a boy, and every day made his yoke more galling. He had raised his hand against his master, and was to be publicly whipped for the offence.[39] I reminded him of the poverty and hardships he must encounter among strangers. I told him he might be caught and brought back; and that was terrible to think of.

He grew vexed, and asked if poverty and hardships with freedom, were not preferable to our treatment in slavery. "Linda," he continued, "we are dogs here; foot-balls, cattle, every thing that's mean. No, I will not stay. Let them bring me back. We don't die but once."

He was right; but it was hard to give him up. "Go," said I, "and break your mother's heart."

I repented of my words ere they were out.

"Linda," said he, speaking as I had not heard him speak that evening, "how *could* you say that? Poor mother! be kind to her, Linda; and you, too, cousin Fanny."

Cousin Fanny was a friend who had lived some years with us.

Farewells were exchanged, and the bright, kind boy, endeared to us by so many acts of love, vanished from our sight.

[38]Joseph's master was Josiah Collins III, who would become one of the three largest slaveholders in North Carolina.

[39]According to Yellin, this was probably a private punishment ordered by Collins. Although several Southern states had laws against mistreating slaves, those who resisted or rebelled were dealt with harshly. In a famous decision in 1829, when North Carolina chief justice Thomas Ruffin ruled that a master could not be charged with battery against a slave, he wrote, "The power of the master must be absolute to render submission to the slave perfect" (Eugene D. Genovese, *Roll, Jordan, Roll: The World the Slaves Made* [New York: Random House, 1974], 35). There was, however, a "natural" check on the master's power to brutalize: A dead slave meant a loss of capital.

It is not necessary to state how he made his escape.[40] Suffice it to say, he was on his way to New York when a violent storm overtook the vessel. The captain said he must put into the nearest port. This alarmed Benjamin, who was aware that he would be advertised in every port near his own town. His embarrassment was noticed by the captain. To port they went. There the advertisement met the captain's eye. Benjamin so exactly answered its description, that the captain laid hold on him, and bound him in chains. The storm passed, and they proceeded to New York. Before reaching that port Benjamin managed to get off his chains and throw them overboard. He escaped from the vessel, but was pursued, captured, and carried back to his master.

When my grandmother returned home and found her youngest child had fled, great was her sorrow; but, with characteristic piety, she said, "God's will be done."[41] Each morning, she inquired if any news had been heard from her boy. Yes, news *was* heard. The master was rejoicing over a letter, announcing the capture of his human chattel.

That day seems but as yesterday, so well do I remember it. I saw him led through the streets in chains, to jail. His face was ghastly pale, yet full of determination. He had begged one of the sailors to go to his mother's house and ask her not to meet him. He said the sight of her distress would take from him all self-control. She yearned to see him, and she went; but she screened herself in the crowd, that it might be as her child had said.

We were not allowed to visit him; but we had known the jailer for years, and he was a kind-hearted man.[42] At midnight he opened the jail door for my grandmother and myself to enter, in disguise. When we entered the cell not a sound broke the stillness. "Benjamin, Benjamin!" whispered my grandmother. No answer. "Benjamin!" she again faltered. There was a jingle of chains. The moon had just risen, and cast an uncertain light through the bars of the window. We knelt down and took Benjamin's cold hands in ours. We did not speak. Sobs were heard, and Benjamin's lips were unsealed; for his mother was weeping on his neck. How vividly does memory bring back that sad night! Mother and son talked together. He asked her pardon for the suffering he had caused her. She said she had nothing to forgive; she could not blame his desire

[40]Slave narrators commonly refused to reveal how they or other slaves escaped in order to protect the fugitives and also to make it possible for a particular escape method to be used again.

[41]The Lord's Prayer from Matthew 6:9–13. Collins's lawyer, Joseph B. Skinner, had recognized Joseph in New York City and had him captured and returned to Edenton.

[42]George Lamb was the jailer. See also John Jacobs's *A True Tale of Slavery*, chap. II (Document 11).

for freedom. He told her that when he was captured, he broke away, and was about casting himself into the river, when thoughts of *her* came over him, and he desisted. She asked if he did not also think of God. I fancied I saw his face grow fierce in the moonlight. He answered, "No, I did not think of him. When a man is hunted like a wild beast he forgets there is a God, a heaven. He forgets every thing in his struggle to get beyond the reach of the bloodhounds."

"Don't talk so, Benjamin," said she. "Put your trust in God. Be humble, my child, and your master will forgive you."

"Forgive me for *what*, mother? For not letting him treat me like a dog? No! I will never humble myself to him. I have worked for him for nothing all my life, and I am repaid with stripes and imprisonment. Here I will stay till I die, or till he sells me."[43]

The poor mother shuddered at his words. I think he felt it; for when he next spoke, his voice was calmer. "Don't fret about me, mother. I ain't worth it," said he. "I wish I had some of your goodness. You bear every thing patiently, just as though you thought it was all right. I wish I could."

She told him she had not always been so; once, she was like him; but when sore troubles came upon her, and she had no arm to lean upon, she learned to call on God, and he lightened her burdens. She besought him to do likewise.

We overstaid our time, and were obliged to hurry from the jail.

Benjamin had been imprisoned three weeks, when my grandmother went to intercede for him with his master. He was immovable. He said Benjamin should serve as an example to the rest of his slaves; he should be kept in jail till he was subdued, or be sold if he got but one dollar for him. However, he afterwards relented in some degree. The chains were taken off, and we were allowed to visit him.

As his food was of the coarsest kind, we carried him as often as possible a warm supper, accompanied with some little luxury for the jailer.

Three months elapsed, and there was no prospect of release or of a purchaser. One day he was heard to sing and laugh. This piece of indecorum was told to his master, and the overseer was ordered to rechain him. He was now confined in an apartment with other prisoners, who were covered with filthy rags. Benjamin was chained near them, and was soon covered with vermin. He worked at his chains till he succeeded in getting out of them. He passed them through the bars of

[43]Molly's resignation and Joseph's defiance echo Jacobs's own internal conflict. Jacobs portrays her uncle, father, and brother as models of defiance, in contrast to her portraits of a more cooperative grandmother and mother.

the window, with a request that they should be taken to his master, and he should be informed that he was covered with vermin.

This audacity was punished with heavier chains, and prohibition of our visits.

My grandmother continued to send him fresh changes of clothes. The old ones were burned up. The last night we saw him in jail his mother still begged him to send for his master, and beg his pardon. Neither persuasion nor argument could turn him from his purpose. He calmly answered, "I am waiting his time."

Those chains were mournful to hear.

Another three months passed, and Benjamin left his prison walls. We that loved him waited to bid him a long and last farewell. A slave trader had bought him. You remember, I told you what price he brought when ten years of age. Now he was more than twenty years old, and sold for three hundred dollars. The master had been blind to his own interest. Long confinement had made his face too pale, his form too thin; moreover, the trader had heard something of his character, and it did not strike him as suitable for a slave. He said he would give any price if the handsome lad was a girl. We thanked God that he was not.[44]

Could you have seen that mother clinging to her child, when they fastened the irons upon his wrists; could you have heard her heartrending groans, and seen her bloodshot eyes wander wildly from face to face, vainly pleading for mercy; could you have witnessed that scene as I saw it, you would exclaim, *Slavery is damnable!*[45]

Benjamin, her youngest, her pet, was forever gone! She could not realize it. She had an interview with the trader for the purpose of ascertaining if Benjamin could be purchased. She was told it was impossible, as he had given bonds not to sell him till he was out of the state. He promised that he would not sell him till he reached New Orleans.

With a strong arm and unvaried trust, my grandmother began her work of love. Benjamin must be free. If she succeeded, she knew they would still be separated; but the sacrifice was not too great. Day and

[44]At age ten, Joseph had been valued at $720. Light-skinned slave women were highly valued for what was called the "fancy trade," where they were sold exclusively for use as prostitutes or concubines. New Orleans was the center of the trade, but Charleston, South Carolina; St. Louis, Missouri; and Lexington, Kentucky, also had flourishing "fancy trades" (White, *Ar'n't I a Woman?*, 37).

[45]On February 25, 1837, in response to proslavery speeches in the Senate maintaining that slavery was a "positive good," Frederick Douglass published an editorial in the *New York Plaindealer* titled "The Blessings of Slavery," in which he wrote, "Slavery is an evil, a deep, detestable, damnable evil." A good online resource for Douglass's writings is http://douglassarchives.org.

night she labored. The trader's price would treble that he gave; but she was not discouraged.

She employed a lawyer to write to a gentleman, whom she knew, in New Orleans. She begged him to interest himself for Benjamin, and he willingly favored her request. When he saw Benjamin, and stated his business, he thanked him; but said he preferred to wait a while before making the trader an offer. He knew he had tried to obtain a high price for him, and had invariably failed. This encouraged him to make another effort for freedom. So one morning, long before day, Benjamin was missing. He was riding over the blue billows, bound for Baltimore.

For once his white face did him a kindly service.[46] They had no suspicion that it belonged to a slave; otherwise, the law would have been followed out to the letter, and the *thing* rendered back to slavery. The brightest skies are often overshadowed by the darkest clouds. Benjamin was taken sick, and compelled to remain in Baltimore three weeks. His strength was slow in returning; and his desire to continue his journey seemed to retard his recovery. How could he get strength without air and exercise? He resolved to venture on a short walk. A by-street was selected, where he thought himself secure of not being met by any one that knew him; but a voice called out, "Halloo, Ben, my boy! what are you doing *here*?"

His first impulse was to run; but his legs trembled so that he could not stir. He turned to confront his antagonist, and behold, there stood his old master's next door neighbor! He thought it was all over with him now; but it proved otherwise. That man was a miracle. He possessed a goodly number of slaves, and yet was not quite deaf to that mystic clock, whose ticking is rarely heard in the slaveholder's breast.

"Ben, you are sick," said he. "Why, you look like a ghost. I guess I gave you something of a start. Never mind, Ben, I am not going to touch you. You had a pretty tough time of it, and you may go on your way rejoicing for all me. But I would advise you to get out of this place plaguy quick, for there are several gentlemen here from our town." He described the nearest and safest route to New York, and added, "I shall be glad to tell your mother I have seen you. Good by, Ben."

Benjamin turned away, filled with gratitude, and surprised that the town he hated contained such a gem—a gem worthy of a purer setting.

[46] Based on the evidence, Yellin speculates that Joseph's father may have been a free black barber named Alfred Churton (Yellin, *Harriet Jacobs*, 25).

This gentleman was a Northerner by birth, and had married a southern lady.[47] On his return, he told my grandmother that he had seen her son, and of the service he had rendered him.

Benjamin reached New York safely, and concluded to stop there until he had gained strength enough to proceed further. It happened that my grandmother's only remaining son had sailed for the same city on business for his mistress. Through God's providence, the brothers met. You may be sure it was a happy meeting. "O Phil," exclaimed Benjamin, "I am here at last."[48] Then he told him how near he came to dying, almost in sight of free land, and how he prayed that he might live to get one breath of free air. He said life was worth something now, and it would be hard to die. In the old jail he had not valued it; once, he was tempted to destroy it; but something, he did not know what, had prevented him; perhaps it was fear. He had heard those who profess to be religious declare there was no heaven for self-murderers; and as his life had been pretty hot here, he did not desire a continuation of the same in another world. "If I die now," he exclaimed, "thank God, I shall die a freeman!"

He begged my uncle Phillip not to return south; but stay and work with him, till they earned enough to buy those at home. His brother told him it would kill their mother if he deserted her in her trouble. She had pledged her house, and with difficulty had raised money to buy him. Would he be bought?

"No, never!" he replied. "Do you suppose, Phil, when I have got so far out of their clutches, I will give them one red cent? No! And do you suppose I would turn mother out of her home in her old age? That I would let her pay all those hard-earned dollars for me, and never to see me? For you know she will stay south as long as her other children are slaves. What a good mother! Tell her to buy you, Phil. You have been a comfort to her, and I have been a trouble. And Linda, poor Linda; what'll become of her? Phil, you don't know what a life they lead her. She has told me something about it, and I wish old Flint was dead, or a better man. When I was in jail, he asked her if she didn't want him to ask my master to forgive me, and take me home again. She told him, No; that I didn't want to go back. He got mad, and said we were all alike. I never despised my own master half as much as I do that man. There is many a worse slaveholder than my master; but for all that I would not be his slave."

[47]Pennsylvania-born Daniel McDowell (ca. 1793–1885) had moved to Edenton in 1825 and married Mary Cox Norfleet, who inherited a portion of her family's estate. Later, he bought a lot next to Molly's house (Jacobs, *Incidents*, ed. Yellin, 264n).

[48]Harriet's uncle Mark was working on an Edenton-New York sloop.

While Benjamin was sick, he had parted with nearly all his clothes to pay necessary expenses. But he did not part with a little pin I fastened in his bosom when we parted. It was the most valuable thing I owned, and I thought none more worthy to wear it. He had it still.

His brother furnished him with clothes, and gave him what money he had.

They parted with moistened eyes; and as Benjamin turned away, he said, "Phil, I part with all my kindred." And so it proved. We never heard from him again.

Uncle Phillip came home; and the first words he uttered when he entered the house were, "Mother, Ben is free! I have seen him in New York." She stood looking at him with a bewildered air. "Mother, don't you believe it?" he said, laying his hand softly upon her shoulder. She raised her hands, and exclaimed, "God be praised! Let us thank him." She dropped on her knees, and poured forth her heart in prayer. Then Phillip must sit down and repeat to her every word Benjamin had said. He told her all; only he forbore to mention how sick and pale her darling looked. Why should he distress her when she could do him no good?

The brave old woman still toiled on, hoping to rescue some of her other children. After a while she succeeded in buying Phillip. She paid eight hundred dollars, and came home with the precious document that secured his freedom.[49] The happy mother and son sat together by the old hearthstone that night, telling how proud they were of each other, and how they would prove to the world that they could take care of themselves, as they had long taken care of others. We all concluded by saying, "He that is *willing* to be a slave, let him be a slave."

V. THE TRIALS OF GIRLHOOD

During the first years of my service in Dr. Flint's family, I was accustomed to share some indulgences with the children of my mistress. Though this seemed to me no more than right, I was grateful for it, and tried to merit the kindness by the faithful discharge of my duties. But I now entered on my fifteenth year—a sad epoch in the life of a slave girl. My master began to whisper foul words in my ear. Young as I was, I could not remain ignorant of their import. I tried to treat them

[49]The "eight hundred dollars" may refer to the total of the purchase prices of Molly, Mark, and her house. The "precious document" was a bill of sale. In November 1842, Molly unsuccessfully petitioned the North Carolina legislature for permission to free Mark, but by the time he married the next year, he was free (Yellin, *Harriet Jacobs*, 254).

with indifference or contempt. The master's age, my extreme youth, and the fear that his conduct would be reported to my grandmother, made him bear this treatment for many months. He was a crafty man, and resorted to many means to accomplish his purposes. Sometimes he had stormy, terrific ways, that made his victims tremble; sometimes he assumed a gentleness that he thought must surely subdue. Of the two, I preferred his stormy moods, although they left me trembling. He tried his utmost to corrupt the pure principles my grandmother had instilled. He peopled my young mind with unclean images, such as only a vile monster could think of. I turned from him with disgust and hatred. But he was my master. I was compelled to live under the same roof with him—where I saw a man forty years my senior daily violating the most sacred commandments of nature.[50] He told me I was his property; that I must be subject to his will in all things. My soul revolted against the mean tyranny. But where could I turn for protection? No matter whether the slave girl be as black as ebony or as fair as her mistress. In either case, there is no shadow of law to protect her from insult, from violence, or even from death; all these are inflicted by fiends who bear the shape of men. The mistress, who ought to protect the helpless victim, has no other feelings towards her but those of jealousy and rage.[51] The degradation, the wrongs, the vices, that grow out of slavery, are more than I can describe. They are greater than you would willingly believe. Surely, if you credited one half the truths that are told you concerning the helpless millions suffering in this cruel bondage, you at the north would not help to tighten the yoke. You surely would refuse to do for the master, on your own soil, the mean and cruel work which trained bloodhounds and the lowest class of whites do for him at the south.[52]

Every where the years bring to all enough of sin and sorrow; but in slavery the very dawn of life is darkened by these shadows. Even the

[50]Norcom was actually thirty-five years older than Jacobs.

[51]By law, slave women could not be raped because they were property. By custom, slave women were considered sexually available, in contrast to white women. In Southern culture, male lust was a fact of life, and although it was considered adultery for a Southern husband to have sex with any white woman other than his wife, sex with a black woman was not considered as such. As Jacobs notes, whatever rage the mistress felt about her husband's behavior, she generally took it out on the slave woman and her mixed-race children. For more on this, as well as for a broader discussion of sexuality in the United States, see John D'Emilio and Estelle B. Freedman, *Intimate Matters: A History of Sexuality in America*, 2nd ed. (Chicago: University of Chicago Press, 1998).

[52]In addressing her Northern audience, Jacobs alludes to their complicity with slaveholders under the fugitive slave laws, most pointedly the Fugitive Slave Act of 1850, which required that runaway slaves found in the free states must be returned to their owners.

little child, who is accustomed to wait on her mistress and her children, will learn, before she is twelve years old, why it is that her mistress hates such and such a one among the slaves. Perhaps the child's own mother is among those hated ones. She listens to violent outbreaks of jealous passion, and cannot help understanding what is the cause. She will become prematurely knowing in evil things. Soon she will learn to tremble when she hears her master's footfall. She will be compelled to realize that she is no longer a child. If God has bestowed beauty upon her, it will prove her greatest curse. That which commands admiration in the white woman only hastens the degradation of the female slave. I know that some are too much brutalized by slavery to feel the humiliation of their position; but many slaves feel it most acutely, and shrink from the memory of it. I cannot tell how much I suffered in the presence of these wrongs, nor how I am still pained by the retrospect. My master met me at every turn, reminding me that I belonged to him, and swearing by heaven and earth that he would compel me to submit to him. If I went out for a breath of fresh air, after a day of unwearied toil, his footsteps dogged me. If I knelt by my mother's grave, his dark shadow fell on me even there. The light heart which nature had given me became heavy with sad forebodings. The other slaves in my master's house noticed the change. Many of them pitied me; but none dared to ask the cause. They had no need to inquire. They knew too well the guilty practices under that roof; and they were aware that to speak of them was an offence that never went unpunished.

I longed for some one to confide in. I would have given the world to have laid my head on my grandmother's faithful bosom, and told her all my troubles. But Dr. Flint swore he would kill me, if I was not as silent as the grave. Then, although my grandmother was all in all to me, I feared her as well as loved her. I had been accustomed to look up to her with a respect bordering upon awe. I was very young, and felt shamefaced about telling her such impure things, especially as I knew her to be very strict on such subjects. Moreover, she was a woman of a high spirit. She was usually very quiet in her demeanor; but if her indignation was once roused, it was not very easily quelled. I had been told that she once chased a white gentleman with a loaded pistol, because he insulted one of her daughters. I dreaded the consequences of a violent outbreak; and both pride and fear kept me silent. But though I did not confide in my grandmother, and even evaded her vigilant watchfulness and inquiry, her presence in the neighborhood was some protection to me. Though she had been a slave, Dr. Flint was afraid of her. He dreaded her scorching rebukes. Moreover, she was known and patronized by many people; and he did not wish to have his villainy made public. It was lucky for me that I did not live on a distant plantation, but in a town not so large that the inhabitants were ignorant of each other's affairs. Bad as are the laws and customs in a slaveholding community, the doctor, as a professional man, deemed it prudent to keep up some outward show of decency.

O, what days and nights of fear and sorrow that man caused me! Reader, it is not to awaken sympathy for myself that I am telling you truthfully what I suffered in slavery. I do it to kindle a flame of compassion in your hearts for my sisters who are still in bondage, suffering as I once suffered.

I once saw two beautiful children playing together. One was a fair white child; the other was her slave, and also her sister. When I saw them embracing each other, and heard their joyous laughter, I turned sadly away from the lovely sight. I foresaw the inevitable blight that would fall on the little slave's heart. I knew how soon her laughter would be changed to sighs. The fair child grew up to be a still fairer woman. From childhood to womanhood her pathway was blooming with flowers, and overarched by a sunny sky. Scarcely one day of her life had been clouded when the sun rose on her happy bridal morning.[53]

How had those years dealt with her slave sister, the little playmate of her childhood? She, also, was very beautiful; but the flowers and sunshine of love were not for her. She drank the cup of sin, and shame, and misery, whereof her persecuted race are compelled to drink.[54]

In view of these things, why are ye silent, ye free men and women of the north? Why do your tongues falter in maintenance of the right? Would that I had more ability! But my heart is so full, and my pen is so weak! There are noble men and women who plead for us, striving to help those who cannot help themselves. God bless them! God give them strength and courage to go on! God bless those, every where, who are laboring to advance the cause of humanity!

[53]One of several set pieces in the narrative in which Jacobs contrasts the fate of free white women with enslaved black women. Her emphasis on their entwined yet antithetical lives was fundamental to her appeal to her Northern audience. When she idealizes the white woman's life within the context of the nineteenth-century cult of domesticity, she not only sets up her rhetorical point about the debasement of black women, but she also affirms the sentimental values of the dominant white culture.

[54]"I will take the cup of salvation, and call upon the name of the Lord" (Psalm 116:13).

VI. THE JEALOUS MISTRESS

I would ten thousand times rather that my children should be the half-starved paupers of Ireland than to be the most pampered among the slaves of America.[55] I would rather drudge out my life on a cotton plantation, till the grave opened to give me rest, than to live with an unprincipled master and a jealous mistress. The felon's home in a penitentiary is preferable. He may repent, and turn from the error of his ways, and so find peace; but it is not so with a favorite slave. She is not allowed to have any pride of character. It is deemed a crime in her to wish to be virtuous.

Mrs. Flint possessed the key to her husband's character before I was born.[56] She might have used this knowledge to counsel and to screen the young and the innocent among her slaves; but for them she had no sympathy. They were the objects of her constant suspicion and malevolence. She watched her husband with unceasing vigilance; but he was well practised in means to evade it. What he could not find opportunity to say in words he manifested in signs. He invented more than were ever thought of in a deaf and dumb asylum. I let them pass, as if I did not understand what he meant; and many were the curses and threats bestowed on me for my stupidity. One day he caught me teaching myself to write.[57] He frowned, as if he was not well pleased; but I suppose he came to the conclusion that such an accomplishment might help to advance his favorite scheme. Before long, notes were often slipped into my hand. I would return them, saying, "I can't read them, sir." "Can't you?" he replied; "then I must read them to you." He always finished the reading by asking, "Do you understand?" Sometimes he would complain of the heat of the tea room, and order his supper to be placed on a small table in the piazza. He would seat himself there with a

[55]A potato famine in Ireland from 1845 to 1849 stimulated Irish immigration to the United States, and abolitionists frequently drew a comparison between Southern slaves and poor Irish. This passage resembles one in a letter Jacobs wrote in 1852 to Amy Post (1802–1889), her white abolitionist, feminist friend, when she was considering whether or not to write her narrative (Document 4).

[56]Mary Matilda Horniblow (1794–1868) was sixteen when she married the divorced Dr. Norcom, who was twice her age. The "jealous mistress" is a typical figure in slave women's narratives.

[57]Laws forbidding slaves to learn to read and write existed throughout the South. Even where anti-literacy laws did not exist, educating slaves was frowned on. "If you give a nigger an inch, he will take an ell," Frederick Douglass remembered his master chiding his mistress when he discovered that she was teaching the young Frederick to read. "Learning would spoil the best nigger in the world" (Douglass, *Narrative of the Life of Frederick Douglass*, chap. V). Significantly, reading and writing did enable Jacobs to outwit Norcom while she was in hiding after her escape and even after she fled north.

well-satisfied smile, and tell me to stand by and brush away the flies. He would eat very slowly, pausing between the mouthfuls. These intervals were employed in describing the happiness I was so foolishly throwing away, and in threatening me with the penalty that finally awaited my stubborn disobedience. He boasted much of the forbearance he had exercised towards me, and reminded me that there was a limit to his patience. When I succeeded in avoiding opportunities for him to talk to me at home, I was ordered to come to his office, to do some errand. When there, I was obliged to stand and listen to such language as he saw fit to address to me. Sometimes I so openly expressed my contempt for him that he would become violently enraged, and I wondered why he did not strike me. Circumstanced as he was, he probably thought it was better policy to be forbearing. But the state of things grew worse and worse daily. In desperation I told him that I must and would apply to my grandmother for protection. He threatened me with death, and worse than death, if I made any complaint to her. Strange to say, I did not despair. I was naturally of a buoyant disposition, and always I had a hope of somehow getting out of his clutches. Like many a poor, simple slave before me, I trusted that some threads of joy would yet be woven into my dark destiny.

I had entered my sixteenth year, and every day it became more apparent that my presence was intolerable to Mrs. Flint. Angry words frequently passed between her and her husband. He had never punished me himself, and he would not allow any body else to punish me. In that respect, she was never satisfied; but, in her angry moods, no terms were too vile for her to bestow upon me. Yet I, whom she detested so bitterly, had far more pity for her than he had, whose duty it was to make her life happy. I never wronged her, or wished to wrong her; and one word of kindness from her would have brought me to her feet.

After repeated quarrels between the doctor and his wife, he announced his intention to take his youngest daughter, then four years old,[58] to sleep in his apartment. It was necessary that a servant should sleep in the same room, to be on hand if the child stirred. I was selected for that office, and informed for what purpose that arrangement had been made. By managing to keep within sight of people, as much as possible, during the day time, I had hitherto succeeded in eluding my master, though a razor was often held to my throat to force me to change this line of policy. At night I slept by the side of my great aunt,[59] where I felt safe.

[58]Elizabeth Hannah Norcom (1826–1849).

[59]Elizabeth Horniblow had given Jacobs's aunt Betty to Mrs. Norcom before her marriage.

He was too prudent to come into her room. She was an old woman, and had been in the family many years. Moreover, as a married man, and a professional man, he deemed it necessary to save appearances in some degree. But he resolved to remove the obstacle in the way of his scheme; and he thought he had planned it so that he should evade suspicion. He was well aware how much I prized my refuge by the side of my old aunt, and he determined to dispossess me of it. The first night the doctor had the little child in his room alone. The next morning, I was ordered to take my station as nurse the following night. A kind Providence interposed in my favor. During the day Mrs. Flint heard of this new arrangement, and a storm followed. I rejoiced to hear it rage.

After a while my mistress sent for me to come to her room. Her first question was, "Did you know you were to sleep in the doctor's room?"

"Yes, ma'am."

"Who told you?"

"My master."

"Will you answer truly all the questions I ask?"

"Yes, ma'am."

"Tell me, then, as you hope to be forgiven, are you innocent of what I have accused you?"

"I am."

She handed me a Bible, and said, "Lay your hand on your heart, kiss this holy book, and swear before God that you tell me the truth."

I took the oath she required, and I did it with a clear conscience.

"You have taken God's holy word to testify your innocence," said she. "If you have deceived me, beware! Now take this stool, sit down, look me directly in the face, and tell me all that has passed between your master and you."

I did as she ordered. As I went on with my account her color changed frequently, she wept, and sometimes groaned. She spoke in tones so sad, that I was touched by her grief. The tears came to my eyes; but I was soon convinced that her emotions arose from anger and wounded pride. She felt that her marriage vows were desecrated, her dignity insulted; but she had no compassion for the poor victim of her husband's perfidy. She pitied herself as a martyr; but she was incapable of feeling for the condition of shame and misery in which her unfortunate, helpless slave was placed.

Yet perhaps she had some touch of feeling for me; for when the conference was ended, she spoke kindly, and promised to protect me. I should have been much comforted by this assurance if I could have had confidence in it; but my experiences in slavery had filled me with distrust.

She was not a very refined woman, and had not much control over her passions. I was an object of her jealousy, and, consequently, of her hatred; and I knew I could not expect kindness or confidence from her under the circumstances in which I was placed. I could not blame her. Slaveholders' wives feel as other women would under similar circumstances. The fire of her temper kindled from small sparks, and now the flame became so intense that the doctor was obliged to give up his intended arrangement.

I knew I had ignited the torch, and I expected to suffer for it afterwards; but I felt too thankful to my mistress for the timely aid she rendered me to care much about that. She now took me to sleep in a room adjoining her own. There I was an object of her especial care, though not of her especial comfort, for she spent many a sleepless night to watch over me. Sometimes I woke up, and found her bending over me. At other times she whispered in my ear, as though it was her husband who was speaking to me, and listened to hear what I would answer. If she startled me, on such occasions, she would glide stealthily away; and the next morning she would tell me I had been talking in my sleep, and ask who I was talking to. At last, I began to be fearful for my life. It had been often threatened; and you can imagine, better than I can describe, what an unpleasant sensation it must produce to wake up in the dead of night and find a jealous woman bending over you.[60] Terrible as this experience was, I had fears that it would give place to one more terrible.

My mistress grew weary of her vigils; they did not prove satisfactory. She changed her tactics. She now tried the trick of accusing my master of crime, in my presence, and gave my name as the author of the accusation. To my utter astonishment, he replied, "I don't believe it; but if she did acknowledge it, you tortured her into exposing me." Tortured into exposing him! Truly, Satan had no difficulty in distinguishing the color of his soul! I understood his object in making this false representation. It was to show me that I gained nothing by seeking the protection of my mistress; that the power was still all in his own hands. I pitied Mrs. Flint. She was a second wife, many years the junior of her husband; and the hoary-headed miscreant was enough to try the patience of a wiser and better woman. She was completely foiled, and knew not how to proceed. She would gladly have had me flogged for my supposed false oath; but, as I have already stated, the doctor never allowed any one to whip me.

[60] This gothic tableau resembles one in Charlotte Brontë's *Jane Eyre* (1847), in which Rochester's raving wife, Bertha, hangs over the sleeping Jane. Like Mrs. Norcom, Bertha is associated with fire and burning. Jacobs's narrative ends with another echo of *Jane Eyre* (see page 207).

The old sinner was politic. The application of the lash might have led to remarks that would have exposed him in the eyes of his children and grandchildren.[61] How often did I rejoice that I lived in a town where all the inhabitants knew each other! If I had been on a remote plantation, or lost among the multitude of a crowded city, I should not be a living woman at this day.

The secrets of slavery are concealed like those of the Inquisition.[62] My master was, to my knowledge, the father of eleven slaves. But did the mothers dare to tell who was the father of their children? Did the other slaves dare to allude to it, except in whispers among themselves? No, indeed! They knew too well the terrible consequences.[63]

My grandmother could not avoid seeing things which excited her suspicions. She was uneasy about me, and tried various ways to buy me; but the never-changing answer was always repeated: "Linda does not belong to *me*. She is my daughter's property, and I have no legal right to sell her." The conscientious man! He was too scrupulous to *sell* me; but he had no scruples whatever about committing a much greater wrong against the helpless young girl placed under his guardianship, as his daughter's property. Sometimes my persecutor would ask me whether I would like to be sold. I told him I would rather be sold to any body than to lead such a life as I did. On such occasions he would assume the air of a very injured individual, and reproach me for my ingratitude. "Did I not take you into the house, and make you the companion of my own children?" he would say. "Have I ever treated you like a negro? I have never allowed you to be punished, not even to please your mistress. And this is the recompense I get, you ungrateful girl!" I answered that he had reasons of his own for screening me from punishment, and that the course he pursued made my mistress hate me and persecute me. If I wept, he would say, "Poor child! Don't cry! don't cry! I will make peace for you with your mistress. Only let me arrange matters in my own way. Poor, foolish girl! you don't know what is for your own good. I would cherish you. I would make a lady of you. Now go, and think of all I have promised you."

[61]Yellin thinks that by this time (1828–1829), Norcom had nine living children, six boys and three girls. Another son would be born in 1836 (Jacobs, *Incidents*, ed. Yellin, 266n).

[62]A judicial institution set up by the papacy in 1232 to prosecute heresy. In 1479, the Spanish crown established the notoriously severe Spanish Inquisition.

[63]Slave births were sometimes recorded, along with other inventory, in plantation diaries and commonplace books, but these entries did not give fathers' names. For a reproduction of a birth list from a mistress's commonplace book, see Fleischner, *Mrs. Lincoln and Mrs. Keckly*, illustrations insert.

I did think of it.

Reader, I draw no imaginary pictures of southern homes. I am telling you the plain truth. Yet when victims make their escape from this wild beast of Slavery, northerners consent to act the part of bloodhounds, and hunt the poor fugitive back into his den, "full of dead men's bones, and all uncleanness."[64] Nay, more, they are not only willing, but proud, to give their daughters in marriage to slaveholders. The poor girls have romantic notions of a sunny clime, and of the flowering vines that all the year round shade a happy home. To what disappointments are they destined! The young wife soon learns that the husband in whose hands she has placed her happiness pays no regard to his marriage vows. Children of every shade of complexion play with her own fair babies, and too well she knows that they are born unto him of his own household. Jealousy and hatred enter the flowery home, and it is ravaged of its loveliness.[65]

Southern women often marry a man knowing that he is the father of many little slaves. They do not trouble themselves about it. They regard such children as property, as marketable as the pigs on the plantation; and it is seldom that they do not make them aware of this by passing them into the slave-trader's hands as soon as possible, and thus getting them out of their sight. I am glad to say there are some honorable exceptions.

I have myself known two southern wives who exhorted their husbands to free those slaves towards whom they stood in a "parental relation"; and their request was granted. These husbands blushed before the superior nobleness of their wives' natures. Though they had only counselled them to do that which it was their duty to do, it commanded their respect, and rendered their conduct more exemplary. Concealment was at an end, and confidence took the place of distrust.

Though this bad institution deadens the moral sense, even in white women, to a fearful extent, it is not altogether extinct.[66] I have heard southern ladies say of Mr. Such a one, "He not only thinks it no disgrace to be the father of those little niggers, but he is not ashamed to call himself their master. I declare, such things ought not to be tolerated in any decent society!"

[64]Reference to Matthew 23:27.

[65]This is quite a different portrait of the white woman's life than the ideal one she imagined in the previous chapter, and it seems more realistic. See note 16 on page 20.

[66]An odd comment, though in keeping with the nineteenth-century notion that (white) women were the moral vessels for society and therefore flattering to her audience.

VII. THE LOVER

Why does the slave ever love? Why allow the tendrils of the heart to twine around objects which may at any moment be wrenched away by the hand of violence? When separations come by the hand of death, the pious soul can bow in resignation, and say, "Not my will, but thine be done, O Lord!"[67] But when the ruthless hand of man strikes the blow, regardless of the misery he causes, it is hard to be submissive. I did not reason thus when I was a young girl. Youth will be youth. I loved, and I indulged the hope that the dark clouds around me would turn out a bright lining. I forgot that in the land of my birth the shadows are too dense for light to penetrate. A land

> Where laughter is not mirth; nor thought the mind;
> Nor words a language; nor e'en men mankind.
> Where cries reply to curses, shrieks to blows,
> And each is tortured in his separate hell.[68]

There was in the neighborhood a young colored carpenter; a free born man. We had been well acquainted in childhood, and frequently met together afterwards. We became mutually attached, and he proposed to marry me. I loved him with all the ardor of a young girl's first love. But when I reflected that I was a slave, and that the laws gave no sanction to the marriage of such, my heart sank within me.[69] My lover wanted to buy me; but I knew that Dr. Flint was too wilful and arbitrary a man to consent to that arrangement. From him, I was sure of experiencing all sorts of opposition, and I had nothing to hope from my mistress. She would have been delighted to have got rid of me, but not in that way. It would have relieved her mind of a burden if she could have seen me sold to some distant state, but if I was married near home I should be just as much in her husband's power as I had previously been,—for the husband of a slave has no power to protect her. Moreover, my mistress, like many others, seemed to think that slaves had no right to any family

[67]Reference to Matthew 26:39.

[68]George Gordon, Lord Byron (1788–1824), "The Lament of Tasso," 4.7–10.

[69]By law, Jacobs needed her master's permission to marry a free man. Marriage between slaves was more common and, though also not recognized by law, was encouraged by masters, who not only expected to gain by the increase in slave population promised by marriage but also felt that married slaves with children were more likely to be stable and cooperative. Marriages between slaves of different owners were called "abroad marriages." For the individual slave, having a family, though not protected by law, was a crucial source of psychological and physical support in an otherwise hostile environment. The classic study of the black family in slavery is Herbert G. Gutman, *The Black Family in Slavery and Freedom, 1750–1925* (New York: Random House, 1976).

ties of their own; that they were created merely to wait upon the family of the mistress. I once heard her abuse a young slave girl, who told her that a colored man wanted to make her his wife. "I will have you peeled and pickled,[70] my lady," said she, "if I ever hear you mention that subject again. Do you suppose that I will have you tending *my* children with the children of that nigger?" The girl to whom she said this had a mulatto child, of course not acknowledged by its father. The poor black man who loved her would have been proud to acknowledge his helpless offspring.

Many and anxious were the thoughts I revolved in my mind. I was at a loss what to do. Above all things, I was desirous to spare my lover the insults that had cut so deeply into my own soul. I talked with my grandmother about it, and partly told her my fears. I did not dare to tell her the worst. She had long suspected all was not right, and if I confirmed her suspicions I knew a storm would rise that would prove the overthrow of all my hopes.

This love-dream had been my support through many trials; and I could not bear to run the risk of having it suddenly dissipated. There was a lady in the neighborhood, a particular friend of Dr. Flint's, who often visited the house. I had a great respect for her, and she had always manifested a friendly interest in me. Grandmother thought she would have great influence with the doctor. I went to this lady, and told her my story. I told her I was aware that my lover's being a freeborn man would prove a great objection; but he wanted to buy me; and if Dr. Flint would consent to that arrangement, I felt sure he would be willing to pay any reasonable price. She knew that Mrs. Flint disliked me; therefore, I ventured to suggest that perhaps my mistress would approve of my being sold, as that would rid her of me. The lady listened with kindly sympathy, and promised to do her utmost to promote my wishes. She had an interview with the doctor, and I believe she pleaded my cause earnestly; but it was all to no purpose.

How I dreaded my master now! Every minute I expected to be summoned to his presence; but the day passed, and I heard nothing from him. The next morning, a message was brought to me: "Master wants you in his study." I found the door ajar, and I stood a moment gazing at the hateful man who claimed a right to rule me, body and soul. I entered, and tried to appear calm. I did not want him to know how my heart was bleeding. He looked fixedly at me, with an expression which seemed to say, "I have half a mind to kill you on the spot." At last he broke the silence, and that was a relief to both of us.

[70]To be "peeled and pickled" was to be whipped and washed with brine, or saltwater, to increase the pain.

"So you want to be married, do you?" said he, "and to a free nigger."

"Yes, sir."

"Well, I'll soon convince you whether I am your master, or the nigger fellow you honor so highly. If you *must* have a husband, you may take up with one of my slaves."

What a situation I should be in, as the wife of one of *his* slaves, even if my heart had been interested!

I replied, "Don't you suppose, sir, that a slave can have some preference about marrying? Do you suppose that all men are alike to her?"

"Do you love this nigger?" said he, abruptly.

"Yes, sir."

"How dare you tell me so!" he exclaimed, in great wrath. After a slight pause, he added, "I supposed you thought more of yourself; that you felt above the insults of such puppies."

I replied, "If he is a puppy I am a puppy, for we are both of the negro race. It is right and honorable for us to love each other. The man you call a puppy never insulted me, sir; and he would not love me if he did not believe me to be a virtuous woman."[71]

He sprang upon me like a tiger, and gave me a stunning blow. It was the first time he had ever struck me; and fear did not enable me to control my anger. When I had recovered a little from the effects, I exclaimed, "You have struck me for answering you honestly. How I despise you!"

There was silence for some minutes. Perhaps he was deciding what should be my punishment; or, perhaps, he wanted to give me time to reflect on what I had said, and to whom I had said it. Finally, he asked, "Do you know what you have said?"

"Yes, sir; but your treatment drove me to it."

"Do you know that I have a right to do as I like with you,—that I can kill you, if I please?"

"You have tried to kill me, and I wish you had; but you have no right to do as you like with me."

"Silence!" he exclaimed, in a thundering voice. "By heavens, girl, you forget yourself too far! Are you mad? If you are, I will soon bring you to your senses. Do you think any other master would bear what I have borne from you this morning? Many masters would have killed you on the spot. How would you like to be sent to jail for your insolence?"

[71]In the nineteenth century, "virtue" in unmarried women meant virginity. Jacobs, however, challenges this definition of virtue in her narrative by exposing how slavery sanctioned the sexual persecution of female slaves.

"I know I have been disrespectful, sir," I replied; "but you drove me to it; I couldn't help it. As for the jail, there would be more peace for me there than there is here."

"You deserve to go there," said he, "and to be under such treatment, that you would forget the meaning of the word peace. It would do you good. It would take some of your high notions out of you. But I am not ready to send you there yet, notwithstanding your ingratitude for all my kindness and forbearance. You have been the plague of my life. I have wanted to make you happy, and I have been repaid with the basest ingratitude; but though you have proved yourself incapable of appreciating my kindness, I will be lenient towards you, Linda. I will give you one more chance to redeem your character. If you behave yourself and do as I require, I will forgive you and treat you as I always have done; but if you disobey me, I will punish you as I would the meanest slave on my plantation. Never let me hear that fellow's name mentioned again. If I ever know of your speaking to him, I will cowhide you both; and if I catch him lurking about my premises, I will shoot him as soon as I would a dog. Do you hear what I say? I'll teach you a lesson about marriage and free niggers! Now go, and let this be the last time I have occasion to speak to you on this subject."

Reader, did you ever hate? I hope not. I never did but once; and I trust I never shall again. Somebody has called it "the atmosphere of hell"; and I believe it is so.

For a fortnight[72] the doctor did not speak to me. He thought to mortify me; to make me feel that I had disgraced myself by receiving the honorable addresses of a respectable colored man, in preference to the base proposals of a white man. But though his lips disdained to address me, his eyes were very loquacious. No animal ever watched its prey more narrowly than he watched me. He knew that I could write, though he had failed to make me read his letters; and he was now troubled lest I should exchange letters with another man. After a while he became weary of silence; and I was sorry for it. One morning, as he passed through the hall, to leave the house, he contrived to thrust a note into my hand. I thought I had better read it, and spare myself the vexation of having him read it to me. It expressed regret for the blow he had given me, and reminded me that I myself was wholly to blame for it. He hoped I had become convinced of the injury I was doing myself by incurring his displeasure. He wrote that he had made up his mind to go to Louisiana; that he should take several slaves with him, and intended I should be one of the number. My mistress would remain where she was; therefore

[72]Two weeks.

I should have nothing to fear from that quarter. If I merited kindness from him, he assured me that it would be lavishly bestowed. He begged me to think over the matter, and answer the following day.

The next morning I was called to carry a pair of scissors to his room. I laid them on the table, with the letter beside them. He thought it was my answer, and did not call me back. I went as usual to attend my young mistress to and from school. He met me in the street, and ordered me to stop at his office on my way back.[73] When I entered, he showed me his letter, and asked me why I had not answered it. I replied, "I am your daughter's property, and it is in your power to send me, or take me, wherever you please." He said he was very glad to find me so willing to go, and that we should start early in the autumn. He had a large practice in the town, and I rather thought he had made up the story merely to frighten me. However that might be, I was determined that I would never go to Louisiana with him.

Summer passed away, and early in the autumn Dr. Flint's eldest son[74] was sent to Louisiana to examine the country, with a view to emigrating. That news did not disturb me. I knew very well that I should not be sent with *him*. That I had not been taken to the plantation before this time, was owing to the fact that his son was there. He was jealous of his son; and jealousy of the overseer had kept him from punishing me by sending me into the fields to work. Is it strange that I was not proud of these protectors? As for the overseer, he was a man for whom I had less respect than I had for a bloodhound.

Young Mr. Flint did not bring back a favorable report of Louisiana, and I heard no more of that scheme. Soon after this, my lover met me at the corner of the street, and I stopped to speak to him. Looking up, I saw my master watching us from his window. I hurried home, trembling with fear. I was sent for, immediately, to go to his room. He met me with a blow. "When is mistress to be married?" said he, in a sneering tone. A shower of oaths and imprecations followed. How thankful I was that my lover was a free man! that my tyrant had no power to flog him for speaking to me in the street!

Again and again I revolved in my mind how all this would end. There was no hope that the doctor would consent to sell me on any terms. He had an iron will, and was determined to keep me, and to conquer me.

[73]Norcom's office was on East King Street, less than a block from Jacobs's grandmother's house.

[74]Dr. John Norcom (1802–1856). Norcom, a born-again Christian, would write a letter to Jacobs after her escape to New York urging her to return because, as he wrote, she must be lonely away from her family and friends (Yellin, *Harriet Jacobs*, 90).

My lover was an intelligent and religious man. Even if he could have obtained permission to marry me while I was a slave, the marriage would give him no power to protect me from my master. It would have made him miserable to witness the insults I should have been subjected to. And then, if we had children, I knew they must "follow the condition of the mother."[75] What a terrible blight that would be on the heart of a free, intelligent father! For *his* sake, I felt that I ought not to link his fate with my own unhappy destiny. He was going to Savannah to see about a little property left him by an uncle; and hard as it was to bring my feelings to it, I earnestly entreated him not to come back. I advised him to go to the Free States, where his tongue would not be tied, and where his intelligence would be of more avail to him. He left me, still hoping the day would come when I could be bought. With me the lamp of hope had gone out. The dream of my girlhood was over. I felt lonely and desolate.

Still I was not stripped of all. I still had my good grandmother, and my affectionate brother. When he put his arms round my neck, and looked into my eyes, as if to read there the troubles I dared not tell, I felt that I still had something to love. But even that pleasant emotion was chilled by the reflection that he might be torn from me at any moment, by some sudden freak of my master. If he had known how we loved each other, I think he would have exulted in separating us. We often planned together how we could get to the north. But, as William remarked, such things are easier said than done. My movements were very closely watched, and we had no means of getting any money to defray our expenses. As for grandmother, she was strongly opposed to her children's undertaking any such project. She had not forgotten poor Benjamin's sufferings, and she was afraid that if another child tried to escape, he would have a similar or a worse fate. To me, nothing seemed more dreadful than my present life. I said to myself, "William *must* be free. He shall go to the north, and I will follow him." Many a slave sister has formed the same plans.

VIII. WHAT SLAVES ARE TAUGHT TO THINK OF THE NORTH

Slaveholders pride themselves upon being honorable men; but if you were to hear the enormous lies they tell their slaves, you would have small respect for their veracity. I have spoken plain English. Pardon me. I cannot use a milder term. When they visit the north, and return home, they tell their slaves of the runaways they have seen, and describe them

[75] Children of slave women were by law slaves, regardless of who the father was.

to be in the most deplorable condition. A slaveholder once told me that he had seen a runaway friend of mine in New York, and that she besought him to take her back to her master, for she was literally dying of starvation; that many days she had only one cold potato to eat, and at other times could get nothing at all. He said he refused to take her, because he knew her master would not thank him for bringing such a miserable wretch to his house. He ended by saying to me, "This is the punishment she brought on herself for running away from a kind master."

This whole story was false. I afterwards staid with that friend in New York, and found her in comfortable circumstances. She had never thought of such a thing as wishing to go back to slavery. Many of the slaves believe such stories, and think it is not worth while to exchange slavery for such a hard kind of freedom. It is difficult to persuade such that freedom could make them useful men, and enable them to protect their wives and children. If those heathen in our Christian land had as much teaching as some Hindoos, they would think otherwise.[76] They would know that liberty is more valuable than life. They would begin to understand their own capabilities, and exert themselves to become men and women.

But while the Free States sustain a law which hurls fugitives back into slavery, how can the slaves resolve to become men?[77] There are some who strive to protect wives and daughters from the insults of their masters; but those who have such sentiments have had advantages above the general mass of slaves. They have been partially civilized and Christianized by favorable circumstances. Some are bold enough to *utter* such sentiments to their masters. O, that there were more of them!

Some poor creatures have been so brutalized by the lash that they will sneak out of the way to give their masters free access to their wives

[76]Jacobs's point about the ignorance of slaves who are "heathens"—that is, non-Christians—is in keeping with nineteenth-century colonialist ideas about the civilizing influence of Christianity, a view she repeats later in this chapter. As a member of the Episcopal Church, she believed firmly in the civilizing tendencies of Christianity. Note, however, that she distinguishes between the true faith and the hypocritical Christianity she witnesses in slaveholders.

[77]The Fugitive Slave Act (see note 52) was part of the Compromise of 1850, a legislative package meant to heal the growing rift between Northerners and Southerners over the expansion of slavery in the West. In addition to enforcing fugitive slave laws that made it illegal not to aid in the return of runaways, the Compromise of 1850 allowed California to be admitted to the Union as a free state, fixed the boundaries of Texas, ended the slave trade in Washington, D.C. (slavery was still legal), and left the question of slavery in the territories of Utah and New Mexico up to the people living there. The compromise satisfied no one for long and indeed inflamed already sectional feelings. For discussions of the legislative battles in the years leading up to the Civil War, see David M. Potter, *The Impending Crisis, 1848–1861* (New York: Harper & Row, 1976), and James M. McPherson, *Battle Cry of Freedom* (New York: Ballantine Books, 1998).

and daughters. Do you think this proves the black man to belong to an inferior order of beings? What would *you* be, if you had been born and brought up a slave, with generations of slaves for ancestors? I admit that the black man *is* inferior. But what is it that makes him so? It is the ignorance in which white men compel him to live; it is the torturing whip that lashes manhood out of him; it is the fierce bloodhounds of the South, and the scarcely less cruel human bloodhounds of the north, who enforce the Fugitive Slave Law. *They* do the work.

Southern gentlemen indulge in the most contemptuous expressions about the Yankees, while they, on their part, consent to do the vilest work for them, such as the ferocious bloodhounds and the despised negro-hunters are employed to do at home. When southerners go to the north, they are proud to do them honor; but the northern man is not welcome south of Mason and Dixon's line,[78] unless he suppresses every thought and feeling at variance with their "peculiar institution." Nor is it enough to be silent. The masters are not pleased, unless they obtain a greater degree of subservience than that; and they are generally accommodated. Do they respect the northerner for this? I trow not.[79] Even the slaves despise "a northern man with southern principles"; and that is the class they generally see. When northerners go to the south to reside, they prove very apt scholars. They soon imbibe the sentiments and disposition of their neighbors, and generally go beyond their teachers. Of the two, they are proverbially the hardest masters.

They seem to satisfy their consciences with the doctrine that God created the Africans to be slaves. What a libel upon the heavenly Father, who "made of one blood all nations of men!" And then who *are* Africans? Who can measure the amount of Anglo-Saxon blood coursing in the veins of American slaves?[80]

[78]This refers to the 1767 survey of the border between Maryland and Pennsylvania, which by the end of the eighteenth century was seen to mark the line between Southern slavery and Northern freedom after states north of the border abolished slavery.

[79]"I believe not." *Trow* is a literary borrowing from Old English, demonstrating, perhaps, Jacobs's literary aspirations.

[80]Jacobs quotes Acts 17:26 in this paragraph. A belief in racialism—biological differences that distinguish races—was common at the time Jacobs was writing her narrative. However, the growing population of interracial Americans made it difficult to sustain ideas about racial differences, notably the notion of racial superiority, the racist foundation upon which slavery by that time was based. Jacobs points up the illogic of laws that identified slaves as "black" when they descended from ancestors on both sides of the color line. In raising this obvious problem, Jacobs emphasizes how racialist beliefs go against faith in God's creation. She also points toward the more radical argument that the logic of "blood," given interracial sex, undermines fantasies about racial purity and white superiority. For a deeper look at interracialism, see Werner Sollors, ed., *Interracialism: Black-White Intermarriage in American History, Literature, and Law* (New York: Oxford University Press, 2000).

I have spoken of the pains slaveholders take to give their slaves a bad opinion of the north; but, not with standing this, intelligent slaves are aware that they have many friends in the Free States. Even the most ignorant have some confused notions about it. They knew that I could read; and I was often asked if I had seen any thing in the newspapers about white folks over in the big north, who were trying to get their freedom for them. Some believe that the abolitionists have already made them free, and that it is established by law, but that their masters prevent the law from going into effect. One woman begged me to get a newspaper and read it over. She said her husband told her that the black people had sent word to the queen of 'Merica that they were all slaves; that she didn't believe it, and went to Washington city to see the president about it. They quarrelled; she drew her sword upon him, and swore that he should help her to make them all free.

That poor, ignorant woman thought that America was governed by a Queen, to whom the President was subordinate. I wish the President was subordinate to Queen Justice.[81]

IX. SKETCHES OF NEIGHBORING SLAVEHOLDERS[82]

There was a planter in the country, not far from us, whom I will call Mr. Litch.[83] He was an ill-bred, uneducated man, but very wealthy. He had six hundred slaves, many of whom he did not know by sight. His extensive plantation was managed by well-paid overseers. There was a jail and a whipping post on his grounds; and whatever cruelties were perpetrated there, they passed without comment. He was so effectually screened by his great wealth that he was called to no account for his crimes, not even for murder.

Various were the punishments resorted to. A favorite one was to tie a rope round a man's body, and suspend him from the ground. A fire was kindled over him, from which was suspended a piece of fatpork. As this cooked, the scalding drops of fat continually fell on the bare flesh.

[81] Jacobs began writing her narrative when Franklin Pierce was president and completed it when James Buchanan was president. Both presidents were Democrats and protectors of slaveholders' interests.

[82] Lydia Maria Child pieced this chapter together from incidents Jacobs had scattered throughout her narrative. Compilations of "sketches" of slavery's outrages were popular forms of antislavery literature, in the mold of Theodore Dwight Weld's *American Slavery as It Is: Testimony of a Thousand Witnesses* (New York: American Anti-Slavery Society, 1839).

[83] Josiah Coffield (d. 1837), a younger brother of Elijah Jacobs's last master, James Coffield.

On his own plantation, he required very strict obedience to the eighth commandment.[84] But depredations on the neighbors were allowable, provided the culprit managed to evade detection or suspicion. If a neighbor brought a charge of theft against any of his slaves, he was browbeaten by the master, who assured him that his slaves had enough of every thing at home, and had no inducement to steal. No sooner was the neighbor's back turned, than the accused was sought out, and whipped for his lack of discretion. If a slave stole from him even a pound of meat or a peck of corn, if detection followed, he was put in chains and imprisoned, and so kept till his form was attenuated by hunger and suffering.

A freshet[85] once bore his wine cellar and meat house miles away from the plantation. Some slaves followed, and secured bits of meat and bottles of wine. Two were detected; a ham and some liquor being found in their huts. They were summoned by their master. No words were used, but a club felled them to the ground. A rough box was their coffin, and their interment was a dog's burial. Nothing was said.

Murder was so common on his plantation that he feared to be alone after nightfall. He might have believed in ghosts.

His brother,[86] if not equal in wealth, was at least equal in cruelty. His bloodhounds were well trained. Their pen was spacious, and a terror to the slaves. They were let loose on a runaway, and, if they tracked him, they literally tore the flesh from his bones. When this slaveholder died, his shrieks and groans were so frightful that they appalled his own friends. His last words were, "I am going to hell; bury my money with me."[87]

After death his eyes remained open. To press the lids down, silver dollars were laid on them. These were buried with him. From this circumstance, a rumor went abroad that his coffin was filled with money. Three times his grave was opened, and his coffin taken out. The last time, his body was found on the ground, and a flock of buzzards were pecking at it. He was again interred, and a sentinel set over his grave. The perpetrators were never discovered.

[84]Reference to Exodus 20:15: "Thou shalt not steal." Yellin believes that the story that follows was based on an incident involving James Coffield in 1823, the year before his marriage made him the owner of Elijah, and two slaves owned by a neighbor (Jacobs, *Incidents*, ed. Yellin, 268n).

[85]A flooded stream.

[86]William Coffield (1800–1829), the youngest of the three Coffield brothers.

[87]Refers, perhaps, to Jesus's admonition "For it is easier for a camel to pass through the eye of a needle than it is for a rich man to enter into the kingdom of God" (Luke 18:25).

Cruelty is contagious in uncivilized communities.[88] Mr. Conant, a neighbor of Mr. Litch, returned from town one evening in a partial state of intoxication. His body servant gave him some offence. He was divested of his clothes, except his shirt, whipped, and tied to a large tree in front of the house. It was a stormy night in winter. The wind blew bitterly cold, and the boughs of the old tree crackled under falling sleet. A member of the family, fearing he would freeze to death, begged that he might be taken down; but the master would not relent. He remained there three hours; and, when he was cut down, he was more dead than alive. Another slave, who stole a pig from this master, to appease his hunger, was terribly flogged. In desperation, he tried to run away. But at the end of two miles, he was so faint with loss of blood, he thought he was dying. He had a wife, and he longed to see her once more. Too sick to walk, he crept back that long distance on his hands and knees. When he reached his master's, it was night. He had not strength to rise and open the gate. He moaned, and tried to call for help. I had a friend living in the same family. At last his cry reached her. She went out and found the prostrate man at the gate. She ran back to the house for assistance, and two men returned with her. They carried him in, and laid him on the floor. The back of his shirt was one clot of blood. By means of lard, my friend loosened it from the raw flesh. She bandaged him, gave him cool drink, and left him to rest. The master said he deserved a hundred more lashes. When his own labor was stolen from him, he had stolen food to appease his hunger. This was his crime.

Another neighbor was a Mrs. Wade. At no hour of the day was there cessation of the lash on her premises. Her labors began with the dawn, and did not cease till long after nightfall. The barn was her particular place of torture. There she lashed the slaves with the might of a man. An old slave of hers once said to me, "It is hell in missis's house. 'Pears I can never get out. Day and night I prays to die."

The mistress died before the old woman, and, when dying, entreated her husband not to permit any one of her slaves to look on her after death. A slave who had nursed her children, and had still a child in her care, watched her chance, and stole with it in her arms to the room where lay her dead mistress. She gazed a while on her, then raised her hand and dealt two blows on her face, saying, as she did so, "The devil is got you *now*!" She forgot that the child was looking on. She had just begun to talk; and she said to her father, "I did see ma, and mammy did strike ma, so," striking her own face with her little hand. The master was startled.

[88]The metaphor of disease to describe slavery's effects was common in antislavery literature.

He could not imagine how the nurse could obtain access to the room where the corpse lay; for he kept the door locked. He questioned her. She confessed that what the child had said was true, and told how she had procured the key. She was sold to Georgia.

In my childhood I knew a valuable slave, named Charity, and loved her, as all children did. Her young mistress married, and took her to Louisiana. Her little boy, James, was sold to a good sort of master. He became involved in debt, and James was sold again to a wealthy slaveholder, noted for his cruelty. With this man he grew up to manhood, receiving the treatment of a dog. After a severe whipping, to save himself from further infliction of the lash, with which he was threatened, he took to the woods. He was in a most miserable condition—cut by the cowskin, half naked, half starved, and without the means of procuring a crust of bread.

Some weeks after his escape, he was captured, tied, and carried back to his master's plantation. This man considered punishment in his jail, on bread and water, after receiving hundreds of lashes, too mild for the poor slave's offence. Therefore he decided, after the overseer should have whipped him to his satisfaction, to have him placed between the screws of the cotton gin,[89] to stay as long as he had been in the woods. This wretched creature was cut with the whip from his head to his feet, then washed with strong brine, to prevent the flesh from mortifying, and make it heal sooner than it otherwise would. He was then put into the cotton gin, which was screwed down, only allowing him room to turn on his side when he could not lie on his back. Every morning a slave was sent with a piece of bread and bowl of water, which were placed within reach of the poor fellow. The slave was charged, under penalty of severe punishment, not to speak to him.

Four days passed, and the slave continued to carry the bread and water. On the second morning, he found the bread gone, but the water untouched. When he had been in the press four days and five nights, the slave informed his master that the water had not been used for four mornings, and that a horrible stench came from the gin house. The overseer was sent to examine into it. When the press was unscrewed, the dead body was found partly eaten by rats and vermin. Perhaps the rats that devoured his bread had gnawed him before life was extinct. Poor Charity! Grandmother and I often asked each other how her affectionate heart would bear the news, if she should ever hear of the murder of her son. We had known her husband, and knew that James

[89]Jacobs probably meant the cotton press, used to compress bales of loosely packed cotton lint, and not the cotton gin.

was like him in manliness and intelligence. These were the qualities that made it so hard for him to be a plantation slave. They put him into a rough box, and buried him with less feeling than would have been manifested for an old house dog. Nobody asked any questions. He was a slave; and the feeling was that the master had a right to do what he pleased with his own property. And what did he care for the value of a slave? He had hundreds of them. When they had finished their daily toil, they must hurry to eat their little morsels, and be ready to extinguish their pine knots before nine o'clock, when the overseer went his patrol rounds. He entered every cabin, to see that men and their wives had gone to bed together, lest the men, from over-fatigue, should fall asleep in the chimney corner, and remain there till the morning horn called them to their daily task. Women are considered of no value, unless they continually increase their owner's stock. They are put on a par with animals. This same master shot a woman through the head, who had run away and been brought back to him. No one called him to account for it. If a slave resisted being whipped, the bloodhounds were unpacked, and set upon him, to tear his flesh from his bones. The master who did these things was highly educated, and styled a perfect gentleman. He also boasted the name and standing of a Christian, though Satan never had a truer follower.

I could tell of more slaveholders as cruel as those I have described. They are not exceptions to the general rule. I do not say there are no humane slaveholders. Such characters do exist, notwithstanding the hardening influences around them. But they are "like angels' visits—few and far between."[90]

I knew a young lady who was one of these rare specimens. She was an orphan, and inherited as slaves a woman and her six children. Their father was a free man. They had a comfortable home of their own, parents and children living together. The mother and eldest daughter served their mistress during the day, and at night returned to their dwelling, which was on the premises. The young lady was very pious, and there was some reality in her religion. She taught her slaves to lead pure lives, and wished them to enjoy the fruit of their own industry. *Her* religion was not a garb put on for Sunday, and laid aside till Sunday returned again. The eldest daughter of the slave mother was promised in marriage to a free man; and the day before the wedding this good mistress emancipated her, in order that her marriage might have the sanction of *law*.

[90]Thomas Campbell (1777–1844), "Pleasures of Hope" (1799), 2.378.

Report said that this young lady cherished an unrequited affection for a man who had resolved to marry for wealth. In the course of time a rich uncle of hers died. He left six thousand dollars to his two sons by a colored woman, and the remainder of his property to this orphan niece. The metal soon attracted the magnet. The lady and her weighty purse became his. She offered to manumit her slaves[91]—telling them that her marriage might make unexpected changes in their destiny, and she wished to insure their happiness. They refused to take their freedom, saying that she had always been their best friend, and they could not be so happy any where as with her. I was not surprised. I had often seen them in their comfortable home, and thought that the whole town did not contain a happier family. They had never felt slavery; and, when it was too late, they were convinced of its reality.

When the new master claimed this family as his property, the father became furious, and went to his mistress for protection. "I can do nothing for you now, Harry," said she. "I no longer have the power I had a week ago. I have succeeded in obtaining the freedom of your wife; but I cannot obtain it for your children." The unhappy father swore that nobody should take his children from him. He concealed them in the woods for some days; but they were discovered and taken. The father was put in jail, and the two oldest boys sold to Georgia. One little girl, too young to be of service to her master, was left with the wretched mother. The other three were carried to their master's plantation. The eldest soon became a mother; and, when the slaveholder's wife looked at the babe, she wept bitterly. She knew that her own husband had violated the purity she had so carefully inculcated. She had a second child by her master, and then he sold her and his offspring to his brother. She bore two children to the brother, and was sold again. The next sister went crazy. The life she was compelled to lead drove her mad. The third one became the mother of five daughters. Before the birth of the fourth the pious mistress died. To the last, she rendered every kindness to the slaves that her unfortunate circumstances permitted. She passed away peacefully, glad to close her eyes on a life which had been made so wretched by the man she loved.

This man squandered the fortune he had received, and sought to retrieve his affairs by a second marriage; but, having retired after a night of drunken debauch, he was found dead in the morning. He was called a good master; for he fed and clothed his slaves better than most masters, and the lash was not heard on his plantation so frequently as

[91]To manumit slaves is to release them from slavery.

on many others. Had it not been for slavery, he would have been a better man, and his wife a happier woman.

No pen can give an adequate description of the all-pervading corruption produced by slavery. The slave girl is reared in an atmosphere of licentiousness and fear. The lash and the foul talk of her master and his sons are her teachers. When she is fourteen or fifteen, her owner, or his sons, or the overseer, or perhaps all of them, begin to bribe her with presents. If these fail to accomplish their purpose, she is whipped or starved into submission to their will. She may have had religious principles inculcated by some pious mother or grandmother, or some good mistress; she may have a lover, whose good opinion and peace of mind are dear to her heart; or the profligate men who have power over her may be exceedingly odious to her. But resistance is hopeless.

> The poor worm
> Shall prove her contest vain. Life's little day
> Shall pass, and she is gone![92]

The slaveholder's sons are, of course, vitiated, even while boys, by the unclean influences every where around them. Nor do the master's daughters always escape. Severe retributions sometimes come upon him for the wrongs he does to the daughters of the slaves. The white daughters early hear their parents quarrelling about some female slave. Their curiosity is excited, and they soon learn the cause. They are attended by the young slave girls whom their father has corrupted; and they hear such talk as should never meet youthful ears, or any other ears. They know that the women slaves are subject to their father's authority in all things; and in some cases they exercise the same authority over the men slaves. I have myself seen the master of such a household whose head was bowed down in shame; for it was known in the neighborhood that his daughter had selected one of the meanest slaves on his plantation to be the father of his first grandchild. She did not make her advances to her equals, nor even to her father's more intelligent servants. She selected the most brutalized, over whom her authority could be exercised with less fear of exposure. Her father, half frantic with rage, sought to revenge himself on the offending black man; but his daughter, foreseeing the storm that would arise, had given him free papers, and sent him out of the state.

In such cases the infant is smothered, or sent where it is never seen by any who know its history. But if the white parent is the father, instead

[92]From *Elegant Extracts. A Copious Selection of Instructive, Moral, and Entertaining Passages, From the Most Eminent Poets, Vol. III, Bk. V.VI, Pindaric, Horatian, and Other Odes* (Boston: Wells and Lilly Court-street, 1826).

of the mother, the offspring are unblushingly reared for the market. If they are girls, I have indicated plainly enough what will be their inevitable destiny.

You may believe what I say; for I write only that whereof I know. I was twenty-one years in that cage of obscene birds.[93] I can testify, from my own experience and observation, that slavery is a curse to the whites as well as to the blacks. It makes the white fathers cruel and sensual; the sons violent and licentious; it contaminates the daughters, and makes the wives wretched.[94] And as for the colored race, it needs an abler pen than mine to describe the extremity of their sufferings, the depth of their degradation.

Yet few slaveholders seem to be aware of the wide-spread moral ruin occasioned by this wicked system. Their talk is of blighted cotton crops—not of the blight on their children's souls.

If you want to be fully convinced of the abominations of slavery, go on a southern plantation, and call yourself a negro trader. Then there will be no concealment; and you will see and hear things that will seem to you impossible among human beings with immortal souls.

X. A PERILOUS PASSAGE IN THE SLAVE GIRL'S LIFE

After my lover went away, Dr. Flint contrived a new plan. He seemed to have an idea that my fear of my mistress was his greatest obstacle. In the blandest tones, he told me that he was going to build a small house for me, in a secluded place, four miles away from the town. I shuddered; but I was constrained to listen, while he talked of his intention to give me a home of my own, and to make a lady of me. Hitherto, I had escaped my dreaded fate, by being in the midst of people. My grandmother had already had high words with my master about me. She had told him pretty plainly what she thought of his character, and there was

[93]Jacobs's "cage of obscene birds" is a reference to Revelations 18:2—that is, to Armageddon and the fall of Babylon. The use of apocalyptic rhetoric to describe the fall of the South and the end of slavery would reach its climax during the Civil War in the speeches of Frederick Douglass and in Abraham Lincoln's second inaugural address. See David Blight, *Frederick Douglass's Civil War: Keeping Faith in Jubilee* (Baton Rouge: Louisiana State University Press, 1989), for a study of Douglass's Civil War rhetoric.

[94]Comments on the grotesque effects of slavery on slaveholders can be found not only in the writings of antislavery authors but also in the papers of leading colonial slaveholders, who helped build and define the institution, among them such eighteenth-century Virginians as William Byrd II, George Washington, and Thomas Jefferson. They reveal the ways in which the Revolutionary-era slaveholders in particular sometimes struggled with the unavoidable contradictions between holding slaves and espousing liberty and equality for "all men."

considerable gossip in the neighborhood about our affairs, to which the open-mouthed jealousy of Mrs. Flint contributed, not a little. When my master said he was going to build a house for me, and that he could do it with little trouble and expense, I was in hopes something would happen to frustrate his scheme; but I soon heard that the house was actually begun. I vowed before my Maker that I would never enter it. I had rather toil on the plantation from dawn till dark; I had rather live and die in jail, than drag on, from day to day, through such a living death. I was determined that the master, whom I so hated and loathed, who had blighted the prospects of my youth, and made my life a desert, should not, after my long struggle with him, succeed at last in trampling his victim under his feet. I would do any thing, every thing, for the sake of defeating him. What *could* I do? I thought and thought, till I became desperate, and made a plunge into the abyss.

And now, reader, I come to a period in my unhappy life, which I would gladly forget if I could. The remembrance fills me with sorrow and shame. It pains me to tell you of it; but I have promised to tell you the truth, and I will do it honestly, let it cost me what it may. I will not try to screen myself behind the plea of compulsion from a master; for it was not so. Neither can I plead ignorance or thoughtlessness. For years, my master had done his utmost to pollute my mind with foul images, and to destroy the pure principles inculcated by my grandmother, and the good mistress of my childhood. The influences of slavery had had the same effect on me that they had on other young girls; they had made me prematurely knowing, concerning the evil ways of the world. I knew what I did, and I did it with deliberate calculation.

But, O, ye happy women, whose purity has been sheltered from childhood, who have been free to choose the objects of your affection, whose homes are protected by law, do not judge the poor desolate slave girl too severely! If slavery had been abolished, I, also, could have married the man of my choice; I could have had a home shielded by the laws; and I should have been spared the painful task of confessing what I am now about to relate; but all my prospects had been blighted by slavery. I wanted to keep myself pure; and, under the most adverse circumstances, I tried hard to preserve my self-respect; but I was struggling alone in the powerful grasp of the demon Slavery; and the monster proved too strong for me. I felt as if I was forsaken by God and man; as if all my efforts must be frustrated; and I became reckless in my despair.[95]

[95]In the phrase "forsaken by God and man" lies an allusion to Jesus's martyrdom in Matthew 27:45–46. Jacobs uses a similar phrase, referring to her grandmother, at the end of this chapter.

I have told you that Dr. Flint's persecutions and his wife's jealousy had given rise to some gossip in the neighborhood. Among others, it chanced that a white unmarried gentleman had obtained some knowledge of the circumstances in which I was placed.[96] He knew my grandmother, and often spoke to me in the street. He became interested for me, and asked questions about my master, which I answered in part. He expressed a great deal of sympathy, and a wish to aid me. He constantly sought opportunities to see me, and wrote to me frequently. I was a poor slave girl, only fifteen years old.

So much attention from a superior person was, of course, flattering; for human nature is the same in all. I also felt grateful for his sympathy, and encouraged by his kind words. It seemed to me a great thing to have such a friend. By degrees, a more tender feeling crept into my heart. He was an educated and eloquent gentleman; too eloquent, alas, for the poor slave girl who trusted in him. Of course I saw whither all this was tending. I knew the impassable gulf between us; but to be an object of interest to a man who is not married, and who is not her master, is agreeable to the pride and feelings of a slave, if her miserable situation has left her any pride or sentiment. It seems less degrading to give one's self, than to submit to compulsion. There is something akin to freedom in having a lover who has no control over you, except that which he gains by kindness and attachment. A master may treat you as rudely as he pleases, and you dare not speak; moreover, the wrong does not seem so great with an unmarried man, as with one who has a wife to be made unhappy. There may be sophistry in all this; but the condition of a slave confuses all principles of morality, and, in fact, renders the practice of them impossible.

When I found that my master had actually begun to build the lonely cottage, other feelings mixed with those I have described. Revenge, and calculations of interest, were added to flattered vanity and sincere gratitude for kindness. I knew nothing would enrage Dr. Flint so much as to know that I favored another; and it was something to triumph over my tyrant even in that small way. I thought he would revenge himself by selling me, and I was sure my friend, Mr. Sands, would buy me. He was a man of more generosity and feeling than my master, and I thought my

[96]Samuel Tredwell Sawyer (1800–1863), a descendant of a colonial governor of North Carolina, was related to the current governor and had been educated at the College of William and Mary before training to become a lawyer. He had just returned to his home on King Street in Edenton to establish a law practice. He became a North Carolina legislator and was elected to Congress in 1844. Sawyer, also "Mr. S ———," became John Jacobs's master. See *A True Tale of Slavery*, chaps. III, IV, VI (Document 11).

freedom could be easily obtained from him.[97] The crisis of my fate now came so near that I was desperate. I shuddered to think of being the mother of children that should be owned by my old tyrant. I knew that as soon as a new fancy took him, his victims were sold far off to get rid of them; especially if they had children. I had seen several women sold, with his babies at the breast. He never allowed his offspring by slaves to remain long in sight of himself and his wife. Of a man who was not my master I could ask to have my children well supported; and in this case, I felt confident I should obtain the boon. I also felt quite sure that they would be made free. With all these thoughts revolving in my mind, and seeing no other way of escaping the doom I so much dreaded, I made a headlong plunge. Pity me, and pardon me, O virtuous reader![98] You never knew what it is to be a slave; to be entirely unprotected by law or custom; to have the laws reduce you to the condition of a chattel, entirely subject to the will of another. You never exhausted your ingenuity in avoiding the snares, and eluding the power of a hated tyrant; you never shuddered at the sound of his footsteps, and trembled within hearing of his voice. I know I did wrong. No one can feel it more sensibly than I do. The painful and humiliating memory will haunt me to my dying day. Still, in looking back, calmly, on the events of my life, I feel that the slave woman ought not to be judged by the same standard as others.

The months passed on. I had many unhappy hours. I secretly mourned over the sorrow I was bringing on my grandmother, who had so tried to shield me from harm. I knew that I was the greatest comfort of her old age, and that it was a source of pride to her that I had not degraded myself, like most of the slaves. I wanted to confess to her that I was no longer worthy of her love; but I could not utter the dreaded words.

As for Dr. Flint, I had a feeling of satisfaction and triumph in the thought of telling *him*. From time to time he told me of his intended arrangements, and I was silent. At last, he came and told me the cottage was completed, and ordered me to go to it. I told him I would never enter it. He said, "I have heard enough of such talk as that. You shall go, if you are carried by force; and you shall remain there."

[97]According to Yellin, Jacobs modeled her plan on the story of a freedwoman in Edenton named Rose, who at age sixteen had become the mistress of her owner, Auguste Carbarrus, a bachelor, with whom she had two children. Carbarrus emancipated Rose and gave her the children (Yellin, *Harriet Jacobs*, 26).

[98]The tone of this exclamation and the passage that follows is ambiguous. It is not clear whether Jacobs is speaking earnestly or ironically, whether she sincerely requests the pardon of the "virtuous reader" or whether she feels, as she suggests in the final sentence, that she needs no pardon and did no wrong.

I replied, "I will never go there. In a few months I shall be a mother."

He stood and looked at me in dumb amazement, and left the house without a word. I thought I should be happy in my triumph over him. But now that the truth was out, and my relatives would hear of it, I felt wretched. Humble as were their circumstances, they had pride in my good character. Now, how could I look them in the face? My self-respect was gone! I had resolved that I would be virtuous, though I was a slave. I had said, "Let the storm beat! I will brave it till I die." And now, how humiliated I felt![99]

I went to my grandmother. My lips moved to make confession, but the words stuck in my throat. I sat down in the shade of a tree at her door and began to sew. I think she saw something unusual was the matter with me. The mother of slaves is very watchful. She knows there is no security for her children. After they have entered their teens she lives in daily expectation of trouble. This leads to many questions. If the girl is of a sensitive nature, timidity keeps her from answering truthfully, and this well-meant course has a tendency to drive her from maternal counsels. Presently, in came my mistress, like a mad woman, and accused me concerning her husband. My grandmother, whose suspicions had been previously awakened, believed what she said. She exclaimed, "O Linda! has it come to this? I had rather see you dead than to see you as you now are. You are a disgrace to your dead mother." She tore from my fingers my mother's wedding ring and her silver thimble. "Go away!" she exclaimed, "and never come to my house, again." Her reproaches fell so hot and heavy, that they left me no chance to answer. Bitter tears, such as the eyes never shed but once, were my only answer. I rose from my seat, but fell back again, sobbing. She did not speak to me; but the tears were running down her furrowed cheeks, and they scorched me like fire. She had always been so kind to me! *So* kind! How I longed to throw myself at her feet, and tell her all the truth! But she had ordered me to go, and never to come there again. After a few minutes, I mustered strength, and started to obey her. With what feelings did I now close that little gate, which I used to open with such an eager hand in my childhood! It closed upon me with a sound I never heard before.

Where could I go? I was afraid to return to my master's. I walked on recklessly, not caring where I went, or what would become of me. When I had gone four or five miles, fatigue compelled me to stop. I sat down

[99]Jacobs adopts the language of the heroines of countless eighteenth- and nineteenth-century works of sentimental fiction beginning with Samuel Richardson's influential *Pamela; or, Virtue Rewarded* (1740). The scene with her grandmother that follows and her hours of desperate wandering are also cast in the language and sentiment typical of the genre.

on the stump of an old tree. The stars were shining through the boughs above me. How they mocked me, with their bright, calm light! The hours passed by, and as I sat there alone a chilliness and deadly sickness came over me. I sank on the ground. My mind was full of horrid thoughts. I prayed to die; but the prayer was not answered. At last, with great effort I roused myself, and walked some distance further, to the house of a woman who had been a friend of my mother. When I told her why I was there, she spoke soothingly to me; but I could not be comforted. I thought I could bear my shame if I could only be reconciled to my grandmother. I longed to open my heart to her. I thought if she could know the real state of the case, and all I had been bearing for years, she would perhaps judge me less harshly. My friend advised me to send for her. I did so; but days of agonizing suspense passed before she came. Had she utterly forsaken me? No. She came at last. I knelt before her, and told her the things that had poisoned my life; how long I had been persecuted; that I saw no way of escape; and in an hour of extremity I had become desperate. She listened in silence. I told her I would bear any thing and do any thing, if in time I had hopes of obtaining her forgiveness. I begged of her to pity me, for my dead mother's sake. And she did pity me. She did not say, "I forgive you"; but she looked at me lovingly, with her eyes full of tears. She laid her old hand gently on my head, and murmured, "Poor child! Poor child!"

XI. THE NEW TIE TO LIFE

I returned to my good grandmother's house. She had an interview with Mr. Sands. When she asked him why he could not have left her one ewe lamb,[100]—whether there were not plenty of slaves who did not care about character,—he made no answer; but he spoke kind and encouraging words. He promised to care for my child, and to buy me, be the conditions what they might.

I had not seen Dr. Flint for five days. I had never seen him since I made the avowal to him. He talked of the disgrace I had brought on myself; how I had sinned against my master, and mortified my old grandmother. He intimated that if I had accepted his proposals, he, as a physician, could have saved me from exposure.[101] He even condescended to pity me.

[100]Allusion to 2 Samuel 12: a female lamb, one's most cherished possession.

[101]Likely a reference to abortion. Plants, vegetable poisons, and oils, such as camphor, were used at the time to induce miscarriages, sometimes deliberately by slave women themselves (Fleischner, *Mrs. Lincoln and Mrs. Keckly*, 30).

Could he have offered wormwood more bitter? He, whose persecutions had been the cause of my sin![102]

"Linda," said he, "though you have been criminal towards me, I feel for you, and I can pardon you if you obey my wishes. Tell me whether the fellow you wanted to marry is the father of your child. If you deceive me, you shall feel the fires of hell."

I did not feel as proud as I had done. My strongest weapon with him was gone. I was lowered in my own estimation, and had resolved to bear his abuse in silence. But when he spoke contemptuously of the lover who had always treated me honorably; when I remembered that but for him I might have been a virtuous, free, and happy wife, I lost my patience. "I have sinned against God and myself," I replied; "but not against you."[103]

He clinched his teeth, and muttered, "Curse you!" He came towards me, with ill-suppressed rage, and exclaimed, "You obstinate girl! I could grind your bones to powder! You have thrown yourself away on some worthless rascal. You are weak-minded, and have been easily persuaded by those who don't care a straw for you. The future will settle accounts between us. You are blinded now; but hereafter you will be convinced that your master was your best friend. My lenity towards you is a proof of it. I might have punished you in many ways. I might have had you whipped till you fell dead under the lash. But I wanted you to live; I would have bettered your condition. Others cannot do it. You are my slave. Your mistress, disgusted by your conduct, forbids you to return to the house; therefore I leave you here for the present; but I shall see you often. I will call tomorrow."

He came with frowning brows, that showed a dissatisfied state of mind. After asking about my health, he inquired whether my board was paid, and who visited me. He then went on to say that he had neglected his duty; that as a physician there were certain things that he ought to have explained to me. Then followed talk such as would have made the most shameless blush. He ordered me to stand up before him. I obeyed. "I command you," said he, "to tell me whether the father of your child is white or black." I hesitated. "Answer me this instant!" he exclaimed. I did answer. He sprang upon me like a wolf, and grabbed my arm as if he would have broken it. "Do you love him?" said he, in a hissing tone.

"I am thankful that I do not despise him," I replied.

[102]Reference to Lamentations 3:15–20, the lament of Jeremiah. "Wormwood" figuratively means a cause of bitterness or grief.

[103]In her rebuke, Jacobs continues her identification with Jeremiah.

He raised his hand to strike me; but it fell again. I don't know what arrested the blow. He sat down, with lips tightly compressed. At last he spoke. "I came here," said he, "to make you a friendly proposition; but your ingratitude chafes me beyond endurance. You turn aside all my good intentions towards you. I don't know what it is that keeps me from killing you." Again he rose, as if he had a mind to strike me.

But he resumed. "On one condition I will forgive your insolence and crime. You must henceforth have no communication of any kind with the father of your child. You must not ask any thing from him, or receive any thing from him. I will take care of you and your child. You had better promise this at once, and not wait till you are deserted by him. This is the last act of mercy I shall show towards you."

I said something about being unwilling to have my child supported by a man who had cursed it and me also. He rejoined, that a woman who had sunk to my level had no right to expect any thing else. He asked, for the last time, would I accept his kindness? I answered that I would not.

"Very well," said he; "then take the consequences of your wayward course. Never look to me for help. You are my slave, and shall always be my slave. I will never sell you, that you may depend upon."

Hope died away in my heart as he closed the door after him. I had calculated that in his rage he would sell me to a slave-trader; and I knew the father of my child was on the watch to buy me.

About this time my uncle Phillip was expected to return from a voyage. The day before his departure I had officiated as bridesmaid to a young friend. My heart was then ill at ease, but my smiling countenance did not betray it. Only a year had passed; but what fearful changes it had wrought! My heart had grown gray in misery. Lives that flash in sunshine, and lives that are born in tears, receive their hue from circumstances. None of us know what a year may bring forth.

I felt no joy when they told me my uncle had come. He wanted to see me, though he knew what had happened. I shrank from him at first; but at last consented that he should come to my room. He received me as he always had done. O, how my heart smote me when I felt his tears on my burning cheeks! The words of my grandmother came to my mind,—"Perhaps your mother and father are taken from the evil days to come."[104] My disappointed heart could now praise God that it was so. But why, thought I, did my relatives ever cherish hopes for me?

[104] Allusion to Ecclesiastes 12:1.

What was there to save me from the usual fate of slave girls? Many more beautiful and more intelligent than I had experienced a similar fate, or a far worse one. How could they hope that I should escape?

My uncle's stay was short, and I was not sorry for it. I was too ill in mind and body to enjoy my friends as I had done. For some weeks I was unable to leave my bed. I could not have any doctor but my master, and I would not have him sent for. At last, alarmed by my increasing illness, they sent for him. I was very weak and nervous; and as soon as he entered the room, I began to scream. They told him my state was very critical. He had no wish to hasten me out of the world, and he withdrew.

When my babe was born, they said it was premature. It weighed only four pounds; but God let it live.[105] I heard the doctor say I could not survive till morning. I had often prayed for death; but now I did not want to die, unless my child could die too. Many weeks passed before I was able to leave my bed. I was a mere wreck of my former self. For a year there was scarcely a day when I was free from chills and fever. My babe also was sickly. His little limbs were often racked with pain. Dr. Flint continued his visits, to look after my health; and he did not fail to remind me that my child was an addition to his stock of slaves.[106]

I felt too feeble to dispute with him, and listened to his remarks in silence. His visits were less frequent; but his busy spirit could not remain quiet. He employed my brother in his office, and he was made the medium of frequent notes and messages to me. William was a bright lad, and of much use to the doctor. He had learned to put up medicines, to leech, cup, and bleed.[107] He had taught himself to read and spell. I was proud of my brother; and the old doctor suspected as much. One day, when I had not seen him for several weeks, I heard his steps approaching the door. I dreaded the encounter, and hid myself. He inquired for me, of course; but I was nowhere to be found. He went to his office, and despatched William with a note. The color mounted to my

[105]Joseph Jacobs (1829–1860?), named after Jacobs's uncle Joseph. After joining Jacobs in the North, Joseph served a brief apprenticeship with a printer and soon ran away to sea, later going with his uncle to find gold in California, then on to Australia, where he died, probably in 1860.

[106]Slaveholders frequently used blunt commercial language when describing their slaves. For instance, Thomas Jefferson observed of his slaves, "A woman who brings a child every two years [is] more profitable than the best man of the farm" (Edmund Morris Betts, ed., *Thomas Jefferson's Farm Book* [Princeton, N.J.: Princeton University Press, 1953], 46).

[107]Using leeches to stimulate bloodletting, then applying warm cups to the skin, was a common treatment for infections.

brother's face when he gave it to me; and he said, "Don't you hate me, Linda, for bringing you these things?" I told him I could not blame him; he was a slave, and obliged to obey his master's will. The note ordered me to come to his office. I went. He demanded to know where I was when he called. I told him I was at home. He flew into a passion, and said he knew better. Then he launched out upon his usual themes,—my crimes against him, and my ingratitude for his forbearance. The laws were laid down to me anew, and I was dismissed. I felt humiliated that my brother should stand by, and listen to such language as would be addressed only to a slave. Poor boy! He was powerless to defend me; but I saw the tears, which he vainly strove to keep back. This manifestation of feeling irritated the doctor. William could do nothing to please him. One morning he did not arrive at the office so early as usual; and that circumstance afforded his master an opportunity to vent his spleen. He was put in jail. The next day my brother sent a trader to the doctor, with a request to be sold. His master was greatly incensed at what he called his insolence. He said he had put him there to reflect upon his bad conduct, and he certainly was not giving any evidence of repentance. For two days he harassed himself to find somebody to do his office work; but every thing went wrong without William. He was released, and ordered to take his old stand, with many threats, if he was not careful about his future behavior.

As the months passed on, my boy improved in health. When he was a year old, they called him beautiful. The little vine was taking deep root in my existence, though its clinging fondness excited a mixture of love and pain. When I was most sorely oppressed I found a solace in his smiles. I loved to watch his infant slumbers; but always there was a dark cloud over my enjoyment. I could never forget that he was a slave. Sometimes I wished that he might die in infancy. God tried me. My darling became very ill. The bright eyes grew dull, and the little feet and hands were so icy cold that I thought death had already touched them. I had prayed for his death, but never so earnestly as I now prayed for his life; and my prayer was heard. Alas, what mockery it is for a slave mother to try to pray back her dying child to life! Death is better than slavery. It was a sad thought that I had no name to give my child. His father caressed him and treated him kindly, whenever he had a chance to see him. He was not unwilling that he should bear his name; but he had no legal claim to it; and if I had bestowed it upon him, my master would have regarded it as a new crime, a new piece of insolence, and would, perhaps, revenge it on the boy. O, the serpent of Slavery has many and poisonous fangs!

XII. FEAR OF INSURRECTION

Not far from this time Nat Turner's insurrection broke out; and the news threw our town into great commotion. Strange that they should be alarmed, when their slaves were so "contented and happy"! But so it was.[108]

It was always the custom to have a muster every year. On that occasion every white man shouldered his musket. The citizens and the so-called country gentlemen wore military uniforms. The poor whites took their places in the ranks in every-day dress, some without shoes, some without hats. This grand occasion had already passed; and when the slaves were told there was to be another muster, they were surprised and rejoiced. Poor creatures! They thought it was going to be a holiday. I was informed of the true state of affairs, and imparted it to the few I could trust. Most gladly would I have proclaimed it to every slave; but I dared not. All could not be relied on. Mighty is the power of the torturing lash.

By sunrise, people were pouring in from every quarter within twenty miles of the town. I knew the houses were to be searched; and I expected it would be done by country bullies and the poor whites. I knew nothing annoyed them so much as to see colored people living in comfort and respectability; so I made arrangements for them with especial care. I arranged every thing in my grandmother's house as neatly as possible. I put white quilts on the beds, and decorated some of the rooms with flowers. When all was arranged, I sat down at the window to watch. Far as my eye could reach, it rested on a motley crowd of soldiers. Drums and fifes were discoursing martial music. The men were divided into companies of sixteen, each headed by a captain. Orders were given, and the wild scouts rushed in every direction, wherever a colored face was to be found.

It was a grand opportunity for the low whites, who had no negroes of their own to scourge.[109] They exulted in such a chance to exercise a little brief authority, and show their subserviency to the slaveholders;

[108]In August 1831, in Southampton, Virginia, about forty miles from Edenton, a group of about fifty or sixty slaves, under the leadership of Nat Turner (1800–1831), rode through eleven farms murdering fifty-seven to sixty white men, women, and children. All of the black insurgents were either killed or captured, and nineteen of them, including Turner, were hanged. Gripped by fear of slave insurrection, white Southerners tightened manumission laws and other laws governing slave conduct—for instance, forbidding the congregation of slaves. They also formed militias to guard against rebellion. No one knows how many blacks were killed in the wave of antiblack violence that followed, but estimates put the number in the hundreds.

[109]Not quite 30 percent of the white families in North Carolina owned slaves, and the average number of slaves each owned was fewer than ten. The highest concentration of slaves and the largest plantations were in the Deep South—South Carolina, Mississippi, Georgia, Alabama, Florida, and Louisiana.

not reflecting that the power which trampled on the colored people also kept themselves in poverty, ignorance, and moral degradation. Those who never witnessed such scenes can hardly believe what I know was inflicted at this time on innocent men, women, and children, against whom there was not the slightest ground for suspicion. Colored people and slaves who lived in remote parts of the town suffered in an especial manner. In some cases the searchers scattered powder and shot among their clothes, and then sent other parties to find them, and bring them forward as proof that they were plotting insurrection. Every where men, women, and children were whipped till the blood stood in puddles at their feet. Some received five hundred lashes; others were tied hands and feet, and tortured with a bucking paddle,[110] which blisters the skin terribly. The dwellings of the colored people, unless they happened to be protected by some influential white person, who was nigh at hand, were robbed of clothing and every thing else the marauders thought worth carrying away. All day long these unfeeling wretches went round, like a troop of demons, terrifying and tormenting the helpless. At night, they formed themselves into patrol bands, and went wherever they chose among the colored people, acting out their brutal will. Many women hid themselves in woods and swamps, to keep out of their way. If any of the husbands or fathers told of these outrages, they were tied up to the public whipping post, and cruelly scourged for telling lies about white men. The consternation was universal. No two people that had the slightest tinge of color in their faces dared to be seen talking together.

I entertained no positive fears about our household, because we were in the midst of white families who would protect us. We were ready to receive the soldiers whenever they came. It was not long before we heard the tramp of feet and the sound of voices. The door was rudely pushed open; and in they tumbled, like a pack of hungry wolves. They snatched at every thing within their reach. Every box, trunk, closet, and corner underwent a thorough examination. A box in one of the drawers containing some silver change was eagerly pounced upon. When I stepped forward to take it from them, one of the soldiers turned and said angrily, "What d'ye foller us fur? D'ye s'pose white folks is come to steal?"

I replied, "You have come to search; but you have searched that box, and I will take it, if you please."

At that moment I saw a white gentleman who was friendly to us; and I called to him, and asked him to have the goodness to come in and

[110]Most likely "backing paddle," described in *A True Tale of Slavery* (Document 11, chap. VII); an oak paddle with a blade.

stay till the search was over. He readily complied. His entrance into the house brought in the captain of the company, whose business it was to guard the outside of the house, and see that none of the inmates left it. This officer was Mr. Litch, the wealthy slaveholder whom I mentioned, in the account of neighboring planters, as being notorious for his cruelty. He felt above soiling his hands with the search. He merely gave orders; and, if a bit of writing was discovered, it was carried to him by his ignorant followers, who were unable to read.

My grandmother had a large trunk of bedding and table cloths. When that was opened, there was a great shout of surprise; and one exclaimed, "Where'd the damned niggers git all dis sheet an' table clarf?"

My grandmother, emboldened by the presence of our white protector, said, "You may be sure we didn't pilfer 'em from *your* houses."

"Look here, mammy," said a grim-looking fellow without any coat, "you seem to feel mighty gran' 'cause you got all them 'ere fixens. White folks oughter have 'em all."

His remarks were interrupted by a chorus of voices shouting, "We's got 'em! We's got 'em! Dis 'ere yaller gal's got letters!"

There was a general rush for the supposed letter, which, upon examination, proved to be some verses written to me by a friend. In packing away my things, I had overlooked them. When their captain informed them of their contents, they seemed much disappointed. He inquired of me who wrote them. I told him it was one of my friends. "Can you read them?" he asked. When I told him I could, he swore, and raved, and tore the paper into bits. "Bring me all your letters!" said he, in a commanding tone. I told him I had none. "Don't be afraid," he continued, in an insinuating way. "Bring them all to me. Nobody shall do you any harm." Seeing I did not move to obey him, his pleasant tone changed to oaths and threats. "Who writes to you? half free niggers?" inquired he. I replied, "O, no; most of my letters are from white people. Some request me to burn them after they are read, and some I destroy without reading."

An exclamation of surprise from some of the company put a stop to our conversation. Some silver spoons which ornamented an old-fashioned buffet had just been discovered. My grandmother was in the habit of preserving fruit for many ladies in the town, and of preparing suppers for parties; consequently she had many jars of preserves. The closet that contained these was next invaded, and the contents tasted. One of them, who was helping himself freely, tapped his neighbor on the shoulder, and said, "Wal done! Don't wonder de niggers want to kill all de white folks, when dey live on 'sarves" [meaning preserves].

I stretched out my hand to take the jar, saying, "You were not sent here to search for sweetmeats."

"And what *were* we sent for?" said the captain, bristling up to me. I evaded the question.

The search of the house was completed, and nothing found to condemn us. They next proceeded to the garden, and knocked about every bush and vine, with no better success. The captain called his men together, and, after a short consultation, the order to march was given. As they passed out of the gate, the captain turned back, and pronounced a malediction on the house. He said it ought to be burned to the ground, and each of its inmates receive thirty-nine lashes.[111] We came out of this affair very fortunately; not losing any thing except some wearing apparel.

Towards evening the turbulence increased. The soldiers, stimulated by drink, committed still greater cruelties. Shrieks and shouts continually rent the air. Not daring to go to the door, I peeped under the window curtain. I saw a mob dragging along a number of colored people, each white man, with his musket upraised, threatening instant death if they did not stop their shrieks. Among the prisoners was a respectable old colored minister. They had found a few parcels of shot in his house, which his wife had for years used to balance her scales. For this they were going to shoot him on Court House Green. What a spectacle was that for a civilized country! A rabble, staggering under intoxication, assuming to be the administrators of justice!

The better class of the community exerted their influence to save the innocent, persecuted people; and in several instances they succeeded, by keeping them shut up in jail till the excitement abated. At last the white citizens found that their own property was not safe from the lawless rabble they had summoned to protect them. They rallied the drunken swarm, drove them back into the country, and set a guard over the town.

The next day, the town patrols were commissioned to search colored people that lived out of the city; and the most shocking outrages were committed with perfect impunity. Every day for a fortnight, if I looked out, I saw horsemen with some poor panting negro tied to their saddles, and compelled by the lash to keep up with their speed, till they arrived at the jail yard. Those who had been whipped too unmercifully to walk were washed with brine, tossed into a cart, and carried to jail.

[111]Giving thirty-nine lashes, a fairly common slave punishment, has a biblical origin in Deuteronomy 25:1–3. Slaveholders drew from biblical as well as English models to establish their criminal code.

One black man, who had not fortitude to endure scourging, promised to give information about the conspiracy. But it turned out that he knew nothing at all. He had not even heard the name of Nat Turner. The poor fellow had, however, made up a story, which augmented his own sufferings and those of the colored people.[112]

The day patrol continued for some weeks, and at sundown a night guard was substituted. Nothing at all was proved against the colored people, bond or free. The wrath of the slaveholders was somewhat appeased by the capture of Nat Turner. The imprisoned were released. The slaves were sent to their masters, and the free were permitted to return to their ravaged homes. Visiting was strictly forbidden on the plantations. The slaves begged the privilege of again meeting at their little church in the woods, with their burying ground around it. It was built by the colored people, and they had no higher happiness than to meet there and sing hymns together, and pour out their hearts in spontaneous prayer. Their request was denied, and the church was demolished. They were permitted to attend the white churches, a certain portion of the galleries being appropriated to their use. There, when every body else had partaken of the communion, and the benediction had been pronounced, the minister said, "Come down, now, my colored friends." They obeyed the summons, and partook of the bread and wine, in commemoration of the meek and lowly Jesus, who said, "God is your Father, and all ye are brethren."[113]

XIII. THE CHURCH AND SLAVERY

After the alarm caused by Nat Turner's insurrection had subsided, the slaveholders came to the conclusion that it would be well to give the slaves enough of religious instruction to keep them from murdering their masters. The Episcopal clergyman offered to hold a separate service on Sundays for their benefit.[114] His colored members were very few, and also very respectable—a fact which I presume had some weight with him. The difficulty was to decide on a suitable place for

[112]This refers to the questioning of one Small's Jim, who named a dozen slaves he said were conspiring to kill whites. Within a month, nineteen slaves were arrested and charged, and although no plot was uncovered and the men were freed, tensions between the races did not abate (Yellin, *Harriet Jacobs*, 38).

[113]Allusion to Matthew 23:8–10.

[114]Northern born and educated, John Avery, D.D. (d. 1837), taught at Edenton Academy and was rector of St. Paul's Episcopal Church (Jacobs, *Incidents*, ed. Yellin, 270).

them to worship.[115] The Methodist and Baptist churches admitted them in the afternoon; but their carpets and cushions were not so costly as those at the Episcopal church. It was at last decided that they should meet at the house of a free colored man, who was a member.

I was invited to attend, because I could read. Sunday evening came, and, trusting to the cover of night, I ventured out. I rarely ventured out by daylight, for I always went with fear, expecting at every turn to encounter Dr. Flint, who was sure to turn me back, or order me to his office to inquire where I got my bonnet, or some other article of dress. When the Rev. Mr. Pike came, there were some twenty persons present. The reverend gentleman knelt in prayer, then seated himself, and requested all present, who could read, to open their books, while he gave out the portions he wished them to repeat or respond to.

His text was, "Servants, be obedient to them that are your masters according to the flesh, with fear and trembling, in singleness of your heart, as unto Christ."[116]

Pious Mr. Pike brushed up his hair till it stood upright, and, in deep, solemn tones, began: "Hearken, ye servants! Give strict heed unto my words. You are rebellious sinners. Your hearts are filled with all manner of evil. 'Tis the devil who tempts you. God is angry with you, and will surely punish you, if you don't forsake your wicked ways. You that live in town are eye-servants[117] behind your master's back. Instead of serving your masters faithfully, which is pleasing in the sight of your heavenly Master, you are idle, and shirk your work. God sees you. You tell lies. God hears you. Instead of being engaged in worshipping him, you are hidden away somewhere, feasting on your master's substance; tossing coffee-grounds with some wicked fortuneteller, or cutting cards with another old hag. Your masters may not find you out, but God sees you, and will punish you. O, the depravity of your hearts! When your master's work is done, are you quietly together, thinking of the goodness of God to such sinful creatures? No; you are quarrelling, and tying up little bags of roots to bury under the door-steps to poison each other with. God sees you. You men steal away to every grog shop to sell your master's corn, that you may buy rum to drink. God sees you. You sneak into the back streets, or among

[115]In 1818, Edenton's free blacks bought a tract of land in the woods, which they called Providence, where they built a graveyard, a small church, and two or three other buildings. It was here that Jacobs's parents were buried. After Nat Turner's insurrection, Edenton's blacks were forbidden to use Providence. The church was torn down, and its members were told to worship from the galleries in the white churches that would permit them (Yellin, *Harriet Jacobs*, 18–19, 39).

[116]Saint Paul's Epistle to the Ephesians 6:5, a favorite text of proslavery ideologues.

[117]Servants who work only when they're being observed; out of sight of their masters they do nothing.

the bushes, to pitch coppers. Although your masters may not find you out, God sees you; and he will punish you. You must forsake your sinful ways, and be faithful servants. Obey your old master and your young master—your old mistress and your young mistress. If you disobey your earthly master, you offend your heavenly Master. You must obey God's commandments. When you go from here, don't stop at the corners of the streets to talk, but go directly home, and let your master and mistress see that you have come."[118]

The benediction was pronounced. We went home, highly amused at brother Pike's gospel teaching, and we determined to hear him again. I went the next Sabbath evening, and heard pretty much a repetition of the last discourse. At the close of the meeting, Mr. Pike informed us that he found it very inconvenient to meet at the friend's house, and he should be glad to see us, every Sunday evening, at his own kitchen.

I went home with the feeling that I had heard the Reverend Mr. Pike for the last time. Some of his members repaired to his house, and found that the kitchen sported two tallow candles; the first time, I am sure, since its present occupant owned it, for the servants never had any thing but pine knots. It was so long before the reverend gentleman descended from his comfortable parlor that the slaves left, and went to enjoy a Methodist shout. They never seem so happy as when shouting and singing at religious meetings.[119] Many of them are sincere, and nearer to the gate of heaven than sanctimonious Mr. Pike, and other long-faced Christians, who see wounded Samaritans, and pass by on the other side.[120]

The slaves generally compose their own songs and hymns; and they do not trouble their heads much about the measure. They often sing the following verses:

> Old Satan is one busy ole man;
> He rolls dem blocks all in my way;
> But Jesus is my bosom friend;
> He rolls dem blocks away.
> If I had died when I was young,
> Den how my stam'ring tongue would have sung;
> But I am ole, and now I stand
> A narrow chance for to tread dat heavenly land.[121]

[118]The theme and tone of this sermon, encountered often in American religious rhetoric, recalls the biblical prophet Jeremiah.

[119]A key feature of early Methodism, the "shout" was a cry of praise and rejoicing. Methodist meetings were filled with emotional displays of singing, dancing, and shouting, which often dismayed more demur worshippers.

[120]Reference to Luke 10:25–37.

[121]Typical of the songs published in Methodist songbooks from the early nineteenth century, such as *Hymns and Spiritual Songs* (1807) and *The Hesperian Harp* (1848).

I well remember one occasion when I attended a Methodist class meeting. I went with a burdened spirit, and happened to sit next [to] a poor, bereaved mother, whose heart was still heavier than mine. The class leader was the town constable—a man who bought and sold slaves, who whipped his brethren and sisters of the church at the public whipping post, in jail or out of jail. He was ready to perform that Christian office any where for fifty cents. This white-faced, black-hearted brother came near us, and said to the stricken woman, "Sister, can't you tell us how the Lord deals with your soul? Do you love him as you did formerly?"

She rose to her feet, and said, in piteous tones, "My Lord and Master, help me! My load is more than I can bear. God has hid himself from me, and I am left in darkness and misery." Then, striking her breast, she continued, "I can't tell you what is in here! They've got all my children. Last week they took the last one. God only knows where they've sold her. They let me have her sixteen years, and then ——— O! O! Pray for her brothers and sisters! I've got nothing to live for now. God make my time short!"

She sat down, quivering in every limb. I saw that constable class leader become crimson in the face with suppressed laughter, while he held up his handkerchief, that those who were weeping for the poor woman's calamity might not see his merriment. Then, with assumed gravity, he said to the bereaved mother, "Sister, pray to the Lord that every dispensation of his divine will may be sanctified to the good of your poor needy soul!"

The congregation struck up a hymn, and sung as though they were as free as the birds that warbled round us,—

> Ole Satan thought he had a mighty aim;
> He missed my soul, and caught my sins.
> Cry Amen, cry Amen, cry Amen to God!
>
> He took my sins upon his back;
> Went muttering and grumbling down to hell.
> Cry Amen, cry Amen, cry Amen to God!
>
> Ole Satan's church is here below.
> Up to God's free church I hope to go.
> Cry Amen, cry Amen, cry Amen to God!

Precious are such moments to the poor slaves. If you were to hear them at such times, you might think they were happy. But can that hour of singing and shouting sustain them through the dreary week, toiling without wages, under constant dread of the lash?

The Episcopal clergyman, who, ever since my earliest recollection, had been a sort of god among the slaveholders, concluded, as his family was large, that he must go where money was more abundant. A very different clergyman took his place.[122] The change was very agreeable to the colored people, who said, "God has sent us a good man this time." They loved him, and their children followed him for a smile or a kind word. Even the slaveholders felt his influence. He brought to the rectory five slaves. His wife taught them to read and write, and to be useful to her and themselves. As soon as he was settled, he turned his attention to the needy slaves around him. He urged upon his parishioners the duty of having a meeting expressly for them every Sunday, with a sermon adapted to their comprehension. After much argument and importunity, it was finally agreed that they might occupy the gallery of the church on Sunday evenings. Many colored people, hitherto unaccustomed to attend church, now gladly went to hear the gospel preached. The sermons were simple, and they understood them. Moreover, it was the first time they had ever been addressed as human beings. It was not long before his white parishioners began to be dissatisfied. He was accused of preaching better sermons to the negroes than he did to them. He honestly confessed that he bestowed more pains upon those sermons than upon any others; for the slaves were reared in such ignorance that it was a difficult task to adapt himself to their comprehension. Dissensions arose in the parish. Some wanted he should preach to them in the evening, and to the slaves in the afternoon. In the midst of these disputings his wife died, after a very short illness. Her slaves gathered round her dying bed in great sorrow. She said, "I have tried to do you good and promote your happiness; and if I have failed, it has not been for want of interest in your welfare. Do not weep for me; but prepare for the new duties that lie before you. I leave you all free. May we meet in a better world." Her liberated slaves were sent away, with funds to establish them comfortably.[123] The colored people will long bless the memory of that truly Christian woman. Soon after her death her husband preached his farewell sermon, and many tears were shed at his departure.

[122] Rev. William D. Cairnes (ca. 1803–1850).

[123] According to Yellin, it was not Dr. Cairnes's wife but a neighbor, Mary Bissell, who had Dr. Cairnes write out her will in 1836 directing that her seven slaves be left to the American Colonization Society, to be freed and sent to Africa. Relatives contested the will, and one year later, her slaves were hired out. Norcom hired one, Maria, in 1838. The white vestrymen of St. Paul's, Norcom among them, later unanimously voted against keeping Dr. Cairnes on as rector (Yellin, *Harriet Jacobs*, 82–83).

Several years after, he passed through our town and preached to his former congregation. In his afternoon sermon he addressed the colored people. "My friends," said he, "it affords me great happiness to have an opportunity of speaking to you again. For two years I have been striving to do something for the colored people of my own parish; but nothing is yet accomplished. I have not even preached a sermon to them. Try to live according to the word of God, my friends. Your skin is darker than mine; but God judges men by their hearts, not by the color of their skins." This was strange doctrine from a southern pulpit. It was very offensive to slaveholders. They said he and his wife had made fools of their slaves, and that he preached like a fool to the negroes.

I knew an old black man, whose piety and child-like trust in God were beautiful to witness. At fifty-three years old he joined the Baptist church. He had a most earnest desire to learn to read. He thought he should know how to serve God better if he could only read the Bible. He came to me, and begged me to teach him. He said he could not pay me, for he had no money; but he would bring me nice fruit when the season for it came. I asked him if he didn't know it was contrary to law; and that slaves were whipped and imprisoned for teaching each other to read. This brought the tears into his eyes. "Don't be troubled, uncle Fred," said I. "I have no thoughts of refusing to teach you. I only told you of the law, that you might know the danger, and be on your guard." He thought he could plan to come three times a week without its being suspected. I selected a quiet nook, where no intruder was likely to penetrate, and there I taught him his A, B, C. Considering his age, his progress was astonishing. As soon as he could spell in two syllables he wanted to spell out words in the Bible. The happy smile that illuminated his face put joy into my heart. After spelling out a few words, he paused, and said, "Honey, it 'pears when I can read dis good book I shall be nearer to God. White man is got all de sense. He can larn easy. It ain't easy for ole black man like me. I only wants to read dis book, dat I may know how to live; den I hab no fear 'bout dying."

I tried to encourage him by speaking of the rapid progress he had made. "Hab patience, child," he replied. "I larns slow."

I had no need of patience. His gratitude, and the happiness I imparted, were more than a recompense for all my trouble.

At the end of six months he had read through the New Testament, and could find any text in it. One day, when he had recited unusually well, I said, "Uncle Fred, how do you manage to get your lessons so well?"

"Lord bress you, chile," he replied. "You nebber gibs me a lesson dat I don't pray to God to help me to understan' what I spells and what I reads. And he *does* help me, chile. Bress his holy name!"

There are thousands, who, like good uncle Fred, are thirsting for the water of life;[124] but the law forbids it, and the churches withhold it. They send the Bible to heathen abroad, and neglect the heathen at home. I am glad that missionaries go out to the dark corners of the earth; but I ask them not to overlook the dark corners at home. Talk to American slaveholders as you talk to savages in Africa. Tell *them* it is wrong to traffic in men. Tell them it is sinful to sell their own children, and atrocious to violate their own daughters. Tell them that all men are brethren, and that man has no right to shut out the light of knowledge from his brother. Tell them they are answerable to God for sealing up the Fountain of Life from souls that are thirsting for it.[125]

There are men who would gladly undertake such missionary work as this; but, alas! their number is small. They are hated by the south, and would be driven from its soil, or dragged to prison to die, as others have been before them. The field is ripe for the harvest, and awaits the reapers.[126] Perhaps the great grandchildren of uncle Fred may have freely imparted to them the divine treasures, which he sought by stealth, at the risk of the prison and the scourge.

Are doctors of divinity blind, or are they hypocrites? I suppose some are the one, and some the other; but I think if they felt the interest in the poor and the lowly, that they ought to feel, they would not be so easily blinded. A clergyman who goes to the south, for the first time, has usually some feeling, however vague, that slavery is wrong. The slaveholder suspects this, and plays his game accordingly. He makes himself as agreeable as possible; talks on theology, and other kindred topics. The reverend gentleman is asked to invoke a blessing on a table loaded with luxuries. After dinner he walks round the premises, and sees the beautiful groves and flowering vines, and the comfortable huts of favored household slaves. The southerner invites him to talk with these slaves. He asks them, if they want to be free, and they say, "O, no, massa." This is sufficient to satisfy him. He comes home to publish a "South-Side View of Slavery," and to complain of the exaggerations of abolitionists. He assures people that he has been to the south, and seen slavery for himself; that it is a beautiful "patriarchal institution"; that the

[124]Reference to Revelation 22:17.
[125]Reference to Psalms 36:9.
[126]Reference to Revelation 14:15.

slaves don't want their freedom; that they have hallelujah meetings, and other religious privileges.[127]

What does *he* know of the half-starved wretches toiling from dawn till dark on the plantations? of mothers shrieking for their children, torn from their arms by slave traders? of young girls dragged down into moral filth? of pools of blood around the whipping post? of hounds trained to tear human flesh? of men screwed into cotton gins to die? The slaveholder showed him none of these things, and the slaves dared not tell of them if he had asked them.

There is a great difference between Christianity and religion at the south. If a man goes to the communion table, and pays money into the treasury of the church, no matter if it be the price of blood, he is called religious. If a pastor has offspring by a woman not his wife, the church dismiss him, if she is a white woman; but if she is colored, it does not hinder his continuing to be their good shepherd.

When I was told that Dr. Flint had joined the Episcopal church, I was much surprised. I supposed that religion had a purifying effect on the character of men; but the worst persecutions I endured from him were after he was a communicant. The conversation of the doctor, the day after he had been confirmed, certainly gave *me* no indication that he had "renounced the devil and all his works." In answer to some of his usual talk, I reminded him that he had just joined the church. "Yes, Linda," said he. "It was proper for me to do so. I am getting in years, and my position in society requires it, and it puts an end to all the damned slang. You would do well to join the church, too, Linda."

"There are sinners enough in it already," rejoined I. "If I could be allowed to live like a Christian, I should be glad."

"You can do what I require; and if you are faithful to me, you will be as virtuous as my wife," he replied.

I answered that the Bible didn't say so.[128]

His voice became hoarse with rage. "How dare you preach to me about your infernal Bible!" he exclaimed. "What right have you, who are my negro, to talk to me about what you would like, and what you wouldn't like? I am your master, and you shall obey me."

No wonder the slaves sing,—

> Ole Satan's church is here below;
> Up to God's free church I hope to go.

[127]The proslavery *A South-Side View of Slavery; or, Three Months in the South in 1854* (Boston: Ticknor and Fields, 1854) was written by the Reverend Nehemiah Adams (1806–1878), pastor of Essex Street Church in Boston.

[128]Jacobs alludes to the seventh commandment against adultery.

XIV. ANOTHER LINK TO LIFE

I had not returned to my master's house since the birth of my child. The old man raved to have me thus removed from his immediate power; but his wife vowed, by all that was good and great, she would kill me if I came back; and he did not doubt her word. Sometimes he would stay away for a season. Then he would come and renew the old threadbare discourse about his forbearance and my ingratitude. He labored, most unnecessarily, to convince me that I had lowered myself. The venomous old reprobate had no need of descanting on that theme. I felt humiliated enough. My unconscious babe was the ever-present witness of my shame. I listened with silent contempt when he talked about my having forfeited *his* good opinion; but I shed bitter tears that I was no longer worthy of being respected by the good and pure. Alas! slavery still held me in its poisonous grasp. There was no chance for me to be respectable. There was no prospect of being able to lead a better life.

Sometimes, when my master found that I still refused to accept what he called his kind offers, he would threaten to sell my child. "Perhaps that will humble you," said he.

Humble *me*! Was I not already in the dust? But his threat lacerated my heart. I knew the law gave him power to fulfil it; for slaveholders have been cunning enough to enact that "the child shall follow the condition of the *mother*," not of the *father*; thus taking care that licentiousness shall not interfere with avarice. This reflection made me clasp my innocent babe all the more firmly to my heart. Horrid visions passed through my mind when I thought of his liability to fall into the slave trader's hands. I wept over him, and said, "O my child! perhaps they will leave you in some cold cabin to die, and then throw you into a hole, as if you were a dog."

When Dr. Flint learned that I was again to be a mother, he was exasperated beyond measure. He rushed from the house, and returned with a pair of shears. I had a fine head of hair; and he often railed about my pride of arranging it nicely. He cut every hair close to my head, storming and swearing all the time. I replied to some of his abuse, and he struck me. Some months before, he had pitched me down stairs in a fit of passion; and the injury I received was so serious that I was unable to turn myself in bed for many days. He then said, "Linda, I swear by God I will never raise my hand against you again"; but I knew that he would forget his promise.

After he discovered my situation, he was like a restless spirit from the pit. He came every day; and I was subjected to such insults as no pen can describe. I would not describe them if I could; they were too low, too revolting. I tried to keep them from my grandmother's knowledge as much as I could. I knew she had enough to sadden her life, without having my troubles to bear. When she saw the doctor treat me with violence, and heard him utter oaths terrible enough to palsy a man's tongue, she could not always hold her peace. It was natural and motherlike that she should try to defend me; but it only made matters worse.

When they told me my new-born babe was a girl,[129] my heart was heavier than it had ever been before. Slavery is terrible for men; but it is far more terrible for women. Superadded to the burden common to all, *they* have wrongs, and sufferings, and mortifications peculiarly their own.

Dr. Flint had sworn that he would make me suffer, to my last day, for this new crime against *him*, as he called it; and as long as he had me in his power he kept his word. On the fourth day after the birth of my babe, he entered my room suddenly, and commanded me to rise and bring my baby to him. The nurse who took care of me had gone out of the room to prepare some nourishment, and I was alone. There was no alternative. I rose, took up my babe, and crossed the room to where he sat. "Now stand there," said he, "till I tell you to go back!" My child bore a strong resemblance to her father, and to the deceased Mrs. Sands, her grandmother.[130] He noticed this; and while I stood before him, trembling with weakness, he heaped upon me and my little one every vile epithet he could think of. Even the grandmother in her grave did not escape his curses. In the midst of his vituperations I fainted at his feet. This recalled him to his senses. He took the baby from my arms, laid it on the bed, dashed cold water in my face, took me up, and shook me violently, to restore my consciousness before any one entered the room. Just then my grandmother came in, and he hurried out of the house. I suffered in consequence of this treatment; but I begged my friends to let me die, rather than send for the doctor. There was nothing I dreaded so much as his presence. My life was spared; and I was glad for the sake of my little ones. Had it not been for these ties to life, I should have been glad to be released by death, though I had lived only nineteen years.

[129]Louisa Matilda Jacobs (ca. 1832/33–1917). In Mount Auburn Cemetery, Cambridge, Massachusetts, the tombstone incorrectly dates her birth as 1836, since Jacobs writes in chapter XVIII that when she went into hiding, which was in June 1835, Louisa was two years old (Yellin, *Harriet Jacobs*, 278n).

[130]Margaret Blair Hosmer Sawyer (d. 1826), Samuel Tredwell Sawyer's mother.

Always it gave me a pang that my children had no lawful claim to a name. Their father offered his; but, if I had wished to accept the offer, I dared not while my master lived. Moreover, I knew it would not be accepted at their baptism. A Christian name they were at least entitled to; and we resolved to call my boy for our dear good Benjamin, who had gone far away from us.

My grandmother belonged to the church; and she was very desirous of having the children christened. I knew Dr. Flint would forbid it, and I did not venture to attempt it. But chance favored me. He was called to visit a patient out of town, and was obliged to be absent during Sunday. "Now is the time," said my grandmother; "we will take the children to church,[131] and have them christened."

When I entered the church, recollections of my mother came over me, and I felt subdued in spirit. There she had presented me for baptism, without any reason to feel ashamed. She had been married, and had such legal rights as slavery allows to a slave. The vows had at least been sacred to *her*, and she had never violated them. I was glad she was not alive, to know under what different circumstances her grandchildren were presented for baptism. Why had my lot been so different from my mother's? *Her* master had died when she was a child; and she remained with her mistress till she married. She was never in the power of any master; and thus she escaped one class of the evils that generally fall upon slaves.

When my baby was about to be christened, the former mistress of my father stepped up to me, and proposed to give it her Christian name.[132] To this I added the surname of my father, who had himself no legal right to it; for my grandfather on the paternal side was a white gentleman. What tangled skeins are the genealogies of slavery! I loved my father; but it mortified me to be obliged to bestow his name on my children.

When we left the church, my father's old mistress invited me to go home with her. She clasped a gold chain round my baby's neck. I thanked her for this kindness; but I did not like the emblem. I wanted no chain to be fastened on my daughter, not even if its links were of gold. How earnestly I prayed that she might never feel the weight of slavery's chain, whose iron entereth into the soul![133]

[131]St. Paul's Episcopal Church in Edenton. After years of attending services there, Molly was listed as a communicant in 1842 (Jacobs, *Incidents*, ed. Yellin, 273n).

[132]Louisa Matilda was named after the younger daughter of her father's master, Dr. Andrew Knox.

[133]Biblical allusion to the binding of Joseph in iron fetters (Psalm 105).

XV. CONTINUED PERSECUTIONS

My children grew finely; and Dr. Flint would often say to me, with an exulting smile, "These brats will bring me a handsome sum of money one of these days."

I thought to myself that, God being my helper, they should never pass into his hands. It seemed to me I would rather see them killed than have them given up to his power.[134] The money for the freedom of myself and my children could be obtained; but I derived no advantage from that circumstance. Dr. Flint loved money, but he loved power more. After much discussion, my friends resolved on making another trial. There was a slaveholder about to leave for Texas, and he was commissioned to buy me. He was to begin with nine hundred dollars, and go up to twelve. My master refused his offers. "Sir," said he, "she don't belong to me. She is my daughter's property, and I have no right to sell her. I mistrust that you come from her paramour. If so, you may tell him that he cannot buy her for any money; neither can he buy her children."

The doctor came to see me the next day, and my heart beat quicker as he entered. I never had seen the old man tread with so majestic a step. He seated himself and looked at me with withering scorn. My children had learned to be afraid of him. The little one would shut her eyes and hide her face on my shoulder whenever she saw him; and Benny, who was now nearly five years old, often inquired, "What makes that bad man come here so many times? Does he want to hurt us?" I would clasp the dear boy in my arms, trusting that he would be free before he was old enough to solve the problem. And now, as the doctor sat there so grim and silent, the child left his play and came and nestled up by me. At last my tormentor spoke. "So you are left in disgust, are you?" said he. "It is no more than I expected. You remember I told you years ago that you would be treated so. So he is tired of you? Ha! ha! ha! The virtuous madam don't like to hear about it, does she? Ha! ha! ha!" There was a sting in his calling me virtuous madam. I no longer had the power of answering him as I had formerly done. He continued: "So it seems you are trying to get up another intrigue. Your new paramour came to me, and offered to buy you; but you may be assured you will not succeed. You are mine; and you shall be mine for life. There lives no human being that can take you out of slavery. I would have done it; but you rejected my kind offer."

[134]In 1856, while Jacobs was writing her narrative, the case of Margaret Garner, a fugitive slave who slit the throat of her daughter rather than allow her to be seized and returned to slavery, became widely known. It is difficult to know how common infanticide was among slaves, but it seems fair to say that it was rarely chosen as a way to resist slavery.

I told him I did not wish to get up any intrigue; that I had never seen the man who offered to buy me.

"Do you tell me I lie?" exclaimed he, dragging me from my chair. "Will you say again that you never saw that man?"

I answered, "I do say so."

He clinched my arm with a volley of oaths. Ben began to scream, and I told him to go to his grandmother.

"Don't you stir a step, you little wretch!" said he. The child drew nearer to me, and put his arms round me, as if he wanted to protect me. This was too much for my enraged master. He caught him up and hurled him across the room. I thought he was dead, and rushed towards him to take him up.

"Not yet!" exclaimed the doctor. "Let him lie there till he comes to."

"Let me go! Let me go!" I screamed, "or I will raise the whole house." I struggled and got away; but he clinched me again. Somebody opened the door, and he released me. I picked up my insensible child, and when I turned my tormentor was gone. Anxiously I bent over the little form, so pale and still; and when the brown eyes at last opened, I don't know whether I was very happy.

All the doctor's former persecutions were renewed. He came morning, noon, and night. No jealous lover ever watched a rival more closely than he watched me and the unknown slaveholder, with whom he accused me of wishing to get up an intrigue. When my grandmother was out of the way he searched every room to find him.

In one of his visits, he happened to find a young girl, whom he had sold to a trader a few days previous. His statement was, that he sold her because she had been too familiar with the overseer. She had had a bitter life with him, and was glad to be sold. She had no mother, and no near ties. She had been torn from all her family years before. A few friends had entered into bonds for her safety, if the trader would allow her to spend with them the time that intervened between her sale and the gathering up of his human stock. Such a favor was rarely granted. It saved the trader the expense of board and jail fees, and though the amount was small, it was a weighty consideration in a slave-trader's mind.

Dr. Flint always had an aversion to meeting slaves after he had sold them. He ordered Rose out of the house; but he was no longer her master, and she took no notice of him. For once the crushed Rose was the conqueror. His gray eyes flashed angrily upon her; but that was the extent of his power. "How came this girl here?" he exclaimed. "What right had you to allow it, when you knew I had sold her?"

I answered "This is my grandmother's house, and Rose came to see her. I have no right to turn any body out of doors, that comes here for honest purposes."

He gave me the blow that would have fallen upon Rose if she had still been his slave. My grandmother's attention had been attracted by loud voices, and she entered in time to see a second blow dealt. She was not a woman to let such an outrage, in her own house, go unrebuked. The doctor undertook to explain that I had been insolent. Her indignant feelings rose higher and higher, and finally boiled over in words. "Get out of my house!" she exclaimed. "Go home, and take care of your wife and children, and you will have enough to do, without watching my family."

He threw the birth of my children in her face, and accused her of sanctioning the life I was leading. She told him I was living with her by compulsion of his wife; that he needn't accuse her, for he was the one to blame; he was the one who had caused all the trouble. She grew more and more excited as she went on. "I tell you what, Dr. Flint," said she, "you ain't got many more years to live, and you'd better be saying your prayers. It will take 'em all, and more too, to wash the dirt off your soul."[135]

"Do you know whom you are talking to?" he exclaimed.

She replied, "Yes, I know very well who I am talking to."

He left the house in a great rage. I looked at my grandmother. Our eyes met. Their angry expression had passed away, but she looked sorrowful and weary—weary of incessant strife. I wondered that it did not lessen her love for me; but if it did she never showed it. She was always kind, always ready to sympathize with my troubles. There might have been peace and contentment in that humble home if it had not been for the demon Slavery.

The winter passed undisturbed by the doctor. The beautiful spring came; and when Nature resumes her loveliness, the human soul is apt to revive also.[136] My drooping hopes came to life again with the flowers. I was dreaming of freedom again; more for my children's sake than my own. I planned and I planned. Obstacles hit against plans. There seemed no way of overcoming them; and yet I hoped.

Back came the wily doctor. I was not at home when he called. A friend had invited me to a small party, and to gratify her I went. To my great

[135]Biblical references to spiritual cleansing are common, as in Psalm 51:2 and Isaiah 1:16.

[136]A typical link between Nature and the soul in Romantic art and literature, often found in slave narratives that draw from this early nineteenth-century tradition.

consternation, a messenger came in haste to say that Dr. Flint was at my grandmother's, and insisted on seeing me. They did not tell him where I was, or he would have come and raised a disturbance in my friend's house. They sent me a dark wrapper; I threw it on and hurried home. My speed did not save me; the doctor had gone away in anger. I dreaded the morning, but I could not delay it; it came, warm and bright. At an early hour the doctor came and asked me where I had been last night. I told him. He did not believe me, and sent to my friend's house to ascertain the facts. He came in the afternoon to assure me he was satisfied that I had spoken the truth. He seemed to be in a facetious mood, and I expected some jeers were coming. "I suppose you need some recreation," said he, "but I am surprised at your being there, among those negroes. It was not the place for *you*. Are you *allowed* to visit such people?"

I understood this covert fling at the white gentleman who was my friend; but I merely replied, "I went to visit my friends, and any company they keep is good enough for me."

He went on to say, "I have seen very little of you of late, but my interest in you is unchanged. When I said I would have no more mercy on you I was rash. I recall my words. Linda, you desire freedom for yourself and your children, and you can obtain it only through me. If you agree to what I am about to propose, you and they shall be free. There must be no communication of any kind between you and their father. I will procure a cottage, where you and the children can live together. Your labor shall be light, such as sewing for my family. Think what is offered you, Linda—a home and freedom! Let the past be forgotten. If I have been harsh with you at times, your wilfulness drove me to it. You know I exact obedience from my own children, and I consider you as yet a child."

He paused for an answer, but I remained silent.

"Why don't you speak?" said he. "What more do you wait for?"

"Nothing, sir."

"Then you accept my offer?"

"No, sir."

His anger was ready to break loose; but he succeeded in curbing it, and replied, "You have answered without thought. But I must let you know there are two sides to my proposition; if you reject the bright side, you will be obliged to take the dark one. You must either accept my offer, or you and your children shall be sent to your young master's plantation, there to remain till your young mistress is married; and your children shall fare like the rest of the negro children. I give you a week to consider of it."

He was shrewd; but I knew he was not to be trusted. I told him I was ready to give my answer now.

"I will not receive it now," he replied. "You act too much from impulse. Remember that you and your children can be free a week from to-day if you choose."

On what a monstrous chance hung the destiny of my children! I knew that my master's offer was a snare, and that if I entered it escape would be impossible. As for his promise, I knew him so well that I was sure if he gave me free papers, they would be so managed as to have no legal value. The alternative was inevitable. I resolved to go to the plantation. But then I thought how completely I should be in his power, and the prospect was apalling. Even if I should kneel before him, and implore him to spare me, for the sake of my children, I knew he would spurn me with his foot, and my weakness would be his triumph.

Before the week expired, I heard that young Mr. Flint was about to be married to a lady of his own stamp.[137] I foresaw the position I should occupy in his establishment. I had once been sent to the plantation for punishment, and fear of the son had induced the father to recall me very soon. My mind was made up; I was resolved that I would foil my master and save my children, or I would perish in the attempt. I kept my plans to myself; I knew that friends would try to dissuade me from them, and I would not wound their feelings by rejecting their advice.

On the decisive day the doctor came, and said he hoped I had made a wise choice.

"I am ready to go to the plantation, sir," I replied.

"Have you thought how important your decision is to your children?" said he.

I told him I had.

"Very well. Go to the plantation, and my curse go with you," he replied. "Your boy shall be put to work, and he shall soon be sold; and your girl shall be raised for the purpose of selling well. Go your own ways!" He left the room with curses, not to be repeated.

As I stood rooted to the spot, my grandmother came and said, "Linda, child, what did you tell him?"

I answered that I was going to the plantation.

"*Must* you go?" said she. "Can't something be done to stop it?"

I told her it was useless to try; but she begged me not to give up. She said she would go to the doctor, and remind him how long and how faithfully she had served in the family, and how she had taken

[137]Penelope Hoskins (1812–1843) married James Norcom Jr. in May 1835.

her own baby from her breast to nourish his wife. She would tell him I had been out of the family so long they would not miss me; that she would pay them for my time, and the money would procure a woman who had more strength for the situation than I had. I begged her not to go; but she persisted in saying, "He will listen to *me*, Linda." She went, and was treated as I expected. He coolly listened to what she said, but denied her request. He told her that what he did was for my good, that my feelings were entirely above my situation, and that on the plantation I would receive treatment that was suitable to my behavior.

My grandmother was much cast down. I had my secret hopes; but I must fight my battle alone. I had a woman's pride, and a mother's love for my children; and I resolved that out of the darkness of this hour a brighter dawn should rise for them. My master had power and law on his side; I had a determined will.[138] There is might in each.

XVI. SCENES AT THE PLANTATION[139]

Early the next morning I left my grandmother's with my youngest child. My boy was ill, and I left him behind. I had many sad thoughts as the old wagon jolted on. Hitherto, I had suffered alone; now, my little one was to be treated as a slave. As we drew near the great house, I thought of the time when I was formerly sent there out of revenge. I wondered for what purpose I was now sent. I could not tell. I resolved to obey orders so far as duty required; but within myself, I determined to make my stay as short as possible. Mr. Flint was waiting to receive us, and told me to follow him up stairs to receive orders for the day. My little Ellen was left below in the kitchen. It was a change for her, who had always been so carefully tended. My young master said she might amuse herself in the yard. This was kind of him, since the child was hateful to his sight. My task was to fit up the house for the reception of the bride. In the midst of sheets, tablecloths, towels, drapery, and carpeting, my head was as busy planning, as were my fingers with the needle. At noon I was allowed to go to Ellen. She had sobbed herself to sleep. I heard Mr. Flint say to a neighbor, "I've got her down here, and

[138]In this important contest between law and will, Jacobs attacks what she sees as the illegitimate law of the master, against which she asserts the legitimacy of her own will. She is also playing against the meaning of *will* as the legal document of inheritance with which slaveholders perpetuated slavery. Slaves, of course, could not write legally enforceable wills.

[139]Auburn, a 435-acre corn and cotton plantation near Albemarle Sound.

I'll soon take the town notions out of her head. My father is partly to blame for her nonsense. He ought to have broke her in long ago." The remark was made within my hearing, and it would have been quite as manly to have made it to my face. He *had* said things to my face which might, or might not, have surprised his neighbor if he had known of them. He was "a chip of the old block."

I resolved to give him no cause to accuse me of being too much of a lady, so far as work was concerned. I worked day and night, with wretchedness before me. When I lay down beside my child, I felt how much easier it would be to see her die than to see her master beat her about, as I daily saw him beat other little ones. The spirit of the mothers was so crushed by the lash, that they stood by, without courage to remonstrate. How much more must I suffer, before I should be "broke in" to that degree?

I wished to appear as contented as possible. Sometimes I had an opportunity to send a few lines home; and this brought up recollections that made it difficult, for a time, to seem calm and indifferent to my lot. Notwithstanding my efforts, I saw that Mr. Flint regarded me with a suspicious eye. Ellen broke down under the trials of her new life. Separated from me, with no one to look after her, she wandered about, and in a few days cried herself sick. One day, she sat under the window where I was at work, crying that weary cry which makes a mother's heart bleed. I was obliged to steel myself to bear it. After a while it ceased. I looked out, and she was gone. As it was near noon, I ventured to go down in search of her. The great house was raised two feet above the ground. I looked under it, and saw her about midway, fast asleep. I crept under and drew her out. As I held her in my arms, I thought how well it would be for her if she never waked up; and I uttered my thought aloud. I was startled to hear some one say, "Did you speak to me?" I looked up, and saw Mr. Flint standing beside me. He said nothing further, but turned, frowning, away. That night he sent Ellen a biscuit and a cup of sweetened milk. This generosity surprised me. I learned afterwards, that in the afternoon he had killed a large snake, which crept from under the house; and I supposed that incident had prompted his unusual kindness.

The next morning the old cart was loaded with shingles for town. I put Ellen into it, and sent her to her grandmother. Mr. Flint said I ought to have asked his permission. I told him the child was sick, and required attention which I had no time to give. He let it pass; for he was aware that I had accomplished much work in a little time.

I had been three weeks on the plantation, when I planned a visit home. It must be at night, after every body was in bed.[140] I was six miles from town, and the road was very dreary. I was to go with a young man, who, I knew, often stole to town to see his mother. One night, when all was quiet, we started. Fear gave speed to our steps, and we were not long in performing the journey. I arrived at my grandmother's. Her bed room was on the first floor, and the window was open, the weather being warm. I spoke to her and she awoke. She let me in and closed the window, lest some late passer-by should see me. A light was brought, and the whole household gathered round me, some smiling and some crying. I went to look at my children, and thanked God for their happy sleep. The tears fell as I leaned over them. As I moved to leave, Benny stirred. I turned back, and whispered, "Mother is here." After digging at his eyes with his little fist, they opened, and he sat up in bed, looking at me curiously. Having satisfied himself that it was I, he exclaimed, "O mother! you ain't dead, are you? They didn't cut off your head at the plantation, did they?"

My time was up too soon, and my guide was waiting for me. I laid Benny back in his bed, and dried his tears by a promise to come again soon. Rapidly we retraced our steps back to the plantation. About half way we were met by a company of four patrols.[141] Luckily we heard their horses' hoofs before they came in sight, and we had time to hide behind a large tree. They passed, hallooing and shouting in a manner that indicated a recent carousal. How thankful we were that they had not their dogs with them! We hastened our footsteps, and when we arrived on the plantation we heard the sound of the hand-mill. The slaves were grinding their corn. We were safely in the house before the horn summoned them to their labor. I divided my little parcel of food with my guide, knowing that he had lost the chance of grinding his corn, and must toil all day in the field.

Mr. Flint often took an inspection of the house, to see that no one was idle. The entire management of the work was trusted to me, because he knew nothing about it; and rather than hire a superintendent he contented himself with my arrangements. He had often urged upon his father the necessity of having me at the plantation to take charge of his affairs, and make clothes for the slaves; but the old man knew him too well to consent to that arrangement.

[140]"Night walking," as it was called, was common among slaves separated from their families.

[141]Volunteers, generally mounted, armed, and with dogs, patrolled areas looking for slaves who were away from their owners without written passes.

When I had been working a month at the plantation, the great aunt of Mr. Flint came to make him a visit. This was the good old lady who paid fifty dollars for my grandmother, for the purpose of making her free, when she stood on the auction block. My grandmother loved this old lady, whom we all called Miss Fanny. She often came to take tea with us. On such occasions the table was spread with a snow-white cloth, and the china cups and silver spoons were taken from the old-fashioned buffet. There were hot muffins, tea rusks, and delicious sweetmeats.[142] My grandmother kept two cows, and the fresh cream was Miss Fanny's delight. She invariably declared that it was the best in town. The old ladies had cosey times together. They would work and chat, and sometimes, while talking over old times, their spectacles would get dim with tears, and would have to be taken off and wiped. When Miss Fanny bade us good by, her bag was filled with grandmother's best cakes, and she was urged to come again soon.

There had been a time when Dr. Flint's wife came to take tea with us, and when her children were also sent to have a feast of "Aunt Marthy's" nice cooking. But after I became an object of her jealousy and spite, she was angry with grandmother for giving a shelter to me and my children. She would not even speak to her in the street. This wounded my grandmother's feelings, for she could not retain ill will against the woman whom she had nourished with her milk when a babe. The doctor's wife would gladly have prevented our intercourse with Miss Fanny if she could have done it, but fortunately she was not dependent on the bounty of the Flints. She had enough to be independent; and that is more than can ever be gained from charity, however lavish it may be.

Miss Fanny was endeared to me by many recollections, and I was rejoiced to see her at the plantation. The warmth of her large, loyal heart made the house seem pleasanter while she was in it. She staid a week, and I had many talks with her. She said her principal object in coming was to see how I was treated, and whether any thing could be done for me. She inquired whether she could help me in any way. I told her I believed not. She condoled with me in her own peculiar way; saying she wished that I and all my grandmother's family were at rest in our graves, for not until then should she feel any peace about us. The good old soul did not dream that I was planning to bestow peace upon her, with regard to myself and my children; not by death, but by securing our freedom.

[142]Tea rusks are light, twice-baked biscuits.

Again and again I had traversed those dreary twelve miles, to and from the town; and all the way, I was meditating upon some means of escape for myself and my children. My friends had made every effort that ingenuity could devise to effect our purchase, but all their plans had proved abortive. Dr. Flint was suspicious, and determined not to loosen his grasp upon us. I could have made my escape alone; but it was more for my helpless children than for myself that I longed for freedom. Though the boon would have been precious to me, above all price, I would not have taken it at the expense of leaving them in slavery. Every trial I endured, every sacrifice I made for their sakes, drew them closer to my heart, and gave me fresh courage to beat back the dark waves that rolled and rolled over me in a seemingly endless night of storms.

The six weeks were nearly completed, when Mr. Flint's bride was expected to take possession of her new home. The arrangements were all completed, and Mr. Flint said I had done well. He expected to leave home on Saturday, and return with his bride the following Wednesday. After receiving various orders from him, I ventured to ask permission to spend Sunday in town. It was granted; for which favor I was thankful. It was the first I had ever asked of him, and I intended it should be the last. I needed more than one night to accomplish the project I had in view; but the whole of Sunday would give me an opportunity. I spent the Sabbath with my grandmother. A calmer, more beautiful day never came down out of heaven. To me it was a day of conflicting emotions. Perhaps it was the last day I should ever spend under that dear, old sheltering roof! Perhaps these were the last talks I should ever have with the faithful old friend of my whole life! Perhaps it was the last time I and my children should be together! Well, better so, I thought, than that they should be slaves. I knew the doom that awaited my fair baby in slavery, and I determined to save her from it, or perish in the attempt. I went to make this vow at the graves of my poor parents, in the burying-ground of the slaves. "There the wicked cease from troubling, and there the weary be at rest. There the prisoners rest together; they hear not the voice of the oppressor; the servant is free from his master."[143] I knelt by the graves of my parents, and thanked God, as I had often done before, that they had not lived to witness my trials, or to mourn over my sins. I had received my mother's blessing when she died; and in many an hour of tribulation I had seemed to hear her voice, sometimes chiding me, sometimes whispering loving words into my wounded heart. I have

[143]Reference to Job 3:17–19.

shed many and bitter tears, to think that when I am gone from my children they cannot remember me with such entire satisfaction as I remembered my mother.

The graveyard was in the woods, and twilight was coming on. Nothing broke the death-like stillness except the occasional twitter of a bird. My spirit was overawed by the solemnity of the scene. For more than ten years I had frequented this spot, but never had it seemed to me so sacred as now. A black stump, at the head of my mother's grave, was all that remained of a tree my father had planted. His grave was marked by a small wooden board, bearing his name, the letters of which were nearly obliterated. I knelt down and kissed them, and poured forth a prayer to God for guidance and support in the perilous step I was about to take. As I passed the wreck of the old meeting house, where, before Nat Turner's time, the slaves had been allowed to meet for worship, I seemed to hear my father's voice come from it, bidding me not to tarry till I reached freedom or the grave. I rushed on with renovated hopes. My trust in God had been strengthened by that prayer among the graves.

My plan was to conceal myself at the house of a friend, and remain there a few weeks till the search was over. My hope was that the doctor would get discouraged, and, for fear of losing my value, and also of subsequently finding my children among the missing, he would consent to sell us; and I knew somebody would buy us. I had done all in my power to make my children comfortable during the time I expected to be separated from them. I was packing my things, when grandmother came into the room, and asked what I was doing. "I am putting my things in order," I replied. I tried to look and speak cheerfully; but her watchful eye detected something beneath the surface. She drew me towards her, and asked me to sit down. She looked earnestly at me, and said, "Linda, do you want to kill your old grandmother? Do you mean to leave your little, helpless children? I am old now, and cannot do for your babies as I once did for you."

I replied, that if I went away, perhaps their father would be able to secure their freedom.

"Ah, my child," said she, "don't trust too much to him. Stand by your own children, and suffer with them till death. Nobody respects a mother who forsakes her children; and if you leave them, you will never have a happy moment. If you go, you will make me miserable the short time I have to live. You would be taken and brought back, and your sufferings would be dreadful. Remember poor Benjamin. Do give it up, Linda. Try to bear a little longer. Things may turn out better than we expect."

My courage failed me, in view of the sorrow I should bring on that faithful, loving old heart. I promised that I would try longer, and that I would take nothing out of her house without her knowledge.

Whenever the children climbed on my knee, or laid their heads on my lap, she would say, "Poor little souls! what would you do without a mother? She don't love you as I do." And she would hug them to her own bosom, as if to reproach me for my want of affection; but she knew all the while that I loved them better than my life. I slept with her that night, and it was the last time. The memory of it haunted me for many a year.

On Monday I returned to the plantation, and busied myself with preparations for the important day. Wednesday came. It was a beautiful day, and the faces of the slaves were as bright as the sunshine. The poor creatures were merry. They were expecting little presents from the bride, and hoping for better times under her administration. I had no such hopes for them. I knew that the young wives of slaveholders often thought their authority and importance would be best established and maintained by cruelty; and what I had heard of young Mrs. Flint gave me no reason to expect that her rule over them would be less severe than that of the master and overseer. Truly, the colored race are the most cheerful and forgiving people on the face of the earth. That their masters sleep in safety is owing to their superabundance of heart; and yet they look upon their sufferings with less pity than they would bestow on those of a horse or a dog.

I stood at the door with others to receive the bride-groom and bride. She was a handsome, delicate-looking girl, and her face flushed with emotion at sight of her new home. I thought it likely that visions of a happy future were rising before her. It made me sad; for I knew how soon clouds would come over her sunshine. She examined every part of the house, and told me she was delighted with the arrangements I had made. I was afraid old Mrs. Flint had tried to prejudice her against me, and I did my best to please her.

All passed off smoothly for me until dinner time arrived. I did not mind the embarrassment of waiting on a dinner party, for the first time in my life, half so much as I did the meeting with Dr. Flint and his wife, who would be among the guests. It was a mystery to me why Mrs. Flint had not made her appearance at the plantation during all the time I was putting the house in order. I had not met her, face to face, for five years, and I had no wish to see her now. She was a praying woman, and, doubtless, considered my present position a special answer to her prayers. Nothing could please her better than to see me humbled and trampled upon. I was just where she would have me—in the power of a hard, unprincipled master. She did not speak to me when she took her seat at table; but her satisfied, triumphant smile, when I handed her [her] plate, was more eloquent than words. The old doctor was not so quiet in his demonstrations. He ordered me here and there, and spoke with peculiar emphasis when he said "your mistress." I was drilled like a disgraced soldier. When all was over, and the last key turned, I sought my pillow, thankful that God had appointed a season of rest for the weary.[144]

The next day my new mistress began her housekeeping. I was not exactly appointed maid of all work; but I was to do whatever I was told. Monday evening came. It was always a busy time. On that night the slaves received their weekly allowance of food. Three pounds of meat, a peck of corn, and perhaps a dozen herring were allowed to each man. Women received a pound and a half of meat, a peck of corn, and the same number of herring. Children over twelve years old had half the allowance of the women. The meat was cut and weighed by the foreman of the field hands, and piled on planks before the meat house. Then the second foreman went behind the building, and when the first foreman called out, "Who takes this piece of meat?" he answered by calling somebody's name. This method was resorted to as a means of preventing partiality in distributing the meat. The young mistress came out to see how things were done on her plantation, and she soon gave a specimen of her character. Among those in waiting for their allowance was a very old slave, who had faithfully served the Flint family through three generations. When he hobbled up to get his bit of meat, the mistress said he was too old to have any allowance; that when niggers were too old to work, they ought to be fed on grass. Poor old man! He suffered much before he found rest in the grave.

My mistress and I got along very well together. At the end of a week, old Mrs. Flint made us another visit, and was closeted a long time with her daughter-in-law. I had my suspicions what was the subject of the conference. The old doctor's wife had been informed that I could leave the plantation on one condition, and she was very desirous to keep me there. If she had trusted me, as I deserved to be trusted by her, she would have had no fears of my accepting that condition. When she entered her carriage to return home, she said to young Mrs. Flint, "Don't neglect to send for them as quick as possible." My heart was on the watch all the time, and I at once concluded that she spoke of my children. The doctor came the next day, and as

[144]Reference to Exodus 20:8–10 and Hebrews 4.

I entered the room to spread the tea table, I heard him say, "Don't wait any longer. Send for them to-morrow." I saw through the plan. They thought my children's being there would fetter me to the spot, and that it was a good place to break us all in to abject submission to our lot as slaves. After the doctor left, a gentleman called, who had always manifested friendly feelings towards my grandmother and her family. Mr. Flint carried him over the plantation to show him the results of labor performed by men and women who were unpaid, miserably clothed, and half famished. The cotton crop was all they thought of. It was duly admired, and the gentleman returned with specimens to show his friends. I was ordered to carry water to wash his hands. As I did so, he said, "Linda, how do you like your new home?" I told him I liked it as well as I expected. He replied, "They don't think you are contented, and to-morrow they are going to bring your children to be with you. I am sorry for you, Linda. I hope they will treat you kindly." I hurried from the room, unable to thank him. My suspicions were correct. My children were to be brought to the plantation to be "broke in."

To this day I feel grateful to the gentleman who gave me this timely information. It nerved me to immediate action.

XVII. THE FLIGHT

Mr. Flint was hard pushed for house servants, and rather than lose me he had restrained his malice. I did my work faithfully, though not, of course, with a willing mind. They were evidently afraid I should leave them. Mr. Flint wished that I should sleep in the great house instead of the servants' quarters. His wife agreed to the proposition, but said I mustn't bring my bed into the house, because it would scatter feathers on her carpet. I knew when I went there that they would never think of such a thing as furnishing a bed of any kind for me and my little one. I therefore carried my own bed, and now I was forbidden to use it. I did as I was ordered. But now that I was certain my children were to be put in their power, in order to give them a stronger hold on me, I resolved to leave them that night. I remembered the grief this step would bring upon my dear old grandmother; and nothing less than the freedom of my children would have induced me to disregard her advice. I went about my evening work with trembling steps. Mr. Flint twice called from his chamber door to inquire why the house was not locked up. I replied that I had not done my work. "You have had time enough to do it," said he. "Take care how you answer me!"

I shut all the windows, locked all the doors, and went up to the third story, to wait till midnight. How long those hours seemed, and how fervently I prayed that God would not forsake me in this hour of utmost need! I was about to risk every thing on the throw of a die; and if I failed, O what would become of me and my poor children? They would be made to suffer for my fault.

At half past twelve I stole softly down stairs. I stopped on the second floor, thinking I heard a noise. I felt my way down into the parlor, and looked out of the window. The night was so intensely dark that I could see nothing. I raised the window very softly and jumped out. Large drops of rain were falling, and the darkness bewildered me. I dropped on my knees, and breathed a short prayer to God for guidance and protection. I groped my way to the road, and rushed towards the town with almost lightning speed. I arrived at my grandmother's house, but dared not see her. She would say, "Linda, you are killing me"; and I knew that would unnerve me. I tapped softly at the window of a room, occupied by a woman, who had lived in the house several years. I knew she was a faithful friend, and could be trusted with my secret. I tapped several times before she heard me. At last she raised the window, and I whispered, "Sally, I have run away. Let me in, quick." She opened the door softly, and said in low tones, "For God's sake, don't. Your grandmother is trying to buy you and de chillern. Mr. Sands was here last week. He tole her he was going away on business, but he wanted her to go ahead about buying you and de chillern, and he would help her all he could. Don't run away, Linda. Your grandmother is all bowed down wid trouble now."

I replied, "Sally, they are going to carry my children to the plantation to-morrow; and they will never sell them to any body so long as they have me in their power. Now, would you advise me to go back?"

"No, chile, no," answered she. "When dey finds you is gone, dey won't want de plague ob de chillern; but where is you going to hide? Dey knows ebery inch ob dis house."

I told her I had a hiding-place, and that was all it was best for her to know. I asked her to go into my room as soon as it was light, and take all my clothes out of my trunk, and pack them in hers; for I knew Mr. Flint and the constable would be there early to search my room. I feared the sight of my children would be too much for my full heart; but I could not go out into the uncertain future without one last look. I bent over the bed where lay my little Benny and baby Ellen. Poor little ones!

fatherless and motherless! Memories of their father came over me. He wanted to be kind to them; but they were not all to him, as they were to my womanly heart. I knelt and prayed for the innocent little sleepers. I kissed them lightly, and turned away.

As I was about to open the street door, Sally laid her hand on my shoulder, and said, "Linda, is you gwine all alone? Let me call your uncle."

"No, Sally," I replied, "I want no one to be brought into trouble on my account."

I went forth into the darkness and rain. I ran on till I came to the house of the friend who was to conceal me.

Early the next morning Mr. Flint was at my grandmother's inquiring for me. She told him she had not seen me, and supposed I was at the plantation. He watched her face narrowly, and said, "Don't you know any thing about her running off?" She assured him that she did not. He went on to say, "Last night she ran off without the least provocation. We had treated her very kindly. My wife liked her. She will soon be found and brought back. Are her children with you?" When told that they were, he said, "I am very glad to hear that. If they are here, she cannot be far off. If I find out that any of my niggers have had any thing to do with this damned business, I'll give 'em five hundred lashes." As he started to go to his father's, he turned round and added, persuasively, "Let her be brought back, and she shall have her children to live with her."

The tidings made the old doctor rave and storm at a furious rate. It was a busy day for them. My grandmother's house was searched from top to bottom. As my trunk was empty, they concluded I had taken my clothes with me. Before ten o'clock every vessel northward bound was thoroughly examined, and the law against harboring fugitives was read to all on board. At night a watch was set over the town. Knowing how distressed my grandmother would be, I wanted to send her a message; but it could not be done. Every one who went in or out of her house was closely watched. The doctor said he would take my children, unless she became responsible for them; which of course she willingly did. The next day was spent in searching. Before night, the following advertisement was posted at every corner, and in every public place for miles round:—

> $300 Reward! Ran away from the subscriber, an intelligent, bright, mulatto girl, named Linda, 21 years of age. Five feet four inches high. Dark eyes, and black hair inclined to curl; but it can be made straight. Has a decayed spot on a front tooth. She can read

and write, and in all probability will try to get to the Free States. All persons are forbidden, under penalty of the law, to harbor or employ said slave. $150 will be given to whoever takes her in the state, and $300 if taken out of the state and delivered to me, or lodged in jail. Dr. Flint.[145]

XVIII. MONTHS OF PERIL

The search for me was kept up with more perseverance than I had anticipated. I began to think that escape was impossible. I was in great anxiety lest I should implicate the friend who harbored me. I knew the consequences would be frightful; and much as I dreaded being caught, even that seemed better than causing an innocent person to suffer for kindness to me. A week had passed in terrible suspense, when my pursuers came into such close vicinity that I concluded they had tracked me to my hiding-place. I flew out of the house, and concealed myself in a thicket of bushes. There I remained in an agony of fear for two hours. Suddenly, a reptile of some kind seized my leg. In my fright, I struck a blow which loosened its hold, but I could not tell whether I had killed it; it was so dark, I could not see what it was; I only knew it was something cold and slimy. The pain I felt soon indicated that the bite was poisonous. I was compelled to leave my place of concealment, and I groped my way back into the house. The pain had become intense, and my friend was startled by my look of anguish. I asked her to prepare a poultice of warm ashes and vinegar, and I applied it to my leg, which was already much swollen. The application gave me some relief, but the swelling did not abate. The dread of being disabled was greater than the physical pain I endured. My friend asked an old woman, who doctored among the slaves, what was good for the bite of a snake or a lizard. She told her to steep a dozen coppers in vinegar, over night, and apply the cankered vinegar to the inflamed part.[146]

I had succeeded in cautiously conveying some messages to my relatives. They were harshly threatened, and despairing of my having

[145]Norcom ran ads in six issues of the daily *American Beacon* in Norfolk, Virginia, from June 30 to July 13, 1835, offering a $100 reward for Jacobs and giving a description of her (Document 3). "She speaks easily and fluently," he wrote, and will likely be "tricked out in gay and fashionable finery." Norcom considered Jacobs's eloquence and style distinguishing characteristics. He also seemed to feel that they were above her station.

[146]The poison of a snake is a powerful acid, and is counteracted by powerful alkalies, such as potash, ammonia, &c. The Indians are accustomed to apply wet ashes, or plunge the limb into strong lie. White men, employed to lay out railroads in snaky places, often carry ammonia with them as an antidote.—[L. Maria Child]

a chance to escape, they advised me to return to my master, ask his forgiveness, and let him make an example of me. But such counsel had no influence with me. When I started upon this hazardous undertaking, I had resolved that, come what would, there should be no turning back. "Give me liberty, or give me death," was my motto.[147] When my friend contrived to make known to my relatives the painful situation I had been in for twenty-four hours, they said no more about my going back to my master. Something must be done, and that speedily; but where to turn for help, they knew not. God in his mercy raised up "a friend in need."[148]

Among the ladies who were acquainted with my grandmother, was one who had known her from childhood, and always been very friendly to her. She had also known my mother and her children, and felt interested for them. At this crisis of affairs she called to see my grandmother, as she not unfrequently did. She observed the sad and troubled expression of her face, and asked if she knew where Linda was, and whether she was safe. My grandmother shook her head, without answering. "Come, Aunt Martha," said the kind lady, "tell me all about it. Perhaps I can do something to help you." The husband of this lady held many slaves, and bought and sold slaves. She also held a number in her own name; but she treated them kindly, and would never allow any of them to be sold. She was unlike the majority of slaveholders' wives. My grandmother looked earnestly at her. Something in the expression of her face said "Trust me!" and she did trust her. She listened attentively to the details of my story, and sat thinking for a while. At last she said, "Aunt Martha, I pity you both. If you think there is any chance of Linda's getting to the Free States, I will conceal her for a time. But first you must solemnly promise that my name shall never be mentioned. If such a thing should become known, it would ruin me and my family. No one in my house must know of it, except the cook. She is so faithful that I would trust my own life with her; and I know she likes Linda. It is a great risk; but I trust no harm will come of it. Get word to Linda to be ready as soon as it is dark, before the patrols are out. I will send the housemaids on errands, and Betty shall go to meet Linda." The place where we were to meet was designated and agreed upon. My grandmother was unable to thank the lady for this noble deed; overcome by her emotions, she sank on her knees and sobbed like a child.

[147]Patrick Henry, speaking before the Virginia Convention in 1775, adapted this line from Joseph Addison's enormously popular 1713 tragedy *Cato* (act 2, scene 4). This play about the stoic Roman statesman profoundly influenced the Revolutionary generation.

[148]Most likely Martha Hoskins Rombough Blount (1777–1858), who lived two blocks from Molly, on Queen Street, with three slaves (Jacobs, *Incidents*, ed. Yellin, 275).

I received a message to leave my friend's house at such an hour, and go to a certain place where a friend would be waiting for me. As a matter of prudence no names were mentioned. I had no means of conjecturing who I was to meet, or where I was going. I did not like to move thus blindfolded, but I had no choice. It would not do for me to remain where I was. I disguised myself, summoned up courage to meet the worst, and went to the appointed place. My friend Betty was there; she was the last person I expected to see. We hurried along in silence. The pain in my leg was so intense that it seemed as if I should drop; but fear gave me strength. We reached the house and entered unobserved. Her first words were: "Honey, now you is safe. Dem devils ain't coming to search *dis* house. When I get you into missis' safe place, I will bring some nice hot supper. I specs you need it after all dis skeering." Betty's vocation led her to think eating the most important thing in life. She did not realize that my heart was too full for me to care much about supper.

The mistress came to meet us, and led me up stairs to a small room over her own sleeping apartment. "You will be safe here, Linda," said she; "I keep this room to store away things that are out of use. The girls are not accustomed to be sent to it, and they will not suspect any thing unless they hear some noise. I always keep it locked, and Betty shall take care of the key. But you must be very careful, for my sake as well as your own; and you must never tell my secret; for it would ruin me and my family. I will keep the girls busy in the morning, that Betty may have a chance to bring your breakfast; but it will not do for her to come to you again till night. I will come to see you sometimes. Keep up your courage. I hope this state of things will not last long." Betty came with the "nice hot supper," and the mistress hastened down stairs to keep things straight till she returned. How my heart overflowed with gratitude! Words choked in my throat; but I could have kissed the feet of my benefactress. For that deed of Christian womanhood, may God forever bless her!

I went to sleep that night with the feeling that I was for the present the most fortunate slave in town. Morning came and filled my little cell with light. I thanked the heavenly Father for this safe retreat. Opposite my window was a pile of feather beds. On the top of these I could lie perfectly concealed, and command a view of the street through which Dr. Flint passed to his office. Anxious as I was, I felt a gleam of satisfaction when I saw him. Thus far I had outwitted him, and I triumphed over it. Who can blame slaves for being cunning? They are constantly compelled to resort to it. It is the only weapon of the weak and oppressed against the strength of their tyrants.

I was daily hoping to hear that my master had sold my children; for I knew who was on the watch to buy them. But Dr. Flint cared even more for revenge than he did for money. My brother William, and the good aunt who had served in his family twenty years, and my little Benny, and Ellen, who was a little over two years old, were thrust into jail, as a means of compelling my relatives to give some information about me.[149] He swore my grandmother should never see one of them again till I was brought back. They kept these facts from me for several days. When I heard that my little ones were in a loathsome jail, my first impulse was to go to them. I was encountering dangers for the sake of freeing them, and must I be the cause of their death? The thought was agonizing. My benefactress tried to soothe me by telling me that my aunt would take good care of the children while they remained in jail. But it added to my pain to think that the good old aunt, who had always been so kind to her sister's orphan children, should be shut up in prison for no other crime than loving them. I suppose my friends feared a reckless movement on my part, knowing, as they did, that my life was bound up in my children. I received a note from my brother William. It was scarcely legible, and ran thus: "Wherever you are, dear sister, I beg of you not to come here. We are all much better off than you are. If you come, you will ruin us all. They would force you to tell where you had been, or they would kill you. Take the advice of your friends; if not for the sake of me and your children, at least for the sake of those you would ruin."

Poor William! He also must suffer for being my brother. I took his advice and kept quiet. My aunt was taken out of jail at the end of a month, because Mrs. Flint could not spare her any longer. She was tired of being her own housekeeper. It was quite too fatiguing to order her dinner and eat it too. My children remained in jail, where brother William did all he could for their comfort. Betty went to see them sometimes, and brought me tidings. She was not permitted to enter the jail; but William would hold them up to the grated window while she chatted with them. When she repeated their prattle, and told me how they wanted to see their ma, my tears would flow. Old Betty would exclaim, "Lors, chile! what's you crying 'bout? Dem young uns vil kill you dead. Don't be so chick'n hearted! If you does, you vil nebber git thro' dis world."

Good old soul! She had gone through the world childless. She had never had little ones to clasp their arms round her neck; she had never seen their soft eyes looking into hers; no sweet little voices had called her mother; she had never pressed her own infants to her heart, with

[149] Aunt Nancy; compare with John S. Jacobs, *A True Tale of Slavery*, chap. II (Document 11).

the feeling that even in fetters there was something to live for. How could she realize my feelings? Betty's husband loved children dearly, and wondered why God had denied them to him. He expressed great sorrow when he came to Betty with the tidings that Ellen had been taken out of jail and carried to Dr. Flint's. She had the measles a short time before they carried her to jail, and the disease had left her eyes affected. The doctor had taken her home to attend to them. My children had always been afraid of the doctor and his wife. They had never been inside of their house. Poor little Ellen cried all day to be carried back to prison. The instincts of childhood are true. She knew she was loved in the jail. Her screams and sobs annoyed Mrs. Flint. Before night she called one of the slaves, and said, "Here, Bill, carry this brat back to the jail. I can't stand her noise. If she would be quiet I should like to keep the little minx. She would make a handy waiting-maid for my daughter by and by. But if she staid here, with her white face, I suppose I should either kill her or spoil her. I hope the doctor will sell them as far as wind and water can carry them. As for their mother, her ladyship will find out yet what she gets by running away. She hasn't so much feeling for her children as a cow has for its calf. If she had, she would have come back long ago, to get them out of jail, and save all this expense and trouble. The good-for-nothing hussy! When she is caught, she shall stay in jail, in irons, for one six months, and then be sold to a sugar plantation.[150] I shall see her broke in yet. What do you stand there for, Bill? Why don't you go off with the brat? Mind, now, that you don't let any of the niggers speak to her in the street!"

When these remarks were reported to me, I smiled at Mrs. Flint's saying that she should either kill my child or spoil her. I thought to myself there was very little danger of the latter. I have always considered it as one of God's special providences that Ellen screamed till she was carried back to jail.

That same night Dr. Flint was called to a patient, and did not return till near morning. Passing my grandmother's, he saw a light in the house, and thought to himself, "Perhaps this has something to do with Linda." He knocked, and the door was opened. "What calls you up so early?" said he. "I saw your light, and I thought I would just stop and tell you that I have found out where Linda is. I know where to put my hands on her, and I shall have her before twelve o'clock." When he had turned away, my grandmother and my uncle looked anxiously at

[150] Slaveholders often used this threat to sell their slaves into a deep Southern state, such as Louisiana, far from family and into particularly brutal labor conditions, to frighten them into compliance.

each other. They did not know whether or not it was merely one of the doctor's tricks to frighten them. In their uncertainty, they thought it was best to have a message conveyed to my friend Betty. Unwilling to alarm her mistress, Betty resolved to dispose of me herself. She came to me, and told me to rise and dress quickly. We hurried down stairs, and across the yard, into the kitchen. She locked the door, and lifted up a plank in the floor. A buffalo skin and a bit of carpet were spread for me to lie on, and a quilt thrown over me. "Stay dar," said she, "till I sees, if dey know 'bout you. Dey say dey vil put thar hans on you afore twelve o'clock. If dey *did* know whar you are, dey won't know *now*. Dey'll be disapinted dis time. Dat's all I got to say. If dey comes rummagin 'mong *my* tings, dey'll get one bressed sarssin from dis 'ere nigger." In my shallow bed I had but just room enough to bring my hands to my face to keep the dust out of my eyes; for Betty walked over me twenty times in an hour, passing from the dresser to the fireplace. When she was alone, I could hear her pronouncing anathemas over Dr. Flint and all his tribe, every now and then saying, with a chuckling laugh, "Dis nigger's too cute for 'em dis time." When the housemaids were about, she had sly ways of drawing them out, that I might hear what they would say. She would repeat stories she had heard about my being in this, or that, or the other place. To which they would answer, that I was not fool enough to be staying round there; that I was in Philadelphia or New York before this time. When all were abed and asleep, Betty raised the plank, and said, "Come out, chile; come out. Dey don't know nottin 'bout you. 'Twas only white folks' lies, to skeer de niggers."

Some days after this adventure I had a much worse fright. As I sat very still in my retreat above stairs, cheerful visions floated through my mind. I thought Dr. Flint would soon get discouraged, and would be willing to sell my children, when he lost all hopes of making them the means of my discovery. I knew who was ready to buy them. Suddenly I heard a voice that chilled my blood. The sound was too familiar to me, it had been too dreadful, for me not to recognize at once my old master. He was in the house, and I at once concluded he had come to seize me. I looked round in terror. There was no way of escape. The voice receded. I supposed the constable was with him, and they were searching the house. In my alarm I did not forget the trouble I was bringing on my generous benefactress. It seemed as if I were born to bring sorrow on all who befriended me, and that was the bitterest drop in the bitter cup of my life. After a while I heard approaching footsteps; the key was turned in my door. I braced myself against the wall to keep from falling. I ventured to look up, and there stood my kind benefactress alone. I was too much overcome to speak, and sunk down upon the floor.

"I thought you would hear your master's voice," she said; "and knowing you would be terrified, I came to tell you there is nothing to fear. You may even indulge in a laugh at the old gentleman's expense. He is so sure you are in New York, that he came to borrow five hundred dollars to go in pursuit of you. My sister had some money to loan on interest. He has obtained it, and proposes to start for New York tonight. So, for the present, you see you are safe. The doctor will merely lighten his pocket hunting after the bird he has left behind."

XIX. THE CHILDREN SOLD

The doctor came back from New York, of course without accomplishing his purpose. He had expended considerable money, and was rather disheartened. My brother and the children had now been in jail two months, and that also was some expense. My friends thought it was a favorable time to work on his discouraged feelings. Mr. Sands sent a speculator to offer him nine hundred dollars for my brother William, and eight hundred for the two children.[151] These were high prices, as slaves were then selling; but the offer was rejected. If it had been merely a question of money, the doctor would have sold any boy of Benny's age for two hundred dollars; but he could not bear to give up the power of revenge. But he was hard pressed for money, and he revolved the matter in his mind. He knew that if he could keep Ellen till she was fifteen, he could sell her for a high price; but I presume he reflected that she might die, or might be stolen away. At all events, he came to the conclusion that he had better accept the slave-trader's offer. Meeting him in the street, he inquired when he would leave town. "To-day, at ten o'clock," he replied. "Ah, do you go so soon?" said the doctor; "I have been reflecting upon your proposition, and I have concluded to let you have the three negroes if you will say nineteen hundred dollars." After some parley, the trader agreed to his terms. He wanted the bill of sale drawn up and signed immediately, as he had a great deal to attend to during the short time he remained in town. The doctor went to the jail and told William he would take him back into his service if he would promise to behave himself; but he replied that he would rather be sold. "And you *shall* be sold, you ungrateful rascal!" exclaimed the doctor.

[151] Sawyer used a speculator to hide his hand in the sale.

In less than an hour the money was paid, the papers were signed, sealed, and delivered, and my brother and children were in the hands of the trader.

It was a hurried transaction; and after it was over, the doctor's characteristic caution returned. He went back to the speculator, and said, "Sir, I have come to lay you under obligations of a thousand dollars not to sell any of those negroes in this state." "You come too late," replied the trader; "our bargain is closed." He had, in fact, already sold them to Mr. Sands, but he did not mention it. The doctor required him to put irons on "that rascal, Bill," and to pass through the back streets when he took his gang out of town. The trader was privately instructed to concede to his wishes. My good old aunt went to the jail to bid the children good by, supposing them to be the speculator's property, and that she should never see them again. As she held Benny in her lap, he said, "Aunt Nancy, I want to show you something." He led her to the door and showed her a long row of marks, saying, "Uncle Will taught me to count. I have made a mark for every day I have been here, and it is sixty days. It is a long time; and the speculator is going to take me and Ellen away. He's a bad man. It's wrong for him to take grandmother's children. I want to go to my mother."

My grandmother was told that the children would be restored to her, but she was requested to act as if they were really to be sent away. Accordingly, she made up a bundle of clothes and went to the jail. When she arrived, she found William handcuffed among the gang, and the children in the trader's cart. The scene seemed too much like reality. She was afraid there might have been some deception or mistake. She fainted, and was carried home.

When the wagon stopped at the hotel, several gentlemen came out and proposed to purchase William, but the trader refused their offers, without stating that he was already sold. And now came the trying hour for that drove of human beings, driven away like cattle, to be sold they knew not where. Husbands were torn from wives, parents from children, never to look upon each other again this side the grave. There was wringing of hands and cries of despair.

Dr. Flint had the supreme satisfaction of seeing the wagon leave town, and Mrs. Flint had the gratification of supposing that my children were going "as far as wind and water would carry them." According to [the] agreement, my uncle followed the wagon some miles, until they came to an old farm house.[152] There the trader took the irons from William, and

[152]Uncle Phillip; compare with John S. Jacobs, *A True Tale of Slavery*, chap. III (Document 11). The farm they stopped at, about a mile outside Edenton, belonged to Joseph B. Skinner.

as he did so, he said, "You are a damned clever fellow. I should like to own you myself. Them gentlemen that wanted to buy you said you was a bright, honest chap, and I must git you a good home. I guess your old master will swear to-morrow, and call himself an old fool for selling the children. I reckon he'll never git their mammy back agin. I expect she's made tracks for the north. Good by, old boy. Remember, I have done you a good turn. You must thank me by coaxing all the pretty gals to go with me next fall. That's going to be my last trip. This trading in niggers is a bad business for a fellow that's got any heart. Move on, you fellows!" And the gang went on, God alone knows where.

Much as I despise and detest the class of slave-traders, whom I regard as the vilest wretches on earth, I must do this man the justice to say that he seemed to have some feeling. He took a fancy to William in the jail, and wanted to buy him. When he heard the story of my children, he was willing to aid them in getting out of Dr. Flint's power, even without charging the customary fee.

My uncle procured a wagon and carried William and the children back to town. Great was the joy in my grandmother's house! The curtains were closed, and the candles lighted. The happy grandmother cuddled the little ones to her bosom. They hugged her, and kissed her, and clapped their hands, and shouted. She knelt down and poured forth one of her heartfelt prayers of thanksgiving to God. The father was present for a while; and though such a "parental relation" as existed between him and my children takes slight hold of the hearts or consciences of slaveholders, it must be that he experienced some moments of pure joy in witnessing the happiness he had imparted.

I had no share in the rejoicings of that evening. The events of the day had not come to my knowledge. And now I will tell you something that happened to me; though you will, perhaps, think it illustrates the superstition of slaves. I sat in my usual place on the floor near the window, where I could hear much that was said in the street without being seen. The family had retired for the night, and all was still. I sat there thinking of my children, when I heard a low strain of music. A band of serenaders were under the window, playing "Home, sweet home."[153] I listened till the sounds did not seem like music, but like the moaning of children. It seemed as if my heart would burst. I rose from my sitting posture, and knelt. A streak of moonlight was on the floor before me, and in the midst of it appeared the forms of my two children. They vanished; but I had seen them distinctly. Some will call it a dream, others a vision. I know

[153]Song from the opera *Clari; or the Maid of Milan* (1823) by John Howard Payne (1791–1852).

not how to account for it, but it made a strong impression on my mind, and I felt certain something had happened to my little ones.[154]

I had not seen Betty since morning. Now I heard her softly turning the key. As soon as she entered, I clung to her, and begged her to let me know whether my children were dead, or whether they were sold; for I had seen their spirits in my room, and I was sure something had happened to them. "Lor, chile," said she, putting her arms round me, "you's got de high-sterics. I'll sleep wid you to-night, 'cause you'll make a noise, and ruin missis. Something has stirred you up mightily. When you is done cryin, I'll talk wid you. De chillern is well, and mighty happy. I seed 'em myself. Does dat satisfy you? Dar, chile, be still! Somebody vill hear you." I tried to obey her. She lay down, and was soon sound asleep; but no sleep would come to my eyelids.

At dawn, Betty was up and off to the kitchen. The hours passed on, and the vision of the night kept constantly recurring to my thoughts. After a while I heard the voices of two women in the entry. In one of them I recognized the housemaid. The other said to her, "Did you know Linda Brent's children was sold to the speculator yesterday. They say ole massa Flint was mighty glad to see 'em drove out of town; but they say they've come back agin. I 'spect it's all their daddy's doings. They say he's bought William too. Lor! how it will take hold of ole massa Flint! I'm going roun' to aunt Marthy's to see 'bout it."

I bit my lips till the blood came to keep from crying out. Were my children with their grandmother, or had the speculator carried them off? The suspense was dreadful. Would Betty *never* come, and tell me the truth about it? At last she came, and I eagerly repeated what I had overheard. Her face was one broad, bright smile. "Lor, you foolish ting!" said she. "I'se gwine to tell you all 'bout it. De gals is eating thar breakfast, and missus tole me to let her tell you; but, poor creeter! t'aint right to keep you waitin', and I'se gwine to tell you. Brudder, chillern, all is bought by de daddy! I'se laugh more

[154]"Varying beliefs in forms of spiritualism were often found among Southern slaves. Jacobs, writing in the 1850s, could also rely on the popularity of spiritualism among her Northern white audience. Spiritualism, a belief that the dead and the living could communicate with one another across the "great divide," emerged in the 1840s after eleven-year-old Kate Fox realized that she could communicate with spirits whose nocturnal rappings had kept the Fox family awake in their small, upstate New York house. One of the earliest messages Kate received was from the spirit of the dead five-year-old daughter of Jacobs's friend Amy Post, after which the Posts became strong supporters of spiritualism. From the start, spiritualism was the domain of women, who found in it a source of power in an age when the pulpit and podium were off-limits to them. Its therapeutic and empowering qualities would have been appealing to a black woman in Jacobs's position.

dan nuff, tinking 'bout ole massa Flint. Lor, how he *vill* swar! He's got ketched dis time, any how; but I must be getting out o' dis, or dem gals vill come and ketch *me*."

Betty went off laughing; and I said to myself, "Can it be true that my children are free? I have not suffered for them in vain. Thank God!"

Great surprise was expressed when it was known that my children had returned to their grandmother's. The news spread through the town, and many a kind word was bestowed on the little ones.

Dr. Flint went to my grandmother's to ascertain who was the owner of my children, and she informed him. "I expected as much," said he. "I am glad to hear it. I have had news from Linda lately, and I shall soon have her. You need never expect to see *her* free. She shall be my slave as long as I live, and when I am dead she shall be the slave of my children. If I ever find out that you or Phillip had any thing to do with her running off I'll kill him. And if I meet William in the street, and he presumes to look at me, I'll flog him within an inch of his life. Keep those brats out of my sight!"

As he turned to leave, my grandmother said something to remind him of his own doings. He looked back upon her, as if he would have been glad to strike her to the ground.

I had my season of joy and thanksgiving. It was the first time since my childhood that I had experienced any real happiness. I heard of the old doctor's threats, but they no longer had the same power to trouble me. The darkest cloud that hung over my life had rolled away. Whatever slavery might do to me, it could not shackle my children. If I fell a sacrifice, my little ones were saved. It was well for me that my simple heart believed all that had been promised for their welfare. It is always better to trust than to doubt.

XX. NEW PERILS

The doctor, more exasperated than ever, again tried to revenge himself on my relatives. He arrested uncle Phillip on the charge of having aided my flight. He was carried before a court, and swore truly that he knew nothing of my intention to escape, and that he had not seen me since I left my master's plantation. The doctor then demanded that he should give bail for five hundred dollars that he would have nothing to do with me. Several gentlemen offered to be security for him; but Mr. Sands told him he had better go back to jail, and he would see that he came out without giving bail.

The news of his arrest was carried to my grandmother, who conveyed it to Betty. In the kindness of her heart, she again stowed me away under the floor; and as she walked back and forth, in the performance of her culinary duties, she talked apparently to herself, but with the intention that I should hear what was going on. I hoped that my uncle's imprisonment would last but few days; still I was anxious. I thought it likely Dr. Flint would do his utmost to taunt and insult him, and I was afraid my uncle might lose control of himself, and retort in some way that would be construed into a punishable offence; and I was well aware that in court his word would not be taken against any white man's. The search for me was renewed. Something had excited suspicions that I was in the vicinity. They searched the house I was in. I heard their steps and their voices. At night, when all were asleep, Betty came to release me from my place of confinement. The fright I had undergone, the constrained posture, and the dampness of the ground, made me ill for several days. My uncle was soon after taken out of prison; but the movements of all my relatives, and of all our friends, were very closely watched.

We all saw that I could not remain where I was much longer. I had already staid longer than was intended, and I knew my presence must be a source of perpetual anxiety to my kind benefactress. During this time, my friends had laid many plans for my escape, but the extreme vigilance of my persecutors made it impossible to carry them into effect.

One morning I was much startled by hearing somebody trying to get into my room. Several keys were tried, but none fitted. I instantly conjectured it was one of the housemaids; and I concluded she must either have heard some noise in the room, or have noticed the entrance of Betty. When my friend came at her usual time, I told her what had happened. "I knows who it was," said she. "'Pend upon it, 'twas dat Jenny. Dat nigger allers got de debble in her." I suggested that she might have seen or heard something that excited her curiosity.

"Tut! tut! chile!" exclaimed Betty, "she ain't seen notin', nor hearn notin'. She only 'spects someting. Dat's all. She wants to fine out who hab cut and make my gownd. But she won't nebber know. Dat's sartin. I'll git missis to fix her."

I reflected a moment, and said, "Betty, I must leave here to-night."

"Do as you tink best, poor chile," she replied. "I'se mighty 'fraid dat 'ere nigger vill pop on you some time."

She reported the incident to her mistress, and received orders to keep Jenny busy in the kitchen till she could see my uncle Phillip. He told her he would send a friend for me that very evening. She told him she hoped I was going to the north, for it was very dangerous for me to remain any where in the vicinity. Alas, it was not an easy thing, for one in my situation, to go to the north. In order to leave the coast quite clear for me, she went into the country to spend the day with her brother, and took Jenny with her. She was afraid to come and bid me good by, but she left a kind message with Betty. I heard her carriage roll from the door, and I never again saw her who had so generously befriended the poor, trembling fugitive! Though she was a slaveholder, to this day my heart blesses her!

I had not the slightest idea where I was going. Betty brought me a suit of sailor's clothes,—jacket, trowsers, and tarpaulin hat.[155] She gave me a small bundle, saying I might need it where I was going. In cheery tones, she exclaimed, "I'se *so* glad you is gwine to free parts! Don't forget ole Betty. P'raps I'll come 'long by and by."

I tried to tell her how grateful I felt for all her kindness, but she interrupted me. "I don't want no tanks, honey. I'se glad I could help you, and I hope de good Lord vill open de path for you. I'se gwine wid you to de lower gate. Put your hands in your pockets, and walk ricketty, like de sailors."

I performed to her satisfaction. At the gate I found Peter, a young colored man, waiting for me. I had known him for years. He had been an apprentice to my father, and had always borne a good character. I was not afraid to trust to him. Betty bade me a hurried good by, and we walked off. "Take courage, Linda," said my friend Peter. "I've got a dagger, and no man shall take you from me, unless he passes over my dead body."

It was a long time since I had taken a walk out of doors, and the fresh air revived me. It was also pleasant to hear a human voice speaking to me above a whisper. I passed several people whom I knew, but they did not recognize me in my disguise. I prayed internally that, for Peter's sake, as well as my own, nothing might occur to bring out his dagger. We walked on till we came to the wharf. My aunt Nancy's husband was a seafaring man, and it had been deemed necessary to let him into our secret.[156] He took me into his boat, rowed out to a vessel not far distant, and hoisted me on board. We three were the only occupants of the vessel. I now ventured to ask what they proposed to do with me. They said I was to remain on board till near dawn, and then they would hide me in Snaky Swamp,

[155]Waterproof canvas hat.

[156]See John S. Jacobs, *A True Tale of Slavery,* chap. III (Document 11), for more on Aunt Nancy's husband, Stephen.

till my uncle Phillip had prepared a place of concealment for me.[157] If the vessel had been bound north, it would have been of no avail to me, for it would certainly have been searched. About four o'clock, we were again seated in the boat, and rowed three miles to the swamp. My fear of snakes had been increased by the venomous bite I had received, and I dreaded to enter this hiding-place. But I was in no situation to choose, and I gratefully accepted the best that my poor, persecuted friends could do for me.

Peter landed first, and with a large knife cut a path through bamboos and briers of all descriptions. He came back, took me in his arms, and carried me to a seat made among the bamboos. Before we reached it, we were covered with hundreds of mosquitos. In an hour's time they had so poisoned my flesh that I was a pitiful sight to behold. As the light increased, I saw snake after snake crawling round us. I had been accustomed to the sight of snakes all my life, but these were larger than any I had ever seen. To this day I shudder when I remember that morning. As evening approached, the number of snakes increased so much that we were continually obliged to thrash them with sticks to keep them from crawling over us. The bamboos were so high and so thick that it was impossible to see beyond a very short distance. Just before it became dark we procured a seat nearer to the entrance of the swamp, being fearful of losing our way back to the boat. It was not long before we heard the paddle of oars, and the low whistle, which had been agreed upon as a signal. We made haste to enter the boat, and were rowed back to the vessel. I passed a wretched night; for the heat of the swamp, the mosquitos, and the constant terror of snakes, had brought on a burning fever. I had just dropped asleep, when they came and told me it was time to go back to that horrid swamp. I could scarcely summon courage to rise. But even those large, venomous snakes were less dreadful to my imagination than the white men in that community called civilized. This time Peter took a quantity of tobacco to burn, to keep off the mosquitos. It produced the desired effect on them, but gave me nausea and severe headache. At dark we returned to the vessel. I had been so sick during the day, that Peter declared I should go home that night, if the devil himself was on patrol. They told me a place of concealment had been provided for me at my grandmother's. I could not imagine how it was possible to hide me in her house, every nook and corner of which was

[157] Cabarrus Pocosin, or "Snaky Swamp," lay southwest of Edenton, thirty miles south of the Great Dismal Swamp, which at ten miles wide and thirty miles long, running from Virginia to North Carolina, was an effective hideout for fugitive slaves (Yellin, *Harriet Jacobs*, 47).

known to the Flint family. They told me to wait and see. We were rowed ashore, and went boldly through the streets, to my grandmother's. I wore my sailor's clothes, and had blackened my face with charcoal. I passed several people whom I knew. The father of my children came so near that I brushed against his arm; but he had no idea who it was.

"You must make the most of this walk," said my friend Peter, "for you may not have another very soon."

I thought his voice sounded sad. It was kind of him to conceal from me what a dismal hole was to be my home for a long, long time.

XXI. THE LOOPHOLE OF RETREAT[158]

A small shed had been added to my grandmother's house years ago. Some boards were laid across the joists at the top, and between these boards and the roof was a very small garret, never occupied by any thing but rats and mice. It was a pent roof, covered with nothing but shingles, according to the southern custom for such buildings. The garret was only nine feet long and seven wide. The highest part was three feet high, and sloped down abruptly to the loose board floor. There was no admission for either light or air. My uncle Phillip, who was a carpenter, had very skilfully made a concealed trap-door, which communicated with the storeroom. He had been doing this while I was waiting in the swamp. The storeroom opened upon a piazza. To this hole I was conveyed as soon as I entered the house. The air was stifling; the darkness total. A bed had been spread on the floor. I could sleep quite comfortably on one side; but the slope was so sudden that I could not turn on the other without hitting the roof. The rats and mice ran over my bed; but I was weary, and I slept such sleep as the wretched may, when a tempest has passed over them. Morning came. I knew it only by the noises I heard; for in my small den day and night were all the same. I suffered for air even more than for light. But I was not comfortless. I heard the voices of my children. There was joy and there was sadness in the sound. It made my tears flow. How I longed to speak to them! I was eager to look on their faces; but there was no hole, no crack, through which I could peep. This continued darkness was oppressive. It seemed horrible to sit or lie in a cramped position day after day, without one gleam of light. Yet I would have chosen this, rather than my lot as a slave, though white people considered it an easy one;

[158]Reference to William Cowper's *The Task* (1785), 4.88–90. Jacobs might have read Cowper (1731–1800) for his religious and antislavery poetry.

and it was so compared with the fate of others. I was never cruelly overworked; I was never lacerated with the whip from head to foot; I was never so beaten and bruised that I could not turn from one side to the other; I never had my heel-strings cut to prevent my running away; I was never chained to a log and forced to drag it about, while I toiled in the fields from morning till night; I was never branded with [a] hot iron, or torn by bloodhounds. On the contrary, I had always been kindly treated, and tenderly cared for, until I came into the hands of Dr. Flint. I had never wished for freedom till then. But though my life in slavery was comparatively devoid of hardships, God pity the woman who is compelled to lead such a life![159]

My food was passed up to me through the trap-door my uncle had contrived; and my grandmother, my uncle Phillip, and aunt Nancy would seize such opportunities as they could, to mount up there and chat with me at the opening. But of course this was not safe in the daytime. It must all be done in darkness. It was impossible for me to move in an erect position, but I crawled about my den for exercise. One day I hit my head against something, and found it was a gimlet. My uncle had left it sticking there when he made the trap-door. I was as rejoiced as Robinson Crusoe could have been at finding such a treasure.[160] It put a lucky thought into my head. I said to myself, "Now I will have some light. Now I will see my children." I did not dare to begin my work during the daytime, for fear of attracting attention. But I groped round; and having found the side next [to] the street, where I could frequently see my children, I stuck the gimlet in and waited for evening. I bored three rows of holes, one above another; then I bored out the interstices between. I thus succeeded in making one hole about an inch long and an inch broad. I sat by it till late into the night, to enjoy the little whiff of air that floated in. In the morning I watched for my children. The first person I saw in the street was Dr. Flint. I had a shuddering, superstitious feeling that it was a bad omen. Several familiar faces passed by. At last I heard the merry laugh of children, and presently two sweet little faces were looking up at me, as though they knew I was there, and were conscious of the joy they imparted. How I longed to *tell* them I was there!

My condition was now a little improved. But for weeks I was tormented by hundreds of little red insects, fine as a needle's point, that pierced through my skin, and produced an intolerable burning.

[159]See John S. Jacobs's description of the cupboard built by their uncle Mark (*A True Tale of Slavery*, chap. IV; see Document 11).

[160]Reference to Daniel Defoe's adventure novel *Robinson Crusoe* (1719) detailing the experiences of a castaway.

The good grandmother gave me herb teas and cooling medicines, and finally I got rid of them. The heat of my den was intense, for nothing but thin shingles protected me from the scorching summer's sun. But I had my consolations. Through my peeping-hole I could watch the children, and when they were near enough, I could hear their talk. Aunt Nancy brought me all the news she could hear at Dr. Flint's. From her I learned that the doctor had written to New York to a colored woman, who had been born and raised in our neighborhood, and had breathed his contaminating atmosphere. He offered her a reward if she could find out any thing about me. I know not what was the nature of her reply; but he soon after started for New York in haste, saying to his family that he had business of importance to transact. I peeped at him as he passed on his way to the steamboat. It was a satisfaction to have miles of land and water between us, even for a little while; and it was a still greater satisfaction to know that he believed me to be in the Free States. My little den seemed less dreary than it had done. He returned, as he did from his former journey to New York, without obtaining any satisfactory information. When he passed our house next morning, Benny was standing at the gate. He had heard them say that he had gone to find me, and he called out, "Dr. Flint, did you bring my mother home? I want to see her." The doctor stamped his foot at him in a rage, and exclaimed, "Get out of the way, you little damned rascal! If you don't, I'll cut off your head."

Benny ran terrified into the house, saying, "You can't put me in jail again. I don't belong to you now." It was well that the wind carried the words away from the doctor's ear. I told my grandmother of it, when we had our next conference at the trap-door; and begged of her not to allow the children to be impertinent to the irascible old man.

Autumn came, with a pleasant abatement of heat.[161] My eyes had become accustomed to the dim light, and by holding my book or work in a certain position near the aperture I contrived to read and sew. That was a great relief to the tedious monotony of my life. But when winter came, the cold penetrated through the thin shingle roof, and I was dreadfully chilled. The winters there are not so long, or so severe, as in northern latitudes; but the houses are not built to shelter from cold, and my little den was peculiarly comfortless. The kind grandmother brought me bed-clothes and warm drinks. Often I was obliged to lie in bed all day to keep comfortable; but with all my precautions, my shoulders and feet were frostbitten. O, those long, gloomy days, with no object for my eye to rest upon,

[161] Jacobs went into hiding in the summer of 1835.

and no thoughts to occupy my mind, except the dreary past and the uncertain future! I was thankful when there came a day sufficiently mild for me to wrap myself up and sit at the loophole to watch the passers by. Southerners have the habit of stopping and talking in the streets, and I heard many conversations not intended to meet my ears. I heard slave-hunters planning how to catch some poor fugitive. Several times I heard allusions to Dr. Flint, myself, and the history of my children, who, perhaps, were playing near the gate. One would say, "I wouldn't move my little finger to catch her, as old Flint's property." Another would say, "I'll catch any nigger for the reward. A man ought to have what belongs to him, if he is a damned brute." The opinion was often expressed that I was in the Free States. Very rarely did any one suggest that I might be in the vicinity. Had the least suspicion rested on my grandmother's house, it would have been burned to the ground. But it was the last place they thought of. Yet there was no place, where slavery existed, that could have afforded me so good a place of concealment.

Dr. Flint and his family repeatedly tried to coax and bribe my children to tell something they had heard said about me. One day the doctor took them into a shop, and offered them some bright little silver pieces and gay handkerchiefs if they would tell where their mother was. Ellen shrank away from him, and would not speak; but Benny spoke up, and said, "Dr. Flint, I don't know where my mother is. I guess she's in New York; and when you go there again, I wish you'd ask her to come home, for I want to see her; but if you put her in jail, or tell her you'll cut her head off, I'll tell her to go right back."

XXII. CHRISTMAS FESTIVITIES

Christmas was approaching. Grandmother brought me materials, and I busied myself making some new garments and little playthings for my children. Were it not that hiring day is near at hand, and many families are fearfully looking forward to the probability of separation in a few days, Christmas might be a happy season for the poor slaves. Even slave mothers try to gladden the hearts of their little ones on that occasion. Benny and Ellen had their Christmas stockings filled. Their imprisoned mother could not have the privilege of witnessing their surprise and joy. But I had the pleasure of peeping at them as they went into the street with their new suits on. I heard Benny ask a little playmate whether Santa Claus brought him any thing. "Yes," replied the boy; "but Santa Claus ain't a real man. It's the children's mothers that put things into the stockings." "No, that can't be," replied Benny, "for Santa Claus brought Ellen and me these new clothes, and my mother has been gone this long time."

How I longed to tell him that his mother made those garments, and that many a tear fell on them while she worked!

Every child rises early on Christmas morning to see the Johnkannaus.[162] Without them, Christmas would be shorn of its greatest attraction. They consist of companies of slaves from the plantations, generally of the lower class. Two athletic men, in calico wrappers, have a net thrown over them, covered with all manner of bright-colored stripes. Cows' tails are fastened to their backs, and their heads are decorated with horns. A box, covered with sheepskin, is called the gumbo box. A dozen beat on this, while others strike triangles and jawbones, to which bands of dancers keep time. For a month previous they are composing songs, which are sung on this occasion. These companies, of a hundred each, turn out early in the morning, and are allowed to go round till twelve o'clock, begging for contributions. Not a door is left unvisited where there is the least chance of obtaining a penny or a glass of rum. They do not drink while they are out, but carry the rum home in jugs, to have a carousal. These Christmas donations frequently amount to twenty or thirty dollars. It is seldom that any white man or child refuses to give them a trifle. If he does, they regale his ears with the following song:—

> Poor massa, so dey say;
> Down in de heel, so dey say;
> Got no money, so dey say;
> Not one shillin, so dey say;
> God A'mighty bress you, so dey say.

Christmas is a day of feasting, both with white and colored people. Slaves, who are lucky enough to have a few shillings, are sure to spend them for good eating; and many a turkey and pig is captured, without saying, "By your leave, sir." Those who cannot obtain these, cook a 'possum, or a raccoon, from which savory dishes can be made. My grandmother raised poultry and pigs for sale; and it was her established custom to have both a turkey and a pig roasted for Christmas dinner.

[162] Also known as Jonkannu or Jon Kuners, this is a carnival celebration based on a masquerade that originates in West African traditions of masking. It was popular in the creolized cultures of the West Indies, New Orleans, Key West, and North Carolina. Under its protection, black slaves dressed as Jonkannu figures openly derided their masters for their stinginess if, during the masquerade, the masters refused to give them rum and money (Jacobs, *Incidents*, ed. Yellin, 277n).

On this occasion, I was warned to keep extremely quiet, because two guests had been invited. One was the town constable, and the other was a free colored man, who tried to pass himself off for white, and who was always ready to do any mean work for the sake of currying favor with white people. My grandmother had a motive for inviting them. She managed to take them all over the house. All the rooms on the lower floor were thrown open for them to pass in and out; and after dinner, they were invited up stairs to look at a fine mocking bird my uncle had just brought home. There, too, the rooms were all thrown open, that they might look in. When I heard them talking on the piazza, my heart almost stood still. I knew this colored man had spent many nights hunting for me. Every body knew he had the blood of a slave father in his veins; but for the sake of passing himself off for white, he was ready to kiss the slaveholders' feet. How I despised him! As for the constable, he wore no false colors. The duties of his office were despicable, but he was superior to his companion, inasmuch as he did not pretend to be what he was not. Any white man, who could raise money enough to buy a slave, would have considered himself degraded by being a constable; but the office enabled its possessor to exercise authority. If he found any slave out after nine o'clock, he could whip him as much as he liked; and that was a privilege to be coveted. When the guests were ready to depart, my grandmother gave each of them some of her nice pudding, as a present for their wives. Through my peep-hole I saw them go out of the gate, and I was glad when it closed after them. So passed the first Christmas in my den.

XXIII. STILL IN PRISON

When spring returned, and I took in the little patch of green the aperture commanded, I asked myself how many more summers and winters I must be condemned to spend thus. I longed to draw in a plentiful draught of fresh air, to stretch my cramped limbs, to have room to stand erect, to feel the earth under my feet again. My relatives were constantly on the lookout for a chance of escape; but none offered that seemed practicable, and even tolerably safe. The hot summer came again, and made the turpentine drop from the thin roof over my head.

During the long nights I was restless for want of air, and I had no room to toss and turn. There was but one compensation; the atmosphere was so stifled that even mosquitos would not condescend to buzz in it. With all my detestation of Dr. Flint, I could hardly wish him a worse punishment, either in this world or that which is to come, than to suffer what I suffered in one single summer. Yet the laws allowed *him* to be out in the free air, while I, guiltless of crime, was pent up here, as the only means of avoiding the cruelties the laws allowed him to inflict upon me! I don't know what kept life within me. Again and again, I thought I should die before long; but I saw the leaves of another autumn whirl through the air, and felt the touch of another winter. In summer the most terrible thunder storms were acceptable, for the rain came through the roof, and I rolled up my bed that it might cool the hot boards under it. Later in the season, storms sometimes wet my clothes through and through, and that was not comfortable when the air grew chilly. Moderate storms I could keep out by filling the chinks with oakum.

But uncomfortable as my situation was, I had glimpses of things out of doors, which made me thankful for my wretched hiding-place. One day I saw a slave pass our gate, muttering, "It's his own, and he can kill it if he will." My grandmother told me that woman's history. Her mistress had that day seen her baby for the first time, and in the lineaments of its fair face she saw a likeness to her husband. She turned the bondwoman and her child out of doors, and forbade her ever to return. The slave went to her master, and told him what had happened. He promised to talk with her mistress, and make it all right. The next day she and her baby were sold to a Georgia trader.

Another time I saw a woman rush wildly by, pursued by two men. She was a slave, the wet nurse of her mistress's children. For some trifling offence her mistress ordered her to be stripped and whipped. To escape the degradation and the torture, she rushed to the river, jumped in, and ended her wrongs in death.

Senator Brown, of Mississippi, could not be ignorant of many such facts as these, for they are of frequent occurrence in every Southern State. Yet he stood up in the Congress of the United States, and declared that slavery was "a great moral, social, and political blessing; a blessing to the master, and a blessing to the slave!"[163]

I suffered much more during the second winter than I did during the first. My limbs were benumbed by inaction, and the cold filled them with cramp. I had a very painful sensation of coldness in my head; even my face and tongue stiffened, and I lost the power of speech.

[163]Albert Gallatin Brown (1813–1880), a Democratic senator from Mississippi, delivered this speech on February 24, 1854, during congressional debate on the Kansas-Nebraska Act. This act effectively repealed the Missouri Compromise of 1820, which had outlawed slavery above latitude 36°30', by opening up all of the land of the Louisiana Purchase to slavery. Its passage radicalized opponents of slavery.

Of course it was impossible, under the circumstances, to summon any physician. My brother William came and did all he could for me. Uncle Phillip also watched tenderly over me; and poor grandmother crept up and down to inquire whether there were any signs of returning life. I was restored to consciousness by the dashing of cold water in my face, and found myself leaning against my brother's arm, while he bent over me with streaming eyes. He afterwards told me he thought I was dying, for I had been in an unconscious state sixteen hours. I next became delirious, and was in great danger of betraying myself and my friends. To prevent this, they stupefied me with drugs. I remained in bed six weeks, weary in body and sick at heart. How to get medical advice was the question. William finally went to a Thomsonian doctor,[164] and described himself as having all my pains and aches. He returned with herbs, roots, and ointment. He was especially charged to rub on the ointment by a fire; but how could a fire be made in my little den? Charcoal in a furnace was tried, but there was no outlet for the gas, and it nearly cost me my life. Afterwards coals, already kindled, were brought up in an iron pan, and placed on bricks. I was so weak, and it was so long since I had enjoyed the warmth of a fire, that those few coals actually made me weep. I think the medicines did me some good; but my recovery was very slow. Dark thoughts passed through my mind as I lay there day after day. I tried to be thankful for my little cell, dismal as it was, and even to love it, as part of the price I had paid for the redemption of my children. Sometimes I thought God was a compassionate Father, who would forgive my sins for the sake of my sufferings. At other times, it seemed to me there was no justice or mercy in the divine government. I asked why the curse of slavery was permitted to exist, and why I had been so persecuted and wronged from youth upward. These things took the shape of mystery, which is to this day not so clear to my soul as I trust it will be hereafter.[165]

In the midst of my illness, grandmother broke down under the weight of anxiety and toil. The idea of losing her, who had always been my best friend and a mother to my children, was the sorest trial I had yet had. O, how earnestly I prayed that she might recover! How hard it seemed,

[164]Samuel Thomson (1769–1843) and his followers treated illnesses by raising the temperature of the body with herbs and steam baths on the theory that heat was the source of life. This was meant to be an alternative treatment to contemporary medicine's use of bleeding, blistering, and purging.

[165]Reference to Mark 4:11, in which "mystery" signifies a divine secret to be revealed to the faithful in God's good time.

that I could not tend upon her, who had so long and so tenderly watched over me!

One day the screams of a child nerved me with strength to crawl to my peeping-hole, and I saw my son covered with blood. A fierce dog, usually kept chained, had seized and bitten him. A doctor was sent for, and I heard the groans and screams of my child while the wounds were being sewed up. O, what torture to a mother's heart, to listen to this and be unable to go to him!

But childhood is like a day in spring, alternately shower and sunshine. Before night Benny was bright and lively, threatening the destruction of the dog; and great was his delight when the doctor told him the next day that the dog had bitten another boy and been shot. Benny recovered from his wounds; but it was long before he could walk.

When my grandmother's illness became known, many ladies, who were her customers, called to bring her some little comforts, and to inquire whether she had every thing she wanted. Aunt Nancy one night asked permission to watch with her sick mother, and Mrs. Flint replied, "I don't see any need of your going. I can't spare you." But when she found other ladies in the neighborhood were so attentive, not wishing to be outdone in Christian charity, she also sallied forth, in magnificent condescension, and stood by the bedside of her who had loved her in her infancy, and who had been repaid by such grievous wrongs. She seemed surprised to find her so ill, and scolded uncle Phillip for not sending for Dr. Flint. She herself sent for him immediately, and he came. Secure as I was in my retreat, I should have been terrified if I had known he was so near me. He pronounced my grandmother in a very critical situation, and said if her attending physician wished it, he would visit her. Nobody wished to have him coming to the house at all hours, and we were not disposed to give him a chance to make out a long bill.

As Mrs. Flint went out, Sally told her the reason Benny was lame was, that a dog had bitten him. "I'm glad of it," replied she. "I wish he had killed him. It would be good news to send to his mother. *Her* day will come. The dogs will grab *her* yet." With these Christian words she and her husband departed, and, to my great satisfaction, returned no more.

I heard from uncle Phillip, with feelings of unspeakable joy and gratitude, that the crisis was passed and grandmother would live. I could now say from my heart, "God is merciful. He has spared me the anguish of feeling that I caused her death."

XXIV. THE CANDIDATE FOR CONGRESS

The summer had nearly ended, when Dr. Flint made a third visit to New York, in search of me. Two candidates were running for Congress, and he returned in season to vote. The father of my children was the Whig candidate. The doctor had hitherto been a stanch Whig; but now he exerted all his energies for the defeat of Mr. Sands. He invited large parties of men to dine in the shade of his trees, and supplied them with plenty of rum and brandy. If any poor fellow drowned his wits in the bowl, and, in the openness of his convivial heart, proclaimed that he did not mean to vote the Democratic ticket, he was shoved into the street without ceremony.

The doctor expended his liquor in vain. Mr. Sands was elected; an event which occasioned me some anxious thoughts.[166] He had not emancipated my children, and if he should die they would be at the mercy of his heirs. Two little voices, that frequently met my ear, seemed to plead with me not to let their father depart without striving to make their freedom secure. Years had passed since I had spoken to him. I had not even seen him since the night I passed him, unrecognized, in my disguise of a sailor. I supposed he would call before he left, to say something to my grandmother concerning the children, and I resolved what course to take.

The day before his departure for Washington I made arrangements, towards evening, to get from my hiding-place into the storeroom below. I found myself so stiff and clumsy that it was with great difficulty I could hitch from one resting place to another. When I reached the storeroom my ankles gave way under me, and I sank exhausted on the floor. It seemed as if I could never use my limbs again. But the purpose I had in view roused all the strength I had. I crawled on my hands and knees to the window, and, screened behind a barrel, I waited for his coming. The clock struck nine, and I knew the steamboat would leave between ten and eleven. My hopes were failing. But presently I heard his voice, saying to some one, "Wait for me a moment. I wish to see aunt Martha." When he came out, as he passed the window, I said, "Stop one moment, and let me speak for my children." He started, hesitated, and then passed on, and went out of the gate. I closed the shutter I had partially opened, and sank down behind the barrel. I had suffered much; but seldom had I experienced a keener pang than I then felt. Had my

[166]Sawyer was elected to Congress in August 1837; the first session he attended opened in September.

children, then, become of so little consequence to him? And had he so little feeling for their wretched mother that he would not listen a moment while she pleaded for them? Painful memories were so busy within me, that I forgot I had not hooked the shutter, till I heard some one opening it. I looked up. He had come back. "Who called me?" said he, in a low tone. "I did," I replied. "Oh, Linda," said he, "I knew your voice; but I was afraid to answer, lest my friend should hear me. Why do you come here? Is it possible you risk yourself in this house? They are mad to allow it. I shall expect to hear that you are all ruined." I did not wish to implicate him, by letting him know my place of concealment; so I merely said, "I thought you would come to bid grandmother good by, and so I came here to speak a few words to you about emancipating my children. Many changes may take place during the six months you are gone to Washington, and it does not seem right for you to expose them to the risk of such changes. I want nothing for myself; all I ask is, that you will free my children, or authorize some friend to do it, before you go."

He promised he would do it, and also expressed a readiness to make any arrangements whereby I could be purchased.

I heard footsteps approaching, and closed the shutter hastily. I wanted to crawl back to my den, without letting the family know what I had done; for I knew they would deem it very imprudent. But he stepped back into the house, to tell my grandmother that he had spoken with me at the storeroom window, and to beg of her not to allow me to remain in the house over night. He said it was the height of madness for me to be there; that we should certainly all be ruined. Luckily, he was in too much of a hurry to wait for a reply, or the dear old woman would surely have told him all.

I tried to go back to my den, but found it more difficult to go up than I had to come down. Now that my mission was fulfilled, the little strength that had supported me through it was gone, and I sank helpless on the floor. My grandmother, alarmed at the risk I had run, came into the storeroom in the dark, and locked the door behind her. "Linda," she whispered, "where are you?"

"I am here by the window," I replied. "I *couldn't* have him go away without emancipating the children. Who knows what may happen?"

"Come, come, child," said she, "it won't do for you to stay here another minute. You've done wrong; but I can't blame you, poor thing!"

I told her I could not return without assistance, and she must call my uncle. Uncle Phillip came, and pity prevented him from scolding me. He carried me back to my dungeon, laid me tenderly on the bed, gave me some medicine, and asked me if there was any thing more he could do.

Then he went away, and I was left with my own thoughts—starless as the midnight darkness around me.

My friends feared I should become a cripple for life; and I was so weary of my long imprisonment that, had it not been for the hope of serving my children, I should have been thankful to die; but, for their sakes, I was willing to bear on.

XXV. COMPETITION IN CUNNING

Dr. Flint had not given me up. Every now and then he would say to my grandmother that I would yet come back, and voluntarily surrender myself; and that when I did, I could be purchased by my relatives, or any one who wished to buy me. I knew his cunning nature too well not to percieve that this was a trap laid for me; and so all my friends understood it. I resolved to match my cunning against his cunning. In order to make him believe that I was in New York, I resolved to write him a letter dated from that place. I sent for my friend Peter, and asked him if he knew any trustworthy seafaring person, who would carry such a letter to New York, and put it in the post office there. He said he knew one that he would trust with his own life to the ends of the world. I reminded him that it was a hazardous thing for him to undertake. He said he knew it, but he was willing to do any thing to help me. I expressed a wish for a New York paper, to ascertain the names of some of the streets. He run his hand into his pocket, and said, "Here is half a one, that was round a cap I bought of a pedler yesterday." I told him the letter would be ready the next evening. He bade me good by, adding, "Keep up your spirits, Linda; brighter days will come by and by."

My uncle Phillip kept watch over the gate until our brief interview was over. Early the next morning, I seated myself near the little aperture to examine the newspaper. It was a piece of the New York Herald; and, for once, the paper that systematically abuses the colored people, was made to render them a service.[167] Having obtained what information I wanted concerning streets and numbers, I wrote two letters, one to my grandmother, the other to Dr. Flint. I reminded him how he, a gray-headed man, had treated a helpless child, who had been placed in his power, and what years of misery he had brought upon her. To my grandmother, I expressed a wish to have my children sent to me at the

[167]A one-cent daily paper, the *New York Herald* was founded in 1835 by editor James Gordon Bennett (1795–1872) and was generally proslavery and antiblack.

north, where I could teach them to respect themselves, and set them a virtuous example; which a slave mother was not allowed to do at the south. I asked her to direct her answer to a certain street in Boston, as I did not live in New York, though I went there sometimes. I dated these letters ahead, to allow for the time it would take to carry them, and sent a memorandum of the date to the messenger. When my friend came for the letters, I said, "God bless and reward you, Peter, for this disinterested kindness. Pray be careful. If you are detected, both you and I will have to suffer dreadfully. I have not a relative who would dare to do it for me." He replied, "You may trust to me, Linda. I don't forget that your father was my best friend, and I will be a friend to his children so long as God lets me live."

It was necessary to tell my grandmother what I had done, in order that she might be ready for the letter, and prepared to hear what Dr. Flint might say about my being at the north. She was sadly troubled. She felt sure mischief would come of it. I also told my plan to aunt Nancy, in order that she might report to us what was said at Dr. Flint's house. I whispered it to her through a crack, and she whispered back, "I hope it will succeed. I shan't mind being a slave all *my* life, if I can only see you and the children free."

I had directed that my letters should be put into the New York post office on the 20th of the month. On the evening of the 24th my aunt came to say that Dr. Flint and his wife had been talking in a low voice about a letter he had received, and that when he went to his office he promised to bring it when he came to tea. So I concluded I should hear my letter read the next morning. I told my grandmother Dr. Flint would be sure to come, and asked her to have him sit near a certain door, and leave it open, that I might hear what he said. The next morning I took my station within sound of that door, and remained motionless as a statue. It was not long before I heard the gate slam, and the well-known footsteps enter the house. He seated himself in the chair that was placed for him, and said, "Well, Martha, I've brought you a letter from Linda. She has sent me a letter, also. I know exactly where to find her; but I don't choose to go to Boston for her. I had rather she would come back of her own accord, in a respectable manner. Her uncle Phillip is the best person to go for her. With *him*, she would feel perfectly free to act. I am willing to pay his expenses going and returning. She shall be sold to her friends. Her children are free; at least I suppose they are; and when you obtain her freedom, you'll make a happy family. I suppose, Martha, you have no objection to my reading to you the letter Linda has written to you."

He broke the seal, and I heard him read it. The old villain! He had suppressed the letter I wrote to grandmother, and prepared a substitute of his own, the purport of which was as follows:—

> Dear Grandmother: I have long wanted to write to you; but the disgraceful manner in which I left you and my children made me ashamed to do it. If you knew how much I have suffered since I ran away, you would pity and forgive me. I have purchased freedom at a dear rate. If any arrangement could be made for me to return to the south without being a slave, I would gladly come. If not, I beg of you to send my children to the north. I cannot live any longer without them. Let me know in time, and I will meet them in New York or Philadelphia, whichever place best suits my uncle's convenience. Write as soon as possible to your unhappy daughter, Linda.

"It is very much as I expected it would be," said the old hypocrite, rising to go. "You see the foolish girl has repented of her rashness, and wants to return. We must help her to do it, Martha. Talk with Phillip about it. If he will go for her, she will trust to him, and come back. I should like an answer tomorrow. Good morning, Martha."

As he stepped out on the piazza, he stumbled over my little girl. "Ah, Ellen, is that you?" he said, in his most gracious manner. "I didn't see you. How do you do?"

"Pretty well, sir," she replied. "I heard you tell grandmother that my mother is coming home. I want to see her."

"Yes, Ellen, I am going to bring her home very soon," rejoined he; "and you shall see her as much as you like, you little curly-headed nigger."

This was as good as a comedy to me, who had heard it all; but grandmother was frightened and distressed, because the doctor wanted my uncle to go for me.

The next evening Dr. Flint called to talk the matter over. My uncle told him that from what he had heard of Massachusetts, he judged he should be mobbed if he went there after a runaway slave.[168] "All stuff and nonsense, Phillip!" replied the doctor. "Do you suppose I want you to kick up a row in Boston? The business can all be done quietly. Linda writes that she wants to come back. You are her relative, and she would

[168]After 1831, when William Lloyd Garrison (1805–1879) founded his abolitionist paper, the *Liberator*, in Boston, the city emerged as a center of the antislavery movement in a fundamentally antislavery state. In 1836, Massachusetts courts ruled that slaves brought into the state by their owners were free. In 1838, the Massachusetts legislature voted to grant runaway slaves in the state the right to a trial by jury.

trust *you*. The case would be different if I went. She might object to coming with *me*; and the damned abolitionists, if they knew I was her master, would not believe me, if I told them she had begged to go back. They would get up a row; and I should not like to see Linda dragged through the streets like a common negro. She has been very ungrateful to me for all my kindness; but I forgive her, and want to act the part of a friend towards her. I have no wish to hold her as my slave. Her friends can buy her as soon as she arrives here."

Finding that his arguments failed to convince my uncle, the doctor "let the cat out of the bag," by saying that he had written to the mayor of Boston, to ascertain whether there was a person of my description at the street and number from which my letter was dated. He had omitted this date in the letter he had made up to read to my grandmother. If I had dated from New York, the old man would probably have made another journey to that city. But even in that dark region, where knowledge is so carefully excluded from the slave, I had heard enough about Massachusetts to come to the conclusion that slaveholders did not consider it a comfortable place to go to in search of a runaway. That was before the Fugitive Slave Law was passed; before Massachusetts had consented to become a "nigger hunter" for the south.

My grandmother, who had become skittish by seeing her family always in danger, came to me with a very distressed countenance, and said, "What will you do if the mayor of Boston sends him word that you haven't been there? Then he will suspect the letter was a trick; and maybe he'll find out something about it, and we shall all get into trouble. O Linda, I wish you had never sent the letters."

"Don't worry yourself, grandmother," said I. "The mayor of Boston won't trouble himself to hunt niggers for Dr. Flint. The letters will do good in the end. I shall get out of this dark hole some time or other."

"I hope you will, child," replied the good, patient old friend. "You have been here a long time; almost five years; but whenever you do go, it will break your old grandmother's heart. I should be expecting every day to hear that you were brought back in irons and put in jail. God help you, poor child! Let us be thankful that some time or other we shall go 'where the wicked cease from troubling, and the weary are at rest.'"[169] My heart responded, Amen.

The fact that Dr. Flint had written to the mayor of Boston convinced me that he believed my letter to be genuine, and of course that he had no suspicion of my being any where in the vicinity. It was a great object

[169]Reference to Job 3:17. This is the second time Jacobs quotes this passage.

to keep up this delusion, for it made me and my friends feel less anxious, and it would be very convenient whenever there was a chance to escape. I resolved, therefore, to continue to write letters from the north from time to time.

Two or three weeks passed, and as no news came from the mayor of Boston, grandmother began to listen to my entreaty to be allowed to leave my cell, sometimes, and exercise my limbs to prevent my becoming a cripple. I was allowed to slip down into the small storeroom, early in the morning, and remain there a little while. The room was all filled up with barrels, except a small open space under my trap-door. This faced the door, the upper part of which was of glass, and purposely left uncurtained, that the curious might look in. The air of this place was close; but it was so much better than the atmosphere of my cell, that I dreaded to return. I came down as soon as it was light, and remained till eight o'clock, when people began to be about, and there was danger that some one might come on the piazza. I had tried various applications to bring warmth and feeling into my limbs, but without avail. They were so numb and stiff that it was a painful effort to move; and had my enemies come upon me during the first mornings I tried to exercise them a little in the small unoccupied space of the storeroom, it would have been impossible for me to have escaped.

XXVI. IMPORTANT ERA IN MY BROTHER'S LIFE

I missed the company and kind attentions of my brother William, who had gone to Washington with his master, Mr. Sands.[170] We received several letters from him, written without any allusion to me, but expressed in such a manner that I knew he did not forget me. I disguised my hand, and wrote to him in the same manner. It was a long session; and when it closed, William wrote to inform us that Mr. Sands was going to the north, to be gone some time, and that he was to accompany him. I knew that his master had promised to give him his freedom, but no time had been specified. Would William trust to a slave's chances? I remembered how we used to talk together, in our young days, about obtaining our freedom, and I thought it very doubtful whether he would come back to us.

Grandmother received a letter from Mr. Sands, saying that William had proved a most faithful servant, and he would also say a valued friend; that no mother had ever trained a better boy. He said he had travelled

[170] See John S. Jacobs, *A True Tale of Slavery*, chap. V (Document 11), for his account of these same events.

through the Northern States and Canada; and though the abolitionists had tried to decoy him away, they had never succeeded. He ended by saying they should be at home shortly.

We expected letters from William, describing the novelties of his journey, but none came. In time, it was reported that Mr. Sands would return late in the autumn, accompanied by a bride.[171] Still no letters from William. I felt almost sure I should never see him again on southern soil; but had he no word of comfort to send to his friends at home? to the poor captive in her dungeon? My thoughts wandered through the dark past, and over the uncertain future. Alone in my cell, where no eye but God's could see me, I wept bitter tears. How earnestly I prayed to him to restore me to my children, and enable me to be a useful woman and a good mother!

At last the day arrived for the return of the travellers. Grandmother had made loving preparations to welcome her absent boy back to the old hearthstone. When the dinner table was laid, William's plate occupied its old place. The stage coach went by empty. My grandmother waited dinner. She thought perhaps he was necessarily detained by his master. In my prison I listened anxiously, expecting every moment to hear my dear brother's voice and step. In the course of the afternoon a lad was sent by Mr. Sands to tell grandmother that William did not return with him; that the abolitionists had decoyed him away. But he begged her not to feel troubled about it, for he felt confident she would see William in a few days. As soon as he had time to reflect he would come back, for he could never expect to be so well off at the north as he had been with him.

If you had seen the tears, and heard the sobs, you would have thought the messenger had brought tidings of death instead of freedom. Poor old grandmother felt that she should never see her darling boy again. And I was selfish. I thought more of what I had lost, than of what my brother had gained. A new anxiety began to trouble me. Mr. Sands had expended a good deal of money, and would naturally feel irritated by the loss he had incurred. I greatly feared this might injure the prospects of my children, who were now becoming valuable property. I longed to have their emancipation made certain. The more so, because their master and father was now married. I was too familiar with slavery not to know that promises made to slaves, though with kind intentions, and sincere at the time, depend upon many contingencies for their fulfilment.

[171] In the summer of 1838, Sawyer married Lavinia Peyton (b. ca. 1818), the niece of the owner of his Washington, D.C., boardinghouse.

Much as I wished William to be free, the step he had taken made me sad and anxious. The following Sabbath was calm and clear; so beautiful that it seemed like a Sabbath in the eternal world. My grandmother brought the children out on the piazza, that I might hear their voices. She thought it would comfort me in my despondency; and it did. They chatted merrily, as only children can. Benny said, "Grandmother, do you think uncle Will has gone for good? Won't he ever come back again? May be he'll find mother. If he does, won't she be glad to see him! Why don't you and uncle Phillip, and all of us, go and live where mother is? I should like it; wouldn't you, Ellen?"

"Yes, I should like it," replied Ellen; "but how could we find her? Do you know the place, grandmother? I don't remember how mother looked—do you, Benny?"

Benny was just beginning to describe me when they were interrupted by an old slave woman, a near neighbor, named Aggie. This poor creature had witnessed the sale of her children, and seen them carried off to parts unknown, without any hopes of ever hearing from them again. She saw that my grandmother had been weeping, and she said, in a sympathizing tone, "What's the matter, aunt Marthy?"

"O Aggie," she replied, "it seems as if I shouldn't have any of my children or grandchildren left to hand me a drink when I'm dying, and lay my old body in the ground. My boy didn't come back with Mr. Sands. He staid at the north."

Poor old Aggie clapped her hands for joy. "Is *dat* what you's crying fur?" she exclaimed. "Git down on your knees and bress de Lord! I don't know whar my poor chillern is, and I nebber 'spect to know. You don't know whar poor Linda's gone to; but you *do* know whar her brudder is. He's in free parts; and dat's de right place. Don't murmur at de Lord's doings, but git down on your knees and tank him for his goodness."

My selfishness was rebuked by what poor Aggie said. She rejoiced over the escape of one who was merely her fellow-bondman, while his own sister was only thinking what his good fortune might cost her children. I knelt and prayed God to forgive me; and I thanked him from my heart, that one of my family was saved from the grasp of slavery.

It was not long before we received a letter from William. He wrote that Mr. Sands had always treated him kindly, and that he had tried to do his duty to him faithfully. But ever since he was a boy, he had longed to be free; and he had already gone through enough to convince him he had better not lose the chance that offered. He concluded by saying, "Don't worry about me, dear grandmother. I shall think of you always; and it will spur me on to work hard and try to do right. When I have earned money enough to give you a home, perhaps you will come to the north, and we can all live happy together."

Mr. Sands told my uncle Phillip the particulars about William's leaving him. He said, "I trusted him as if he were my own brother, and treated him as kindly. The abolitionists talked to him in several places; but I had no idea they could tempt him. However, I don't blame William. He's young and inconsiderate, and those Northern rascals decoyed him. I must confess the scamp was very bold about it. I met him coming down the steps of the Astor House[172] with his trunk on his shoulder, and I asked him where he was going. He said he was going to change his old trunk. I told him it was rather shabby, and asked if he didn't need some money. He said, No, thanked me, and went off. He did not return so soon as I expected; but I waited patiently. At last I went to see if our trunks were packed, ready for our journey. I found them locked, and a sealed note on the table informed me where I could find the keys. The fellow even tried to be religious. He wrote that he hoped God would always bless me, and reward me for my kindness; that he was not unwilling to serve me; but he wanted to be a free man; and that if I thought he did wrong, he hoped I would forgive him. I intended to give him his freedom in five years. He might have trusted me. He has shown himself ungrateful; but I shall not go for him, or send for him. I feel confident that he will soon return to me."

I afterwards heard an account of the affair from William himself. He had not been urged away by abolitionists. He needed no information they could give him about slavery to stimulate his desire for freedom. He looked at his hands, and remembered that they were once in irons. What security had he that they would not be so again? Mr. Sands was kind to him; but he might indefinitely postpone the promise he had made to give him his freedom. He might come under pecuniary embarrassments, and his property be seized by creditors; or he might die, without making any arrangements in his favor. He had too often known such accidents to happen to slaves who had kind masters, and he wisely resolved to make sure of the present opportunity to own himself. He was scrupulous about taking any money from his master on false pretences; so he sold his best clothes to pay for his passage to Boston. The slaveholders pronounced him a base, ungrateful wretch, for thus requiting his master's indulgence. What would *they* have done under similar circumstances?

When Dr. Flint's family heard that William had deserted Mr. Sands, they chuckled greatly over the news. Mrs. Flint made her usual

[172]Founded in 1836, the popular Astor House hotel was on lower Broadway in Manhattan.

manifestations of Christian feeling, by saying, "I'm glad of it. I hope he'll never get him again. I like to see people paid back in their own coin. I reckon Linda's children will have to pay for it. I should be glad to see them in the speculator's hands again, for I'm tired of seeing those little niggers march about the streets."

XXVII. NEW DESTINATION FOR THE CHILDREN

Mrs. Flint proclaimed her intention of informing Mrs. Sands who was the father of my children. She likewise proposed to tell her what an artful devil I was; that I had made a great deal of trouble in her family; that when Mr. Sands was at the north, she didn't doubt I had followed him in disguise, and persuaded William to run away. She had some reason to entertain such an idea; for I had written from the north, from time to time, and I dated my letters from various places. Many of them fell into Dr. Flint's hands, as I expected they would; and he must have come to the conclusion that I travelled about a good deal. He kept a close watch over my children, thinking they would eventually lead to my detection.

A new and unexpected trial was in store for me. One day, when Mr. Sands and his wife were walking in the street, they met Benny. The lady took a fancy to him, and exclaimed, "What a pretty little negro! Whom does he belong to?"

Benny did not hear the answer; but he came home very indignant with the stranger lady, because she had called him a negro.[173] A few days afterwards, Mr. Sands called on my grandmother, and told her he wanted her to take the children to his house. He said he had informed his wife of his relation to them, and told her they were motherless; and she wanted to see them.

When he had gone, my grandmother came and asked what I would do. The question seemed a mockery. What *could* I do? They were Mr. Sands's slaves, and their mother was a slave, whom he had represented to be dead. Perhaps he thought I was. I was too much pained and puzzled to come to any decision; and the children were carried without my knowledge.

Mrs. Sands had a sister from Illinois staying with her. This lady, who had no children of her own, was so much pleased with Ellen, that she offered to adopt her, and bring her up as she would a daughter.[174]

[173]This puzzling detail perhaps suggests that Joseph, like his namesake, was light enough to pass for white.

[174]The sister, Cornelia Peyton Russell (b. ca. 1810), later had her own child.

Mrs. Sands wanted to take Benjamin. When grandmother reported this to me, I was tried almost beyond endurance. Was this all I was to gain by what I had suffered for the sake of having my children free? True, the prospect *seemed* fair; but I knew too well how lightly slaveholders held such "parental relations." If pecuniary troubles should come, or if the new wife required more money than could conveniently be spared, my children might be thought of as a convenient means of raising funds. I had no trust in thee, O Slavery! Never should I know peace till my children were emancipated with all due formalities of law.

I was too proud to ask Mr. Sands to do any thing for my own benefit; but I could bring myself to become a supplicant for my children. I resolved to remind him of the promise he had made me, and to throw myself upon his honor for the performance of it. I persuaded my grandmother to go to him, and tell him I was not dead, and that I earnestly entreated him to keep the promise he had made me; that I had heard of the recent proposals concerning my children, and did not feel easy to accept them; that he had promised to emancipate them, and it was time for him to redeem his pledge. I knew there was some risk in thus betraying that I was in the vicinity; but what will not a mother do for her children? He received the message with surprise, and said, "The children are free. I have never intended to claim them as slaves. Linda may decide their fate. In my opinion, they had better be sent to the north. I don't think they are quite safe here. Dr. Flint boasts that they are still in his power. He says they were his daughter's property, and as she was not of age when they were sold, the contract is not legally binding."

So, then, after all I had endured for their sakes, my poor children were between two fires; between my old master and their new master! And I was powerless. There was no protecting arm of the law for me to invoke. Mr. Sands proposed that Ellen should go, for the present, to some of his relatives, who had removed to Brooklyn, Long Island. It was promised that she should be well taken care of, and sent to school. I consented to it, as the best arrangement I could make for her. My grandmother, of course, negotiated it all; and Mrs. Sands knew of no other person in the transaction. She proposed that they should take Ellen with them to Washington, and keep her till they had a good chance of sending her, with friends, to Brooklyn. She had an infant daughter. I had had a glimpse of it, as the nurse passed with it in her arms. It was not a pleasant thought to me, that the bondwoman's child should tend her free-born sister; but there was no alternative.[175] Ellen was made

[175]Laura, the Sawyers' oldest daughter, was born in January 1840. This recalls the fate of Jacobs's own mother, who was the slave of her "foster sister," underlining the cycle of distorted familial relations that slavery perpetuated.

ready for the journey. O, how it tried my heart to send her away, so young, alone, among strangers! Without a mother's love to shelter her from the storms of life; almost without memory of a mother! I doubted whether she and Benny would have for me the natural affection that children feel for a parent. I thought to myself that I might perhaps never see my daughter again, and I had a great desire that she should look upon me, before she went, that she might take my image with her in her memory. It seemed to me cruel to have her brought to my dungeon. It was sorrow enough for her young heart to know that her mother was a victim of slavery, without seeing the wretched hiding-place to which it had driven her. I begged permission to pass the last night in one of the open chambers, with my little girl. They thought I was crazy to think of trusting such a young child with my perilous secret. I told them I had watched her character, and I felt sure she would not betray me; that I was determined to have an interview, and if they would not facilitate it, I would take my own way to obtain it. They remonstrated against the rashness of such a proceeding; but finding they could not change my purpose, they yielded. I slipped through the trap-door into the storeroom, and my uncle kept watch at the gate, while I passed into the piazza and went up stairs, to the room I used to occupy. It was more than five years since I had seen it; and how the memories crowded on me! There I had taken shelter when my mistress drove me from her house; there came my old tyrant, to mock, insult, and curse me; there my children were first laid in my arms; there I had watched over them, each day with a deeper and sadder love; there I had knelt to God, in anguish of heart, to forgive the wrong I had done. How vividly it all came back! And after this long, gloomy interval, I stood there such a wreck!

In the midst of these meditations, I heard footsteps on the stairs. The door opened, and my uncle Phillip came in, leading Ellen by the hand. I put my arms round her, and said, "Ellen, my dear child, I am your mother." She drew back a little, and looked at me; then, with sweet confidence, she laid her cheek against mine, and I folded her to the heart that had been so long desolated. She was the first to speak. Raising her head, she said, inquiringly, "You really *are* my mother?" I told her I really was; that during all the long time she had not seen me, I had loved her most tenderly; and that now she was going away, I wanted to see her and talk with her, that she might remember me. With a sob in her voice, she said, "I'm glad you've come to see me; but why didn't you ever come before? Benny and I have wanted so much to see you! He remembers you, and sometimes he tells me about you. Why didn't you come home when Dr. Flint went to bring you?"

I answered, "I couldn't come before, dear. But now that I am with you, tell me whether you [would] like to go away." "I don't know," said she, crying. "Grandmother says I ought not to cry; that I am going to a good place, where I can learn to read and write, and that by and by I can write her a letter. But I shan't have Benny, or grandmother, or uncle Phillip, or any body to love me. Can't you go with me? O, *do* go, dear mother!"

I told her I couldn't go now; but sometime I would come to her, and then she and Benny and I would live together, and have happy times. She wanted to run and bring Benny to see me now. I told her he was going to the north, before long, with uncle Phillip, and then I would come to see him before he went away. I asked if she would like to have me stay all night and sleep with her. "O, yes," she replied. Then, turning to her uncle, she said, pleadingly, "*May* I stay? Please, uncle! She is my own mother." He laid his hand on her head, and said, solemnly, "Ellen, this is the secret you have promised grandmother never to tell. If you ever speak of it to any body, they will never let you see your grandmother again, and your mother can never come to Brooklyn." "Uncle," she replied, "I will never tell." He told her she might stay with me; and when he had gone, I took her in my arms and told her I was a slave, and that was the reason she must never say she had seen me. I exhorted her to be a good child, to try to please the people where she was going, and that God would raise her up friends. I told her to say her prayers, and remember always to pray for her poor mother, and that God would permit us to meet again. She wept, and I did not check her tears. Perhaps she would never again have a chance to pour her tears into a mother's bosom. All night she nestled in my arms, and I had no inclination to slumber. The moments were too precious to lose any of them. Once, when I thought she was asleep, I kissed her forehead softly, and she said, "I am not asleep, dear mother."

Before dawn they came to take me back to my den. I drew aside the window curtain, to take a last look of my child. The moonlight shone on her face, and I bent over her, as I had done years before, that wretched night when I ran away. I hugged her close to my throbbing heart; and tears, too sad for such young eyes to shed, flowed down her cheeks, as she gave her last kiss, and whispered in my ear, "Mother, I will never tell." And she never did.

When I got back to my den, I threw myself on the bed and wept there alone in the darkness. It seemed as if my heart would burst. When the time for Ellen's departure drew nigh, I could hear neighbors and friends saying to her, "Good by, Ellen. I hope your poor mother will find you out. *Won't* you be glad to see her!" She replied, "Yes, ma'am"; and they little dreamed of the weighty secret that weighed down her young heart. She was an affectionate child, but naturally very reserved, except with those she loved, and I felt secure that my secret would be safe with her. I heard the gate close after her, with such feelings as only a slave mother can experience. During the day my meditations were very sad. Sometimes I feared I had been very selfish not to give up all claim to her, and let her go to Illinois, to be adopted by Mrs. Sands's sister. It was my experience of slavery that decided me against it. I feared that circumstances might arise that would cause her to be sent back. I felt confident that I should go to New York myself; and then I should be able to watch over her, and in some degree protect her.

Dr. Flint's family knew nothing of the proposed arrangement till after Ellen was gone, and the news displeased them greatly. Mrs. Flint called on Mrs. Sands's sister to inquire into the matter. She expressed her opinion very freely as to the respect Mr. Sands showed for his wife, and for his own character, in acknowledging those "young niggers." And as for sending Ellen away, she pronounced it to be just as much stealing as it would be for him to come and take a piece of furniture out of her parlor. She said her daughter was not of age to sign the bill of sale, and the children were her property; and when she became of age, or was married, she could take them, wherever she could lay hands on them.

Miss Emily Flint, the little girl to whom I had been bequeathed, was now in her sixteenth year.[176] Her mother considered it all right and honorable for her, or her future husband, to steal my children; but she did not understand how any body could hold up their heads in respectable society, after they had purchased their own children, as Mr. Sands had done. Dr. Flint said very little. Perhaps he thought that Benny would be less likely to be sent away if he kept quiet. One of my letters, that fell into his hands, was dated from Canada; and he seldom spoke of me now. This state of things enabled me to slip down into the storeroom more frequently, where I could stand upright, and move my limbs more freely.

Days, weeks, and months passed, and there came no news of Ellen. I sent a letter to Brooklyn, written in my grandmother's name, to inquire whether she had arrived there. Answer was returned that she

[176]In fact, Mary Matilda Norcom turned eighteen in 1840.

had not. I wrote to her in Washington; but no notice was taken of it. There was one person there, who ought to have had some sympathy with the anxiety of the child's friends at home; but the links of such relations as he had formed with me, are easily broken and cast away as rubbish. Yet how protectingly and persuasively he once talked to the poor, helpless slave girl! And how entirely I trusted him! But now suspicions darkened my mind. Was my child dead, or had they deceived me, and sold her?

If the secret memoirs of many members of Congress should be published, curious details would be unfolded. I once saw a letter from a member of Congress to a slave, who was the mother of six of his children. He wrote to request that she would send her children away from the great house before his return, as he expected to be accompanied by friends. The woman could not read, and was obliged to employ another to read the letter. The existence of the colored children did not trouble this gentleman, it was only the fear that friends might recognize in their features a resemblance to him.

At the end of six months, a letter came to my grandmother, from Brooklyn. It was written by a young lady in the family, and announced that Ellen had just arrived. It contained the following message from her: "I do try to do just as you told me to, and I pray for you every night and morning." I understood that these words were meant for me; and they were a balsam to my heart. The writer closed her letter by saying, "Ellen is a nice little girl, and we shall like to have her with us. My cousin, Mr. Sands, has given her to me, to be my little waiting-maid. I shall send her to school, and I hope some day she will write to you herself."[177] This letter perplexed and troubled me. Had my child's father merely placed her there till she was old enough to support herself? Or had he given her to his cousin, as a piece of property? If the last idea was correct, his cousin might return to the south at any time, and hold Ellen as a slave. I tried to put away from me the painful thought that such a foul wrong could have been done to us. I said to myself, "Surely there must be *some* justice in man"; then I remembered, with a sigh, how slavery perverted all the natural feelings of the human heart. It gave me a pang to look on my light-hearted boy. He believed himself free; and to have him brought under the yoke of slavery, would be more than I could bear. How I longed to have him safely out of the reach of its power!

[177]Sawyer sent Louisa to the family home of his cousin James Tredwell and his wife, Mary. The Tredwells had four young daughters.

XXVIII. AUNT NANCY

I have mentioned my great-aunt, who was a slave in Dr. Flint's family, and who had been my refuge during the shameful persecutions I suffered from him. This aunt had been married at twenty years of age; that is, as far as slaves *can* marry. She had the consent of her master and mistress, and a clergyman performed the ceremony. But it was a mere form, without any legal value. Her master or mistress could annul it any day they pleased. She had always slept on the floor in the entry, near Mrs. Flint's chamber door, that she might be within call. When she was married, she was told she might have the use of a small room in an outhouse. Her mother and her husband furnished it. He was a seafaring man, and was allowed to sleep there when he was at home. But on the wedding evening, the bride was ordered to her old post on the entry floor.

Mrs. Flint, at that time, had no children; but she was expecting to be a mother, and if she should want a drink of water in the night, what could she do without her slave to bring it? So my aunt was compelled to lie at her door, until one midnight she was forced to leave, to give premature birth to a child. In a fortnight she was required to resume her place on the entry floor, because Mrs. Flint's babe needed her attentions. She kept her station there through summer and winter, until she had given premature birth to six children; and all the while she was employed as night-nurse to Mrs. Flint's children. Finally, toiling all day, and being deprived of rest at night, completely broke down her constitution, and Dr. Flint declared it was impossible she could ever become the mother of a living child. The fear of losing so valuable a servant by death, now induced them to allow her to sleep in her little room in the out-house, except when there was sickness in the family. She afterwards had two feeble babes, one of whom died in a few days, and the other in four weeks. I well remember her patient sorrow as she held the last dead baby in her arms. "I wish it could have lived," she said; "it is not the will of God that any of my children should live. But I will try to be fit to meet their little spirits in heaven."

Aunt Nancy was housekeeper and waiting-maid in Dr. Flint's family. Indeed, she was the *factotum* of the household. Nothing went on well without her. She was my mother's twin sister, and, as far as was in her power, she supplied a mother's place to us orphans.[178] I slept with her

[178]The statement that her mother and aunt were twins is not consistent with what Jacobs says elsewhere. According to Yellin, this seemingly inaccurate claim is "an exception to the generally striking accuracy in *Incidents*" (Jacobs, *Incidents*, ed. Yellin, 281n).

all the time I lived in my old master's house, and the bond between us was very strong. When my friends tried to discourage me from running away, she always encouraged me. When they thought I had better return and ask my master's pardon, because there was no possibility of escape, she sent me word never to yield. She said if I persevered I might, perhaps, gain the freedom of my children; and even if I perished in doing it, that was better than to leave them to groan under the same persecutions that had blighted my own life. After I was shut up in my dark cell, she stole away, whenever she could, to bring me the news and say something cheering. How often did I kneel down to listen to her words of consolation, whispered through a crack! "I am old, and have not long to live," she used to say; "and I could die happy if I could only see you and the children free. You must pray to God, Linda, as I do for you, that he will lead you out of this darkness." I would beg her not to worry herself on my account; that there was an end of all suffering sooner or later, and that whether I lived in chains or in freedom, I should always remember her as the good friend who had been the comfort of my life. A word from her always strengthened me; and not me only. The whole family relied upon her judgment, and were guided by her advice.

I had been in my cell six years when my grandmother was summoned to the bedside of this, her last remaining daughter. She was very ill, and they said she would die. Grandmother had not entered Dr. Flint's house for several years. They had treated her cruelly, but she thought nothing of that now. She was grateful for permission to watch by the death-bed of her child. They had always been devoted to each other; and now they sat looking into each other's eyes, longing to speak of the secret that had weighed so much on the hearts of both. My aunt had been stricken with paralysis. She lived but two days, and the last day she was speechless. Before she lost the power of utterance, she told her mother not to grieve if she could not speak to her; that she would try to hold up her hand, to let her know that all was well with her. Even the hard-hearted doctor was a little softened when he saw the dying woman try to smile on the aged mother, who was kneeling by her side. His eyes moistened for a moment, as he said she had always been a faithful servant, and they should never be able to supply her place. Mrs. Flint took to her bed, quite overcome by the shock. While my grandmother sat alone with the dead, the doctor came in, leading his youngest son, who had always been a great pet with aunt Nancy, and was much attached to her.[179] "Martha," said he, "aunt Nancy loved this child, and when he comes

[179] In 1842, the Norcoms' youngest son was William Augustus Norcom (b. 1836).

where you are, I hope you will be kind to him, for her sake." She replied, "Your wife was my foster-child, Dr. Flint, the foster-sister of my poor Nancy, and you little know me if you think I can feel any thing but good will for her children."

"I wish the past could be forgotten, and that we might never think of it," said he; "and that Linda would come to supply her aunt's place. She would be worth more to us than all the money that could be paid for her. I wish it for your sake also, Martha. Now that Nancy is taken away from you, she would be a great comfort to your old age."

He knew he was touching a tender chord. Almost choking with grief, my grandmother replied, "It was not I that drove Linda away. My grandchildren are gone; and of my nine children only one is left. God help me!"

To me, the death of this kind relative was an inexpressible sorrow. I knew that she had been slowly murdered; and I felt that my troubles had helped to finish the work. After I heard of her illness, I listened constantly to hear what news was brought from the great house; and the thought that I could not go to her made me utterly miserable. At last, as uncle Phillip came into the house, I heard some one inquire, "How is she?" and he answered, "She is dead." My little cell seemed whirling round, and I knew nothing more till I opened my eyes and found uncle Phillip bending over me. I had no need to ask any questions. He whispered, "Linda, she died happy." I could not weep. My fixed gaze troubled him. "Don't look *so*," he said. "Don't add to my poor mother's trouble. Remember how much she has to bear, and that we ought to do all we can to comfort her." Ah, yes, that blessed old grandmother, who for seventy-three years had borne the pelting storms of a slave-mother's life. She did indeed need consolation!

Mrs. Flint had rendered her poor foster-sister childless, apparently without any compunction; and with cruel selfishness had ruined her health by years of incessant, unrequited toil, and broken rest. But now she became very sentimental. I suppose she thought it would be a beautiful illustration of the attachment existing between slaveholder and slave, if the body of her old worn-out servant was buried at her feet. She sent for the clergyman and asked if he had any objection to burying aunt Nancy in the doctor's family burial-place. No colored person had ever been allowed interment in the white people's burying-ground, and the minister knew that all the deceased of our family reposed together in the old graveyard of the slaves. He therefore replied, "I have no objection to complying with your wish; but perhaps aunt Nancy's *mother* may have some choice as to where her remains shall be deposited."

It had never occurred to Mrs. Flint that slaves could have any feelings. When my grandmother was consulted, she at once said she wanted Nancy to lie with all the rest of her family, and where her own old body would be buried. Mrs. Flint graciously complied with her wish, though she said it was painful to her to have Nancy buried away from her. She might have added with touching pathos, "I was so long used to sleep with her lying near me, on the entry floor."

My uncle Phillip asked permission to bury his sister at his own expense; and slaveholders are always ready to grant *such* favors to slaves and their relatives. The arrangements were very plain, but perfectly respectable. She was buried on the Sabbath, and Mrs. Flint's minister read the funeral service. There was a large concourse of colored people, bond and free, and a few white persons who had always been friendly to our family. Dr. Flint's carriage was in the procession; and when the body was deposited in its humble resting place, the mistress dropped a tear, and returned to her carriage, probably thinking she had performed her duty nobly.

It was talked of by the slaves as a mighty grand funeral. Northern travellers, passing through the place, might have described this tribute of respect to the humble dead as a beautiful feature in the "patriarchal institution"; a touching proof of the attachment between slaveholders and their servants; and tender-hearted Mrs. Flint would have confirmed this impression, with handkerchief at her eyes.[180] *We* could have told them a different story. We could have given them a chapter of wrongs and sufferings, that would have touched their hearts, if they *had* any hearts to feel for the colored people. We could have told them how the poor old slave-mother had toiled, year after year, to earn eight hundred dollars to buy her son Phillip's right to his own earnings; and how that same Phillip paid the expenses of the funeral, which they regarded as doing so much credit to the master. We could also have told them of a poor, blighted young creature, shut up in a living grave for years, to avoid the tortures that would be inflicted on her, if she ventured to come out and look on the face of her departed friend.

All this, and much more, I thought of, as I sat at my loophole, waiting for the family to return from the grave; sometimes weeping, sometimes falling asleep, dreaming strange dreams of the dead and the living.

[180]Proslavery ideologues relied heavily on the argument that slavery was a benign system of paternalism, in which the patriarch, or master, presided over a happy household of his wife, children, and slaves. For a contemporary statement of this view, see George Fitzhugh (1806–1881), "The Blessings of Slavery" (1857), http://occawlonline.pearsoned.com/bookbind/pubbooks/divine5e/medialib/timeline/docs/sources/theme_primarysources_Slavery_16.html. Fitzhugh's title echoes the title of Frederick Douglass's bitter 1837 editorial, although Douglass used it sarcastically (see note 45).

It was sad to witness the grief of my bereaved grandmother. She had always been strong to bear, and now, as ever, religious faith supported her. But her dark life had become still darker, and age and trouble were leaving deep traces on her withered face. She had four places to knock for me to come to the trap-door, and each place had a different meaning. She now came oftener than she had done, and talked to me of her dead daughter, while tears trickled slowly down her furrowed cheeks. I said all I could to comfort her; but it was a sad reflection, that instead of being able to help her, I was a constant source of anxiety and trouble. The poor old back was fitted to its burden. It bent under it, but did not break.

XXIX. PREPARATIONS FOR ESCAPE

I hardly expect that the reader will credit me, when I affirm that I lived in that little dismal hole, almost deprived of light and air, and with no space to move my limbs, for nearly seven years.[181] But it is a fact; and to me a sad one, even now; for my body still suffers from the effects of that long imprisonment, to say nothing of my soul. Members of my family, now living in New York and Boston, can testify to the truth of what I say.

Countless were the nights that I sat late at the little loophole scarcely large enough to give me a glimpse of one twinkling star. There, I heard the patrols and slave-hunters conferring together about the capture of runaways, well knowing how rejoiced they would be to catch me.

Season after season, year after year, I peeped at my children's faces, and heard their sweet voices, with a heart yearning all the while to say, "Your mother is here." Sometimes it appeared to me as if ages had rolled away since I entered upon that gloomy, monotonous existence. At times, I was stupefied and listless; at other times I became very impatient to know when these dark years would end, and I should again be allowed to feel the sunshine, and breathe the pure air.

After Ellen left us, this feeling increased. Mr. Sands had agreed that Benny might go to the north whenever his uncle Phillip could go with him; and I was anxious to be there also, to watch over my children, and protect them so far as I was able. Moreover, I was likely to be drowned out of my den, if I remained much longer; for the slight roof was getting badly out of repair, and uncle Phillip was afraid to remove the shingles,

[181] According to John Jacobs, Harriet hid for six years and eleven months, from August 1835 through June 1842 (John S. Jacobs, *A True Tale of Slavery*, chap. IV; see Document 11).

lest some one should get a glimpse of me. When storms occurred in the night, they spread mats and bits of carpet, which in the morning appeared to have been laid out to dry; but to cover the roof in the daytime might have attracted attention. Consequently, my clothes and bedding were often drenched; a process by which the pains and aches in my cramped and stiffened limbs were greatly increased. I revolved various plans of escape in my mind, which I sometimes imparted to my grandmother, when she came to whisper with me at the trap-door. The kind-hearted old woman had an intense sympathy for runaways. She had known too much of the cruelties inflicted on those who were captured. Her memory always flew back at once to the sufferings of her bright and handsome son, Benjamin, the youngest and dearest of her flock. So, whenever I alluded to the subject, she would groan out, "O, don't think of it, child. You'll break my heart." I had no good old aunt Nancy now to encourage me; but my brother William and my children were continually beckoning me to the north.

And now I must go back a few months in my story. I have stated that the first of January was the time for selling slaves, or leasing them out to new masters. If time were counted by heart-throbs, the poor slaves might reckon years of suffering during that festival so joyous to the free. On the New Year's day preceding my aunt's death, one of my friends, named Fanny, was to be sold at auction, to pay her master's debts. My thoughts were with her during all the day, and at night I anxiously inquired what had been her fate. I was told that she had been sold to one master, and her four little girls to another master, far distant; that she had escaped from her purchaser, and was not to be found. Her mother was the old Aggie I have spoken of. She lived in a small tenement belonging to my grandmother, and built on the same lot with her own house. Her dwelling was searched and watched, and that brought the patrols so near me that I was obliged to keep very close in my den. The hunters were somehow eluded; and not long afterwards Benny accidentally caught sight of Fanny in her mother's hut. He told his grandmother, who charged him never to speak of it, explaining to him the frightful consequences; and he never betrayed the trust. Aggie little dreamed that my grandmother knew where her daughter was concealed, and that the stooping form of her old neighbor was bending under a similar burden of anxiety and fear; but these dangerous secrets deepened the sympathy between the two old persecuted mothers.

My friend Fanny and I remained many weeks hidden within call of each other; but she was unconscious of the fact. I longed to have her share my den, which seemed a more secure retreat than her own;

but I had brought so much trouble on my grandmother, that it seemed wrong to ask her to incur greater risks. My restlessness increased. I had lived too long in bodily pain and anguish of spirit. Always I was in dread that by some accident, or some contrivance, slavery would succeed in snatching my children from me. This thought drove me nearly frantic, and I determined to steer for the North Star at all hazards. At this crisis, Providence opened an unexpected way for me to escape. My friend Peter came one evening, and asked to speak with me. "Your day has come, Linda," said he. "I have found a chance for you to go to the Free States. You have a fortnight to decide." The news seemed too good to be true; but Peter explained his arrangements, and told me all that was necessary was for me to say I would go. I was going to answer him with a joyful yes, when the thought of Benny came to my mind. I told him the temptation was exceedingly strong, but I was terribly afraid of Dr. Flint's alleged power over my child, and that I could not go and leave him behind. Peter remonstrated earnestly. He said such a good chance might never occur again; that Benny was free, and could be sent to me; and that for the sake of my children's welfare I ought not to hesitate a moment. I told him I would consult with uncle Phillip. My uncle rejoiced in the plan, and bade me go by all means. He promised, if his life was spared, that he would either bring or send my son to me as soon as I reached a place of safety. I resolved to go, but thought nothing had better be said to my grandmother till very near the time of departure. But my uncle thought she would feel it more keenly if I left her so suddenly. "I will reason with her," said he, "and convince her how necessary it is, not only for your sake, but for hers also. You cannot be blind to the fact that she is sinking under her burdens." I was not blind to it. I knew that my concealment was an ever-present source of anxiety, and that the older she grew the more nervously fearful she was of discovery. My uncle talked with her, and finally succeeded in persuading her that it was absolutely necessary for me to seize the chance so unexpectedly offered.

The anticipation of being a free woman proved almost too much for my weak frame. The excitement stimulated me, and at the same time bewildered me. I made busy preparations for my journey, and for my son to follow me. I resolved to have an interview with him before I went, that I might give him cautions and advice, and tell him how anxiously I should be waiting for him at the north. Grandmother stole up to me as often as possible to whisper words of counsel. She insisted upon my writing to Dr. Flint, as soon as I arrived in the Free States, and asking him to sell me to her. She said she would sacrifice her house, and all she had in the world, for the sake of having me safe with my children in any part of the world. If she could only live to know *that* she could die in peace. I promised the dear old faithful friend that I would write to her as soon as I arrived, and put the letter in a safe way to reach her; but in my own mind I resolved that not another cent of her hard earnings should be spent to pay rapacious slaveholders for what they called their property. And even if I had not been unwilling to buy what I had already a right to possess, common humanity would have prevented me from accepting the generous offer, at the expense of turning my aged relative out of house and home, when she was trembling on the brink of the grave.

I was to escape in a vessel; but I forbear to mention any further particulars. I was in readiness, but the vessel was unexpectedly detained several days. Meantime, news came to town of a most horrible murder committed on a fugitive slave, named James. Charity, the mother of this unfortunate young man, had been an old acquaintance of ours. I have told the shocking particulars of his death, in my description of some of the neighboring slaveholders. My grandmother, always nervously sensitive about runaways, was terribly frightened. She felt sure that a similar fate awaited me, if I did not desist from my enterprise. She sobbed, and groaned, and entreated me not to go. Her excessive fear was somewhat contagious, and my heart was not proof against her extreme agony. I was grievously disappointed, but I promised to relinquish my project.

When my friend Peter was apprised of this, he was both disappointed and vexed. He said, that judging from our past experience, it would be a long time before I had such another chance to throw away. I told him it need not be thrown away; that I had a friend concealed near by, who would be glad enough to take the place that had been provided for me. I told him about poor Fanny, and the kind-hearted, noble fellow, who never turned his back upon any body in distress, white or black, expressed his readiness to help her. Aggie was much surprised when she found that we knew her secret. She was rejoiced to hear of such a chance for Fanny, and arrangements were made for her to go on board the vessel the next night. They both supposed that I had long been at the north, therefore my name was not mentioned in the transaction. Fanny was carried on board at the appointed time, and stowed away in a very small cabin. This accommodation had been purchased at a price that would pay for a voyage to England. But when one proposes to go to fine old England, they stop to calculate whether they can afford the cost of the pleasure; while in making a bargain to escape from slavery, the trembling victim is ready to say, "Take all I have, only don't betray me!"

The next morning I peeped through my loophole, and saw that it was dark and cloudy. At night I received news that the wind was ahead, and the vessel had not sailed. I was exceedingly anxious about Fanny, and Peter too, who was running a tremendous risk at my instigation. Next day the wind and weather remained the same. Poor Fanny had been half dead with fright when they carried her on board, and I could readily imagine how she must be suffering now. Grandmother came often to my den, to say how thankful she was I did not go. On the third morning she rapped for me to come down to the storeroom. The poor old sufferer was breaking down under her weight of trouble. She was easily flurried now. I found her in a nervous, excited state, but I was not aware that she had forgotten to lock the door behind her, as usual. She was exceedingly worried about the detention of the vessel. She was afraid all would be discovered, and then Fanny, and Peter, and I, would all be tortured to death, and Phillip would be utterly ruined, and her house would be torn down. Poor Peter! If he should die such a horrible death as the poor slave James had lately done, and all for his kindness in trying to help me, how dreadful it would be for us all! Alas, the thought was familiar to me, and had sent many a sharp pang through my heart. I tried to suppress my own anxiety, and speak soothingly to her. She brought in some allusion to aunt Nancy, the dear daughter she had recently buried, and then she lost all control of herself. As she stood there, trembling and sobbing, a voice from the piazza called out, "Whar is you, aunt Marthy?" Grandmother was startled, and in her agitation opened the door, without thinking of me. In stepped Jenny, the mischievous housemaid, who had tried to enter my room, when I was concealed in the house of my white benefactress. "I's bin huntin ebery whar for you, aunt Marthy," said she. "My missis wants you to send her some crackers." I had slunk down behind a barrel, which entirely screened me, but I imagined that Jenny was looking directly at the spot, and my heart beat violently. My grandmother immediately thought what she had done, and went out quickly with Jenny to count the crackers, locking the door after her. She returned to me, in a few minutes, the perfect picture of despair. "Poor child!" she exclaimed, "my carelessness has ruined you. The boat ain't gone yet. Get ready immediately, and go with Fanny. I ain't got another word to say against it now; for there's no telling what may happen this day."

Uncle Phillip was sent for, and he agreed with his mother in thinking that Jenny would inform Dr. Flint in less than twenty-four hours. He advised getting me on board the boat, if possible; if not, I had better keep very still in my den, where they could not find me without tearing the house down. He said it would not do for him to move in the matter, because suspicion would be immediately excited; but he promised to communicate with Peter. I felt reluctant to apply to him again, having implicated him too much already; but there seemed to be no alternative. Vexed as Peter had been by my indecision, he was true to his generous nature, and said at once that he would do his best to help me, trusting I should show myself a stronger woman this time.

He immediately proceeded to the wharf, and found that the wind had shifted, and the vessel was slowly beating down stream. On some pretext of urgent necessity, he offered two boatmen a dollar apiece to catch up with her. He was of lighter complexion than the boatmen he hired, and when the captain saw them coming so rapidly, he thought officers were pursuing his vessel in search of the runaway slave he had on board. They hoisted sails, but the boat gained upon them, and the indefatigable Peter sprang on board.

The captain at once recognized him. Peter asked him to go below, to speak about a bad bill he had given him. When he told his errand, the captain replied, "Why, the woman's here already; and I've put her where you or the devil would have a tough job to find her."

"But it is another woman I want to bring," said Peter. "*She* is in great distress, too, and you shall be paid any thing within reason, if you'll stop and take her."

"What's her name?" inquired the captain.

"Linda," he replied.

"That's the name of the woman already here," rejoined the captain. "By George! I believe you mean to betray me."

"O!" exclaimed Peter, "God knows I wouldn't harm a hair of your head. I am too grateful to you. But there really *is* another woman in great danger. Do have the humanity to stop and take her!"

After a while they came to an understanding. Fanny, not dreaming I was any where about in that region, had assumed my name, though she called herself Johnson. "Linda is a common name," said Peter, "and the woman I want to bring is Linda Brent."

The captain agreed to wait at a certain place till evening, being handsomely paid for his detention.

Of course, the day was an anxious one for us all. But we concluded that if Jenny had seen me, she would be too wise to let her mistress know of it; and that she probably would not get a chance to see Dr. Flint's family till evening, for I knew very well what were the rules in that household. I afterwards believed that she did not see me;

for nothing ever came of it, and she was one of those base characters that would have jumped to betray a suffering fellow being for the sake of thirty pieces of silver.[182]

I made all my arrangements to go on board as soon as it was dusk. The intervening time I resolved to spend with my son. I had not spoken to him for seven years, though I had been under the same roof, and seen him every day, when I was well enough to sit at the loophole. I did not dare to venture beyond the storeroom; so they brought him there, and locked us up together, in a place concealed from the piazza door. It was an agitating interview for both of us. After we had talked and wept together for a little while, he said, "Mother, I'm glad you're going away. I wish I could go with you. I knew you was here; and I have been *so* afraid they would come and catch you!"

I was greatly surprised, and asked him how he had found it out.

He replied, "I was standing under the eaves, one day, before Ellen went away, and I heard somebody cough up over the wood shed. I don't know what made me think it was you, but I did think so. I missed Ellen, the night before she went away; and grandmother brought her back into the room in the night; and I thought maybe she'd been to see you, before she went, for I heard grandmother whisper to her, 'Now go to sleep; and remember never to tell.'"

I asked him if he ever mentioned his suspicions to his sister. He said he never did; but after he heard the cough, if he saw her playing with other children on that side of the house, he always tried to coax her round to the other side, for fear they would hear me cough, too. He said he had kept a close lookout for Dr. Flint, and if he saw him speak to a constable, or a patrol, he always told grandmother. I now recollected that I had seen him manifest uneasiness, when people were on that side of the house, and I had at the time been puzzled to conjecture a motive for his actions. Such prudence may seem extraordinary in a boy of twelve years, but slaves, being surrounded by mysteries, deceptions, and dangers, early learn to be suspicious and watchful, and prematurely cautious and cunning. He had never asked a question of grandmother, or uncle Phillip, and I had often heard him chime in with other children, when they spoke of my being at the north.

I told him I was now really going to the Free States, and if he was a good, honest boy, and a loving child to his dear old grandmother, the Lord would bless him, and bring him to me, and we and Ellen would live together. He began to tell me that grandmother had not eaten any

[182] Reference to the betrayal of Jesus by Judas Iscariot, Matthew 26:14–15.

thing all day. While he was speaking, the door was unlocked, and she came in with a small bag of money, which she wanted me to take. I begged her to keep a part of it, at least, to pay for Benny's being sent to the north; but she insisted, while her tears were falling fast, that I should take the whole. "You may be sick among strangers," she said, "and they would send you to the poorhouse to die." Ah, that good grandmother!

For the last time I went up to my nook. Its desolate appearance no longer chilled me, for the light of hope had risen in my soul. Yet, even with the blessed prospect of freedom before me, I felt very sad at leaving forever that old homestead, where I had been sheltered so long by the dear old grandmother; where I had dreamed my first young dream of love; and where, after that had faded away, my children came to twine themselves so closely round my desolate heart. As the hour approached for me to leave, I again descended to the storeroom. My grandmother and Benny were there. She took me by the hand, and said, "Linda, let us pray." We knelt down together, with my child pressed to my heart, and my other arm round the faithful, loving old friend I was about to leave forever. On no other occasion has it ever been my lot to listen to so fervent a supplication for mercy and protection. It thrilled through my heart, and inspired me with trust in God.

Peter was waiting for me in the street. I was soon by his side, faint in body, but strong of purpose. I did not look back upon the old place, though I felt that I should never see it again.

XXX. NORTHWARD BOUND

I never could tell how we reached the wharf. My brain was all of a whirl, and my limbs tottered under me. At an appointed place we met my uncle Phillip, who had started before us on a different route, that he might reach the wharf first, and give us timely warning if there was any danger. A row-boat was in readiness. As I was about to step in, I felt something pull me gently, and turning round I saw Benny, looking pale and anxious. He whispered in my ear, "I've been peeping into the doctor's window, and he's at home. Good by, mother. Don't cry; I'll come." He hastened away. I clasped the hand of my good uncle, to whom I owed so much, and of Peter, the brave, generous friend who had volunteered to run such terrible risks to secure my safety. To this day I remember how his bright face beamed with joy, when he told me he had discovered a safe method for me to escape. Yet that intelligent, enterprising, noble-hearted man was a chattel! liable, by the laws of a country that calls itself civilized, to be sold with horses and pigs! We parted in silence. Our hearts were all too full for words!

Swiftly the boat glided over the water. After a while, one of the sailors said, "Don't be down-hearted, madam. We will take you safely to your husband, in ____." At first I could not imagine what he meant; but I had presence of mind to think that it probably referred to something the captain had told him; so I thanked him, and said I hoped we should have pleasant weather.

When I entered the vessel the captain came forward to meet me. He was an elderly man, with a pleasant countenance. He showed me to a little box of a cabin, where sat my friend Fanny. She started as if she had seen a spectre. She gazed on me in utter astonishment, and exclaimed, "Linda, can this be *you*? or is it your ghost?" When we were locked in each other's arms, my overwrought feelings could no longer be restrained. My sobs reached the ears of the captain, who came and very kindly reminded us, that for his safety, as well as our own, it would be prudent for us not to attract any attention. He said that when there was a sail in sight he wished us to keep below; but at other times, he had no objection to our being on deck. He assured us that he would keep a good lookout, and if we acted prudently, he thought we should be in no danger. He had represented us as women going to meet our husbands in ____. We thanked him, and promised to observe carefully all the directions he gave us.

Fanny and I now talked by ourselves, low and quietly, in our little cabin. She told me of the sufferings she had gone through in making her escape, and of her terrors while she was concealed in her mother's house. Above all, she dwelt on the agony of separation from all her children on that dreadful auction day. She could scarcely credit me, when I told her of the place where I had passed nearly seven years. "We have the same sorrows," said I. "No," replied she, "you are going to see your children soon, and there is no hope that I shall ever even hear from mine."

The vessel was soon under way, but we made slow progress. The wind was against us. I should not have cared for this, if we had been out of sight of the town; but until there were miles of water between us and our enemies, we were filled with constant apprehensions that the constables would come on board. Neither could I feel quite at ease with the captain and his men. I was an entire stranger to that class of people, and I had heard that sailors were rough, and sometimes cruel. We were so completely in their power, that if they were bad men, our situation would be dreadful. Now that the captain was paid for our passage, might he not be tempted to make more money by giving us up to those who claimed us as property? I was naturally of a confiding disposition, but slavery had made me suspicious of every body. Fanny did not share my distrust of the captain or his men. She said she was afraid at first, but she had been on board three days while the vessel lay in the dock, and nobody had betrayed her, or treated her otherwise than kindly.

The captain soon came to advise us to go on deck for fresh air. His friendly and respectful manner, combined with Fanny's testimony, reassured me, and we went with him. He placed us in a comfortable seat, and occasionally entered into conversation. He told us he was a Southerner by birth, and had spent the greater part of his life in the Slave States, and that he had recently lost a brother who traded in slaves. "But," said he, "it is a pitiable and degrading business, and I always felt ashamed to acknowledge my brother in connection with it." As we passed Snaky Swamp, he pointed to it, and said, "There is a slave territory that defies all the laws." I thought of the terrible days I had spent there, and though it was not called Dismal Swamp, it made me feel very dismal as I looked at it.

I shall never forget that night. The balmy air of spring was so refreshing! And how shall I describe my sensations when we were fairly sailing on Chesapeake Bay? O, the beautiful sunshine! the exhilarating breeze! and I could enjoy them without fear or restraint. I had never realized what grand things air and sunlight are till I had been deprived of them.

Ten days after we left land we were approaching Philadelphia.[183] The captain said we should arrive there in the night, but he thought we had better wait till morning, and go on shore in broad daylight, as the best way to avoid suspicion.

I replied, "You know best. But will you stay on board and protect us?"

He saw that I was suspicious, and he said he was sorry, now that he had brought us to the end of our voyage, to find I had so little confidence in him. Ah, if he had ever been a slave he would have known how difficult it was to trust a white man. He assured us that we might sleep through the night without fear; that he would take care we were not left unprotected. Be it said to the honor of this captain, Southerner as he was, that if Fanny and I had been white ladies, and our passage lawfully

[183]The Mason-Dixon Line ran along the border between free Pennsylvania and slave Maryland. Philadelphia, home to 19,000 free blacks in 1842, had the largest free black population in the United States at the time. It was a first stop for many fugitive slaves from the Southeast.

engaged, he could not have treated us more respectfully. My intelligent friend, Peter, had rightly estimated the character of the man to whose honor he had intrusted us.

The next morning I was on deck as soon as the day dawned. I called Fanny to see the sun rise, for the first time in our lives, on free soil; for such I *then* believed it to be. We watched the reddening sky, and saw the great orb come up slowly out of the water, as it seemed. Soon the waves began to sparkle, and every thing caught the beautiful glow. Before us lay the city of strangers.[184] We looked at each other, and the eyes of both were moistened with tears. We had escaped from slavery, and we supposed ourselves to be safe from the hunters. But we were alone in the world, and we had left dear ties behind us; ties cruelly sundered by the demon Slavery.

XXXI. INCIDENTS IN PHILADELPHIA

I had heard that the poor slave had many friends at the north. I trusted we should find some of them. Meantime, we would take it for granted that all were friends, till they proved to the contrary. I sought out the kind captain, thanked him for his attentions, and told him I should never cease to be grateful for the service he had rendered us. I gave him a message to the friends I had left at home, and he promised to deliver it. We were placed in a row-boat, and in about fifteen minutes were landed on a wood wharf in Philadelphia. As I stood looking round, the friendly captain touched me on the shoulder, and said, "There is a respectable-looking colored man behind you. I will speak to him about the New York trains, and tell him you wish to go directly on." I thanked him, and asked him to direct me to some shops where I could buy gloves and veils. He did so, and said he would talk with the colored man till I returned. I made what haste I could. Constant exercise on board the vessel, and frequent rubbing with salt water, had nearly restored the use of my limbs. The noise of the great city confused me, but I found the shops, and bought some double veils and gloves for Fanny and myself. The shopman told me they were so many levies.[185] I had never heard the word before, but I did not tell him so. I thought if he knew I was a stranger he might ask me where I came from. I gave him a gold piece, and when he returned the change, I counted it, and found

[184] A play on Philadelphia's motto, "the City of Brotherly Love," given by one of its seventeenth-century founders, the Quaker William Penn, who envisioned the city as a place where people from all backgrounds and races could live together harmoniously.

[185] A levy was a coin that was worth between eleven and twelve and a half cents.

out how much a levy was. I made my way back to the wharf, where the captain introduced me to the colored man, as the Rev. Jeremiah Durham, minister of Bethel church.[186] He took me by the hand, as if I had been an old friend. He told us we were too late for the morning cars to New York, and must wait until the evening, or the next morning. He invited me to go home with him, assuring me that his wife would give me a cordial welcome; and for my friend he would provide a home with one of his neighbors. I thanked him for so much kindness to strangers, and told him if I must be detained, I should like to hunt up some people who formerly went from our part of the country. Mr. Durham insisted that I should dine with him, and then he would assist me in finding my friends. The sailors came to bid us good by. I shook their hardy hands, with tears in my eyes. They had all been kind to us, and they had rendered us a greater service than they could possibly conceive of.

I had never seen so large a city, or been in contact with so many people in the streets. It seemed as if those who passed looked at us with an expression of curiosity. My face was so blistered and peeled, by sitting on deck, in wind and sunshine, that I thought they could not easily decide to what nation I belonged.

Mrs. Durham met me with a kindly welcome, without asking any questions. I was tired, and her friendly manner was a sweet refreshment. God bless her! I was sure that she had comforted other weary hearts, before I received her sympathy. She was surrounded by her husband and children, in a home made sacred by protecting laws.[187] I thought of my own children, and sighed.

After dinner Mr. Durham went with me in quest of the friends I had spoken of. They went from my native town, and I anticipated much pleasure in looking on familiar faces. They were not at home, and we retraced our steps through streets delightfully clean. On the way, Mr. Durham observed that I had spoken to him of a daughter I expected to meet; that he was surprised, for I looked so young he had taken me for a single woman. He was approaching a subject on which I was extremely sensitive. He would ask about my husband next, I thought, and if I answered him truly, what would he think of me? I told him I had two children, one in New York the other at the south. He asked some

[186]Founded in 1794 for African American worshippers, Bethel Church was one of fifteen churches serving Philadelphia's black community. It was an active supporter of the Philadelphia Vigilance Committee, founded by black abolitionist Robert Purvis (1810–1898) to help fugitive slaves. Between June 9 and September 8, 1842, the Vigilance Committee helped 117 runaways, one of them Harriet Jacobs (Jacobs, *Incidents*, ed. Yellin, 282–83n).

[187]Legal protection is a key theme in Jacobs's narrative.

further questions, and I frankly told him some of the most important events of my life. It was painful for me to do it; but I would not deceive him. If he was desirous of being my friend, I thought he ought to know how far I was worthy of it. "Excuse me, if I have tried your feelings," said he. "I did not question you from idle curiosity. I wanted to understand your situation, in order to know whether I could be of any service to you, or your little girl. Your straightforward answers do you credit; but don't answer every body so openly. It might give some heartless people a pretext for treating you with contempt."

That word *contempt* burned me like coals of fire. I replied, "God alone knows how I have suffered; and He, I trust, will forgive me. If I am permitted to have my children, I intend to be a good mother, and to live in such a manner that people cannot treat me with contempt."

"I respect your sentiments," said he. "Place your trust in God, and be governed by good principles, and you will not fail to find friends."

When we reached home, I went to my room, glad to shut out the world for a while. The words he had spoken made an indelible impression upon me. They brought up great shadows from the mournful past. In the midst of my meditations I was startled by a knock at the door. Mrs. Durham entered, her face all beaming with kindness, to say that there was an antislavery friend down stairs, who would like to see me. I overcame my dread of encountering strangers, and went with her. Many questions were asked concerning my experiences, and my escape from slavery; but I observed how careful they all were not to say any thing that might wound my feelings. How gratifying this was, can be fully understood only by those who have been accustomed to be treated as if they were not included within the pale of human beings. The antislavery friend had come to inquire into my plans, and to offer assistance, if needed. Fanny was comfortably established, for the present, with a friend of Mr. Durham. The Anti-Slavery Society agreed to pay her expenses to New York. The same was offered to me, but I declined to accept it; telling them that my grandmother had given me sufficient to pay my expenses to the end of my journey. We were urged to remain in Philadelphia a few days, until some suitable escort could be found for us. I gladly accepted the proposition, for I had a dread of meeting slaveholders, and some dread also of railroads. I had never entered a railroad car in my life, and it seemed to me quite an important event.

That night I sought my pillow with feelings I had never carried to it before. I verily believed myself to be a free woman. I was wakeful for a long time, and I had no sooner fallen asleep, than I was roused by fire-bells. I jumped up, and hurried on my clothes. Where I came from, every body hastened to dress themselves on such occasions. The white people thought a great fire might be used as a good opportunity for insurrection, and that it was best to be in readiness; and the colored people were ordered out to labor in extinguishing the flames. There was but one engine in our town, and colored women and children were often required to drag it to the river's edge and fill it. Mrs. Durham's daughter slept in the same room with me, and seeing that she slept through all the din, I thought it was my duty to wake her. "What's the matter?" said she, rubbing her eyes.

"They're screaming fire in the streets, and the bells are ringing," I replied.

"What of that?" said she, drowsily. "We are used to it. We never get up, without the fire is very near. What good would it do?"

I was quite surprised that it was not necessary for us to go and help fill the engine. I was an ignorant child, just beginning to learn how things went on in great cities.

At daylight, I heard women crying fresh fish, berries, radishes, and various other things. All this was new to me. I dressed myself at an early hour, and sat at the window to watch that unknown tide of life. Philadelphia seemed to me a wonderfully great place. At the breakfast table, my idea of going out to drag the engine was laughed over, and I joined in the mirth.

I went to see Fanny, and found her so well contented among her new friends that she was in no haste to leave. I was also very happy with my kind hostess. She had had advantages for education, and was vastly my superior. Every day, almost every hour, I was adding to my little stock of knowledge. She took me out to see the city as much as she deemed prudent. One day she took me to an artist's room, and showed me the portraits of some of her children.[188] I had never seen any paintings of colored people before, and they seemed to me beautiful.

At the end of five days, one of Mrs. Durham's friends offered to accompany us to New York the following morning.[189] As I held the hand of my good hostess in a parting clasp, I longed to know whether her husband had repeated to her what I had told him. I supposed he had, but she never made any allusion to it. I presume it was the delicate silence of womanly sympathy.

[188]The artist was Robert Douglass Jr. (1809–1887), a portrait painter and lithographer (Yellin, *Harriet Jacobs*, 67).

[189]Yellin says that Jacobs met a number of prominent activists during her stay in Philadelphia, including Joshua Coffin, a founder of the American Anti-Slavery Society, who would describe Jacobs's remarkable escape to Lydia Maria Child, then editor of the *National Anti-Slavery Standard*; the Reverend Daniel A. Payne, who would suggest that Jacobs write her narrative; Robert Purvis; and Elizabeth Chew, a member of the Philadelphia Female Anti-Slavery Society, who would become a lifelong friend (Yellin, *Harriet Jacobs*, 67).

When Mr. Durham handed us our tickets, he said, "I am afraid you will have a disagreeable ride; but I could not procure tickets for the first class cars."

Supposing I had not given him money enough, I offered more. "O, no," said he, "they could not be had for any money. They don't allow colored people to go in the first-class cars."

This was the first chill to my enthusiasm about the Free States. Colored people were allowed to ride in a filthy box, behind white people, at the south, but there they were not required to pay for the privilege. It made me sad to find how the north aped the customs of slavery.

We were stowed away in a large, rough car, with windows on each side, too high for us to look out without standing up. It was crowded with people, apparently of all nations. There were plenty of beds and cradles, containing screaming and kicking babies. Every other man had a cigar or pipe in his mouth, and jugs of whiskey were handed round freely. The fumes of the whiskey and the dense tobacco smoke were sickening to my senses, and my mind was equally nauseated by the coarse jokes and ribald songs around me. It was a very disagreeable ride. Since that time there has been some improvement in these matters.[190]

XXXII. THE MEETING OF MOTHER AND DAUGHTER

When we arrived in New York, I was half crazed by the crowd of coachmen calling out, "Carriage, ma'am?" We bargained with one to take us to Sullivan Street for twelve shillings. A burly Irishman stepped up and said, "I'll tak' ye for sax shillings." The reduction of half the price was an object to us, and we asked if he could take us right away. "Troth an I will, ladies," he replied. I noticed that the hackmen smiled at each other, and I inquired whether his conveyance was decent. "Yes, it's dacent it is, marm. Devil a bit would I be after takin' ladies in a cab that was not dacent." We gave him our checks. He went for the baggage, and soon reappeared, saying, "This way, if you plase, ladies." We followed, and found our trunks on a truck, and we were invited to take our seats on them. We told him that was not what we bargained for, and he must take the trunks off. He swore they should not be touched till we had paid him six shillings. In our situation it was not prudent to attract attention, and I was about to pay him what he required, when a man near by shook his head for me not to do it. After a great ado we

[190]Jacobs's descriptions of discrimination in the North reinforce a common abolitionist theme that slavery's shadow was cast not merely in the South. Legal segregation persisted throughout the United States until the 1954 desegregation decision in *Brown v. Board of Education of Topeka* (Jacobs, *Incidents*, ed. Yellin, 283–84n).

got rid of the Irishman, and had our trunks fastened on a hack. We had been recommended to a boarding-house in Sullivan Street, and thither we drove. There Fanny and I separated. The Anti-Slavery Society[191] provided a home for her, and I afterwards heard of her in prosperous circumstances. I sent for an old friend from my part of the country, who had for some time been doing business in New York. He came immediately. I told him I wanted to go to my daughter, and asked him to aid me in procuring an interview.

I cautioned him not to let it be known to the family that I had just arrived from the south, because they supposed I had been at the north seven years. He told me there was a colored woman in Brooklyn who came from the same town I did, and I had better go to her house, and have my daughter meet me there. I accepted the proposition thankfully, and he agreed to escort me to Brooklyn. We crossed Fulton ferry, went up Myrtle Avenue, and stopped at the house he designated.[192] I was just about to enter, when two girls passed. My friend called my attention to them. I turned, and recognized in the eldest, Sarah, the daughter of a woman who used to live with my grandmother, but who had left the south years ago. Surprised and rejoiced at this unexpected meeting, I threw my arms round her, and inquired concerning her mother.

"You take no notice of the other girl," said my friend. I turned, and there stood my Ellen! I pressed her to my heart, then held her away from me to take a look at her. She had changed a good deal in the two years since I parted from her. Signs of neglect could be discerned by eyes less observing than a mother's. My friend invited us all to go into the house; but Ellen said she had been sent of an errand, which she would do as quickly as possible, and go home and ask Mrs. Hobbs to let her come and see me. It was agreed that I should send for her the next day. Her companion, Sarah, hastened to tell her mother of my arrival. When I entered the house, I found the mistress of it absent, and I waited for her return. Before I saw her, I heard her saying, "Where is Linda Brent? I used to know her father and mother." Soon Sarah came with her mother. So there was quite a company of us, all from my grandmother's neighborhood. These friends gathered round me and questioned me eagerly. They laughed, they cried, and they shouted. They thanked God that I had got away from my persecutors and was safe

[191] It is not clear whether this was the Ladies' New York City Anti-Slavery Society, which according to Yellin was an all-white organization. However, black New Yorkers organized a number of associations devoted to aiding fugitives, including the New York Ladies Literary Society, the Manhattan Abolition Society, the all-male New York Vigilance Committee, and the Colored Female Vigilance Committee (Yellin, *Harriet Jacobs*, 69–70).

[192] Until 1883, when the Brooklyn Bridge was finished, a ferry crossing the East River connected New York and Brooklyn.

on Long Island. It was a day of great excitement. How different from the silent days I had passed in my dreary den!

The next morning was Sunday. My first waking thoughts were occupied with the note I was to send to Mrs. Hobbs, the lady with whom Ellen lived.[193] That I had recently come into that vicinity was evident; otherwise I should have sooner inquired for my daughter. It would not do to let them know I had just arrived from the south, for that would involve the suspicion of my having been harbored there, and might bring trouble, if not ruin, on several people.

I like a straightforward course, and am always reluctant to resort to subterfuges. So far as my ways have been crooked, I charge them all upon slavery. It was that system of violence and wrong which now left me no alternative but to enact a falsehood. I began my note by stating that I had recently arrived from Canada, and was very desirous to have my daughter come to see me. She came and brought a message from Mrs. Hobbs, inviting me to her house, and assuring me that I need not have any fears. The conversation I had with my child did not leave my mind at ease. When I asked if she was well treated, she answered yes; but there was no heartiness in the tone, and it seemed to me that she said it from an unwillingness to have me troubled on her account. Before she left me, she asked very earnestly, "Mother, when will you take me to live with you?" It made me sad to think that I could not give her a home till I went to work and earned the means; and that might take me a long time. When she was placed with Mrs. Hobbs, the agreement was that she should be sent to school. She had been there two years, and was now nine years old, and she scarcely knew her letters. There was no excuse for this, for there were good public schools in Brooklyn, to which she could have been sent without expense.[194]

She staid with me till dark, and I went home with her. I was received in a friendly manner by the family, and all agreed in saying that Ellen was a useful, good girl. Mrs. Hobbs looked me coolly in the face, and said, "I suppose you know that my cousin, Mr. Sands, has *given* her to my eldest daughter. She will make a nice waiting-maid for her when she grows up." I did not answer a word. How could she, who knew by experience the strength of a mother's love, and who was perfectly aware of the relation Mr. Sands bore to my children,—how *could* she look me in the face, while she thrust such a dagger into my heart?

[193]According to Yellin, Louisa had been living apart from her mother for two years, five months of which were spent with her father in Washington, D.C., and the rest with the Tredwells in Brooklyn (Jacobs, *Incidents*, ed. Yellin, 284n).

[194]Brooklyn had two African Free Schools that Louisa could have attended.

I was no longer surprised that they had kept her in such a state of ignorance. Mr. Hobbs had formerly been wealthy, but he had failed, and afterwards obtained a subordinate situation in the Custom House. Perhaps they expected to return to the south some day; and Ellen's knowledge was quite sufficient for a slave's condition. I was impatient to go to work and earn money, that I might change the uncertain position of my children. Mr. Sands had not kept his promise to emancipate them. I had also been deceived about Ellen. What security had I with regard to Benjamin? I felt that I had none.

I returned to my friend's house in an uneasy state of mind. In order to protect my children, it was necessary that I should own myself. I called myself free, and sometimes felt so; but I knew I was insecure. I sat down that night and wrote a civil letter to Dr. Flint, asking him to state the lowest terms on which he would sell me; and as I belonged by law to his daughter, I wrote to her also, making a similar request.

Since my arrival at the north I had not been unmindful of my dear brother William. I had made diligent inquiries for him, and having heard of him in Boston, I went thither. When I arrived there, I found he had gone to New Bedford. I wrote to that place, and was informed he had gone on a whaling voyage, and would not return for some months.[195] I went back to New York to get employment near Ellen. I received an answer from Dr. Flint, which gave me no encouragement. He advised me to return and submit myself to my rightful owners, and then any request I might make would be granted. I lent this letter to a friend, who lost it; otherwise I would present a copy to my readers.

XXXIII. A HOME FOUND

My greatest anxiety now was to obtain employment. My health was greatly improved, though my limbs continued to trouble me with swelling whenever I walked much. The greatest difficulty in my way was, that those who employed strangers required a recommendation; and in my peculiar position, I could, of course, obtain no certificates from the families I had so faithfully served.

One day an acquaintance told me of a lady who wanted a nurse for her babe, and I immediately applied for the situation.[196] The lady told me she preferred to have one who had been a mother, and accustomed to the care of infants. I told her I had nursed two babes of my own.

[195] See John S. Jacobs, *A True Tale of Slavery*, chap. VI (Document 11).

[196] Mary Stace Willis (ca. 1816–1845) had one daughter, Imogen, in the spring of 1842.

She asked me many questions, but, to my great relief, did not require a recommendation from my former employers. She told me she was an English woman, and that was a pleasant circumstance to me, because I had heard they had less prejudice against color than Americans entertained. It was agreed that we should try each other for a week. The trial proved satisfactory to both parties, and I was engaged for a month.

The heavenly Father had been most merciful to me in leading me to this place. Mrs. Bruce was a kind and gentle lady, and proved a true and sympathizing friend. Before the stipulated month expired, the necessity of passing up and down stairs frequently, caused my limbs to swell so painfully, that I became unable to perform my duties. Many ladies would have thoughtlessly discharged me; but Mrs. Bruce made arrangements to save me steps, and employed a physician to attend upon me. I had not yet told her that I was a fugitive slave. She noticed that I was often sad, and kindly inquired the cause. I spoke of being separated from my children, and from relatives who were dear to me; but I did not mention the constant feeling of insecurity which oppressed my spirits. I longed for some one to confide in; but I had been so deceived by white people, that I had lost all confidence in them. If they spoke kind words to me, I thought it was for some selfish purpose. I had entered this family with the distrustful feelings I had brought with me out of slavery; but ere six months had passed, I found that the gentle deportment of Mrs. Bruce and the smiles of her lovely babe were thawing my chilled heart. My narrow mind also began to expand under the influences of her intelligent conversation, and the opportunities for reading, which were gladly allowed me whenever I had leisure from my duties. I gradually became more energetic and more cheerful.

The old feeling of insecurity, especially with regard to my children, often threw its dark shadow across my sunshine. Mrs. Bruce offered me a home for Ellen; but pleasant as it would have been, I did not dare to accept it, for fear of offending the Hobbs family. Their knowledge of my precarious situation placed me in their power; and I felt that it was important for me to keep on the right side of them, till, by dint of labor and economy, I could make a home for my children. I was far from feeling satisfied with Ellen's situation. She was not well cared for. She sometimes came to New York to visit me; but she generally brought a request from Mrs. Hobbs that I would buy her a pair of shoes, or some article of clothing. This was accompanied by a promise of payment when Mr. Hobbs's salary at the Custom House became due; but some how or other the pay-day never came. Thus many dollars of my earnings were expended to keep my child comfortably clothed.

That, however, was a slight trouble, compared with the fear that their pecuniary embarrassments might induce them to sell my precious young daughter. I knew they were in constant communication with Southerners, and had frequent opportunities to do it. I have stated that when Dr. Flint put Ellen in jail, at two years old, she had an inflammation of the eyes, occasioned by measles. This disease still troubled her; and kind Mrs. Bruce proposed that she should come to New York for a while, to be under the care of Dr. Elliott, a well known oculist.[197] It did not occur to me that there was any thing improper in a mother's making such a request; but Mrs. Hobbs was very angry, and refused to let her go. Situated as I was, it was not politic to insist upon it. I made no complaint, but I longed to be entirely free to act a mother's part towards my children. The next time I went over to Brooklyn, Mrs. Hobbs, as if to apologize for her anger, told me she had employed her own physician to attend to Ellen's eyes, and that she had refused my request because she did not consider it safe to trust her in New York. I accepted the explanation in silence; but she had told me that my child belonged to her daughter, and I suspected that her real motive was a fear of my conveying her property away from her. Perhaps I did her injustice; but my knowledge of Southerners made it difficult for me to feel otherwise.

Sweet and bitter were mixed in the cup of my life, and I was thankful that it had ceased to be entirely bitter. I loved Mrs. Bruce's babe. When it laughed and crowed in my face, and twined its little tender arms confidingly about my neck, it made me think of the time when Benny and Ellen were babies, and my wounded heart was soothed. One bright morning, as I stood at the window, tossing baby in my arms, my attention was attracted by a young man in sailor's dress, who was closely observing every house as he passed. I looked at him earnestly. Could it be my brother William? It *must* be he—and yet, how changed! I placed the baby safely, flew down stairs, opened the front door, beckoned to the sailor, and in less than a minute I was clasped in my brother's arms. How much we had to tell each other! How we laughed, and how we cried, over each other's adventures! I took him to Brooklyn, and again saw him with Ellen, the dear child whom he had loved and tended so carefully, while I was shut up in my miserable den.

[197]Samuel McKenzie Elliott had treated Mrs. Willis's husband, Nathaniel Parker Willis (1806–1867), and was indeed the most famous oculist (eye doctor) in New York. Elliott's patients also included Henry Wadsworth Longfellow, Francis Parkman, and James Russell Lowell. Willis, associate editor of the *New York Mirror*, was a well-known journalist and essayist. Personally, he was a vain and ambitious man, a society journalist who had as many detractors as friends, and Jacobs correctly pegged him as being sympathetic to slavery.

He staid in New York a week. His old feelings of affection for me and Ellen were as lively as ever. There are no bonds so strong as those which are formed by suffering together.[198]

XXXIV. THE OLD ENEMY AGAIN

My young mistress, Miss Emily Flint, did not return any answer to my letter requesting her to consent to my being sold. But after a while, I received a reply, which purported to be written by her younger brother. In order rightly to enjoy the contents of this letter, the reader must bear in mind that the Flint family supposed I had been at the north many years. They had no idea that I knew of the doctor's three excursions to New York in search of me; that I had heard his voice, when he came to borrow five hundred dollars for that purpose; and that I had seen him pass on his way to the steamboat. Neither were they aware that all the particulars of aunt Nancy's death and burial were conveyed to me at the time they occurred. I have kept the letter, of which I herewith subjoin a copy:—

> Your letter to sister was received a few days ago. I gather from it that you are desirous of returning to your native place, among your friends and relatives. We were all gratified with the contents of your letter; and let me assure you that if any members of the family have had any feeling of resentment towards you, they feel it no longer. We all sympathize with you in your unfortunate condition, and are ready to do all in our power to make you contented and happy. It is difficult for you to return home as a free person. If you were purchased by your grandmother, it is doubtful whether you would be permitted to remain, although it would be lawful for you to do so. If a servant should be allowed to purchase herself, after absenting herself so long from her owners, and return free, it would have an injurious effect. From your letter, I think your situation must be hard and uncomfortable. Come home. You have it in your power to be reinstated in our affections. We would receive you with open arms and tears of joy. You need not apprehend any unkind treatment, as we have not put ourselves to any trouble or expense to get you. Had we done so, perhaps we should feel otherwise.

[198] Compare with John Jacobs's account of their reunion at Astor House, where Harriet lived with the Willis family (*A True Tale of Slavery*, chap. VI; see Document 11). John's pained remark about how much her years of hiding had changed her reminds us of the intense physical suffering she endured and its permanent effects.

You know my sister was always attached to you, and that you were never treated as a slave. You were never put to hard work, nor exposed to field labor. On the contrary, you were taken into the house, and treated as one of us, and almost as free; and we, at least, felt that you were above disgracing yourself by running away. Believing you may be induced to come home voluntarily has induced me to write for my sister. The family will be rejoiced to see you; and your poor old grandmother expressed a great desire to have you come, when she heard your letter read. In her old age she needs the consolation of having her children round her. Doubtless you have heard of the death of your aunt. She was a faithful servant, and a faithful member of the Episcopal church. In her Christian life she taught us how to live—and, O, too high the price of knowledge, she taught us how to die! Could you have seen us round her death bed, with her mother, all mingling our tears in one common stream, you would have thought the same heartfelt tie existed between a master and his servant, as between a mother and her child. But this subject is too painful to dwell upon. I must bring my letter to a close. If you are contented to stay away from your old grandmother, your child, and the friends who love you, stay where you are. We shall never trouble ourselves to apprehend you. But should you prefer to come home, we will do all that we can to make you happy. If you do not wish to remain in the family, I know that father, by our persuasion, will be induced to let you be purchased by any person you may choose in our community. You will please answer this as soon as possible, and let us know your decision. Sister sends much love to you. In the mean time believe me your sincere friend and well wisher.

This letter was signed by Emily's brother, who was as yet a mere lad. I knew, by the style, that it was not written by a person of his age, and though the writing was disguised, I had been made too unhappy by it, in former years, not to recognize at once the hand of Dr. Flint. O, the hypocrisy of slaveholders! Did the old fox suppose I was goose enough to go into such a trap? Verily, he relied too much on "the stupidity of the African race." I did not return the family of Flints any thanks for their cordial invitation—a remissness for which I was, no doubt, charged with base ingratitude.

Not long afterwards I received a letter from one of my friends at the south, informing me that Dr. Flint was about to visit the north. The letter had been delayed, and I supposed he might be already on the way. Mrs. Bruce did not know I was a fugitive. I told her that important business called me to Boston, where my brother then was, and asked permission to bring a friend to supply my place as nurse, for a fortnight. I started on my journey immediately; and as soon as I arrived, I wrote to my grandmother that if Benny came, he must be sent to Boston. I knew she was only waiting for a good chance to send him north, and, fortunately, she had the legal power to do so, without asking leave of any body. She was a free woman; and when my children were purchased, Mr. Sands preferred to have the bill of sale drawn up in her name. It was conjectured that he advanced the money, but it was not known. At the south, a gentleman may have a shoal of colored children without any disgrace; but if he is known to purchase them, with the view of setting them free, the example is thought to be dangerous to their "peculiar institution," and he becomes unpopular.

There was a good opportunity to send Benny in a vessel coming directly to New York. He was put on board with a letter to a friend, who was requested to see him off to Boston. Early one morning, there was a loud rap at my door, and in rushed Benjamin, all out of breath. "O mother!" he exclaimed, "here I am! I run all the way; and I come all alone. How d'you do?"

O reader, can you imagine my joy? No, you cannot, unless you have been a slave mother. Benjamin rattled away as fast as his tongue could go. "Mother, why don't you bring Ellen here? I went over to Brooklyn to see her, and she felt very bad when I bid her good by. She said, 'O Ben, I wish I was going too.' I thought she'd know ever so much; but she don't know so much as I do; for I can read, and she can't. And, mother, I lost all my clothes coming. What can I do to get some more? I 'spose free boys can get along here at the north as well as white boys."

I did not like to tell the sanguine, happy little fellow how much he was mistaken. I took him to a tailor, and procured a change of clothes. The rest of the day was spent in mutual asking and answering of questions, with the wish constantly repeated that the good old grandmother was with us, and frequent injunctions from Benny to write to her immediately, and be sure to tell her every thing about his voyage, and his journey to Boston.

Dr. Flint made his visit to New York, and made every exertion to call upon me, and invite me to return with him; but not being able to ascertain where I was, his hospitable intentions were frustrated, and the affectionate family, who were waiting for me with "open arms," were doomed to disappointment.

As soon as I knew he was safely at home, I placed Benjamin in the care of my brother William, and returned to Mrs. Bruce. There I remained through the winter and spring, endeavoring to perform my duties faithfully, and finding a good degree of happiness in the attractions of baby Mary, the considerate kindness of her excellent mother, and occasional interviews with my darling daughter.

But when summer came, the old feeling of insecurity haunted me. It was necessary for me to take little Mary out daily, for exercise and fresh air, and the city was swarming with Southerners, some of whom might recognize me. Hot weather brings out snakes and slaveholders, and I like one class of the venomous creatures as little as I do the other. What a comfort it is, to be free to *say* so!

XXXV. PREJUDICE AGAINST COLOR

It was a relief to my mind to see preparations for leaving the city. We went to Albany in the steamboat Knickerbocker. When the gong sounded for tea, Mrs. Bruce said, "Linda, it is late, and you and baby had better come to the table with me." I replied, "I know it is time baby had her supper, but I had rather not go with you, if you please. I am afraid of being insulted." "O no, not if you are with me," she said. I saw several white nurses go with their ladies, and I ventured to do the same. We were at the extreme end of the table. I was no sooner seated, than a gruff voice said, "Get up! You know you are not allowed to sit here." I looked up, and, to my astonishment and indignation, saw that the speaker was a colored man. If his office required him to enforce the by-laws of the boat, he might, at least, have done it politely. I replied, "I shall not get up, unless the captain comes and takes me up." No cup of tea was offered me, but Mrs. Bruce handed me hers and called for another. I looked to see whether the other nurses were treated in a similar manner. They were all properly waited on.

Next morning, when we stopped at Troy for breakfast, every body was making a rush for the table. Mrs. Bruce said, "Take my arm, Linda, and we'll go in together." The landlord heard her, and said, "Madam, will you allow your nurse and baby to take breakfast with my family?" I knew this was to be attributed to my complexion; but he spoke courteously, and therefore I did not mind it.

At Saratoga we found the United States Hotel crowded, and Mr. Bruce took one of the cottages belonging to the hotel. I had thought, with gladness, of going to the quiet of the country, where I should meet few people, but here I found myself in the midst of a swarm of Southerners. I looked round me with fear and trembling, dreading to see some one who would recognize me. I was rejoiced to find that we were to stay but a short time.

We soon returned to New York, to make arrangements for spending the remainder of the summer at Rockaway. While the laundress was putting the clothes in order, I took an opportunity to go over to Brooklyn to see Ellen. I met her going to a grocery store, and the first words she said, were, "O, mother, don't go to Mrs. Hobbs's. Her brother, Mr. Thorne, has come from the south, and may be he'll tell where you are." I accepted the warning. I told her I was going away with Mrs. Bruce the next day, and would try to see her when I came back.

Being in servitude to the Anglo-Saxon race, I was not put into a "Jim Crow car,"[199] on our way to Rockaway, neither was I invited to ride through the streets on the top of trunks in a truck; but every where I found the same manifestations of that cruel prejudice, which so discourages the feelings, and represses the energies of the colored people. We reached Rockaway before dark, and put up at the Pavilion—a large hotel, beautifully situated by the sea-side—a great resort of the fashionable world. Thirty or forty nurses were there, of a great variety of nations. Some of the ladies had colored waiting-maids and coachmen, but I was the only nurse tinged with the blood of Africa. When the tea bell rang, I took little Mary and followed the other nurses. Supper was served in a long hall. A young man, who had the ordering of things, took the circuit of the table two or three times, and finally pointed me to a seat at the lower end of it. As there was but one chair, I sat down and took the child in my lap. Whereupon the young man came to me and said, in the blandest manner possible, "Will you please to seat the little girl in the chair, and stand behind it and feed her? After they have done, you will be shown to the kitchen, where you will have a good supper."

This was the climax! I found it hard to preserve my self-control, when I looked round, and saw women who were nurses, as I was, and only one shade lighter in complexion, eyeing me with a defiant look, as if my presence were a contamination. However, I said nothing. I quietly took the child in my arms, went to our room, and refused to go to the table again. Mr. Bruce ordered meals to be sent to the room for little Mary and I. This answered for a few days; but the waiters of the establishment were white, and they soon began to complain, saying they were not

[199]"Jim Crow" comes from the popular minstrel performer Thomas D. Rice, a white man who performed, in blackface, a song-and-dance act featuring a character named Jim Crow.

hired to wait on negroes. The landlord requested Mr. Bruce to send me down to my meals, because his servants rebelled against bringing them up, and the colored servants of other boarders were dissatisfied because all were not treated alike.

My answer was that the colored servants ought to be dissatisfied with *themselves*, for not having too much self-respect to submit to such treatment; that there was no difference in the price of board for colored and white servants, and there was no justification for difference of treatment. I staid a month after this, and finding I was resolved to stand up for my rights, they concluded to treat me well. Let every colored man and woman do this, and eventually we shall cease to be trampled under foot by our oppressors.

XXXVI. THE HAIRBREADTH ESCAPE

After we returned to New York, I took the earliest opportunity to go and see Ellen. I asked to have her called down stairs; for I supposed Mrs. Hobbs's southern brother might still be there, and I was desirous to avoid seeing him, if possible. But Mrs. Hobbs came to the kitchen, and insisted on my going up stairs. "My brother wants to see you," said she, "and he is sorry you seem to shun him. He knows you are living in New York. He told me to say to you that he owes thanks to good old aunt Martha for too many little acts of kindness for him to be base enough to betray her grandchild."

This Mr. Thorne had become poor and reckless long before he left the south, and such persons had much rather go to one of the faithful old slaves to borrow a dollar, or get a good dinner, than to go to one whom they consider an equal. It was such acts of kindness as these for which he professed to feel grateful to my grandmother. I wished he had kept at a distance, but as he was here, and knew where I was, I concluded there was nothing to be gained by trying to avoid him; on the contrary, it might be the means of exciting his ill will. I followed his sister up stairs. He met me in a very friendly manner, congratulated me on my escape from slavery, and hoped I had a good place, where I felt happy.

I continued to visit Ellen as often as I could. She, good thoughtful child, never forgot my hazardous situation, but always kept a vigilant lookout for my safety. She never made any complaint about her own inconveniences and troubles; but a mother's observing eye easily perceived that she was not happy. On the occasion of one of my visits I found her unusually serious. When I asked her what was the matter, she said nothing was the matter. But I insisted upon knowing what made her look so very grave. Finally, I ascertained that she felt troubled about the dissipation that was continually going on in the house. She was sent to the store very often for rum and brandy, and she felt ashamed to ask for it so often; and Mr. Hobbs and Mr. Thorne drank a great deal, and their hands trembled so that they had to call her to pour out the liquor for them. "But for all that," said she, "Mr. Hobbs is good to me, and I can't help liking him. I feel sorry for him." I tried to comfort her, by telling her that I had laid up a hundred dollars, and that before long I hoped to be able to give her and Benjamin a home, and send them to school. She was always desirous not to add to my troubles more than she could help, and I did not discover till years afterwards that Mr. Thorne's intemperance was not the only annoyance she suffered from him. Though he professed too much gratitude to my grandmother to injure any of her descendants, he had poured vile language into the ears of her innocent great-grandchild.

I usually went to Brooklyn to spend Sunday afternoon. One Sunday, I found Ellen, anxiously waiting for me near the house. "O, mother," said she, "I've been waiting for you this long time. I'm afraid Mr. Thorne has written to tell Dr. Flint where you are. Make haste and come in. Mrs. Hobbs will tell you all about it!"

The story was soon told. While the children were playing in the grape-vine arbor, the day before, Mr. Thorne came out with a letter in his hand, which he tore up and scattered about. Ellen was sweeping the yard at the time, and having her mind full of suspicions of him, she picked up the pieces and carried them to the children, saying, "I wonder who Mr. Thorne has been writing to."

"I'm sure I don't know, and don't care," replied the oldest of the children; "and I don't see how it concerns you."

"But it does concern me," replied Ellen; "for I'm afraid he's been writing to the south about my mother."

They laughed at her, and called her a silly thing, but good-naturedly put the fragments of writing together, in order to read them to her. They were no sooner arranged, than the little girl exclaimed, "I declare, Ellen, I believe you are right."

The contents of Mr. Thorne's letter, as nearly as I can remember, were as follows: "I have seen your slave, Linda, and conversed with her. She can be taken very easily, if you manage prudently. There are enough of us here to swear to her identity as your property. I am a patriot, a lover of my country, and I do this as an act of justice to the laws." He concluded by informing the doctor of the street and number where I lived. The children carried the pieces to Mrs. Hobbs, who immediately went to her brother's room for an explanation. He was not to be found. The servants said they saw him go out with a letter in his hand, and they supposed he had gone to the post office. The natural inference was, that he had sent to Dr. Flint a copy of those fragments. When he returned, his sister accused him of it, and he did not deny the charge. He went immediately to his room, and the next morning he was missing. He had gone over to New York, before any of the family were astir.

It was evident that I had no time to lose; and I hastened back to the city with a heavy heart. Again I was to be torn from a comfortable home, and all my plans for the welfare of my children were to be frustrated by that demon Slavery! I now regretted that I never told Mrs. Bruce my story. I had not concealed it merely on account of being a fugitive; that would have made her anxious, but it would have excited sympathy in her kind heart. I valued her good opinion, and I was afraid of losing it, if I told her all the particulars of my sad story. But now I felt that it was necessary for her to know how I was situated. I had once left her abruptly, without explaining the reason, and it would not be proper to do it again. I went home resolved to tell her in the morning. But the sadness of my face attracted her attention, and, in answer to her kind inquiries, I poured out my full heart to her, before bed time. She listened with true womanly sympathy, and told me she would do all she could to protect me. How my heart blessed her!

Early the next morning, Judge Vanderpool and Lawyer Hopper were consulted.[200] They said I had better leave the city at once, as the risk would be great if the case came to trial. Mrs. Bruce took me in a carriage to the house of one of her friends, where she assured me I should be safe until my brother could arrive, which would be in a few days. In the interval my thoughts were much occupied with Ellen. She was mine by birth, and she was also mine by Southern law, since my grandmother held the bill of sale that made her so. I did not feel that she was safe unless I had her with me. Mrs. Hobbs, who felt badly about her brother's treachery, yielded to my entreaties, on condition that she should return in ten days. I avoided making any promise. She came to me clad in very thin garments, all outgrown, and with a school satchel on her arm, containing a few articles. It was late in October, and I knew the child must suffer; and not daring to go out in the streets to purchase

[200] Antislavery judge Arent Van der Poel (1799–1870) of the New York Superior Court and abolitionist lawyer John Hooper (1815–1864). Hooper's father was the Quaker abolitionist Isaac T. Hooper.

any thing, I took off my own flannel skirt and converted it into one for her. Kind Mrs. Bruce came to bid me good by, and when she saw that I had taken off my clothing for my child, the tears came to her eyes. She said, "Wait for me, Linda," and went out. She soon returned with a nice warm shawl and hood for Ellen. Truly, of such souls as hers are the kingdom of heaven.[201]

My brother reached New York on Wednesday. Lawyer Hopper advised us to go to Boston by the Stonington route, as there was less Southern travel in that direction. Mrs. Bruce directed her servants to tell all inquirers that I formerly lived there, but had gone from the city.

We reached the steamboat Rhode Island in safety. That boat employed colored hands, but I knew that colored passengers were not admitted to the cabin. I was very desirous for the seclusion of the cabin, not only on account of exposure to the night air, but also to avoid observation. Lawyer Hopper was waiting on board for us. He spoke to the stewardess, and asked, as a particular favor, that she would treat us well. He said to me, "Go and speak to the captain yourself by and by. Take your little girl with you, and I am sure that he will not let her sleep on deck." With these kind words and a shake of the hand he departed.

The boat was soon on her way, bearing me rapidly from the friendly home where I had hoped to find security and rest. My brother had left me to purchase the tickets, thinking that I might have better success than he would. When the stewardess came to me, I paid what she asked, and she gave me three tickets with clipped corners. In the most unsophisticated manner I said, "You have made a mistake; I asked you for cabin tickets. I cannot possibly consent to sleep on deck with my little daughter." She assured me there was no mistake. She said on some of the routes colored people were allowed to sleep in the cabin, but not on this route, which was much travelled by the wealthy. I asked her to show me to the captain's office, and she said she would after tea. When the time came, I took Ellen by the hand and went to the captain, politely requesting him to change our tickets, as we should be very uncomfortable on deck. He said it was contrary to their custom, but he would see that we had berths below; he would also try to obtain comfortable seats for us in the cars; of that he was not certain, but he would speak to the conductor about it, when the boat arrived. I thanked him, and returned to the ladies' cabin. He came afterwards and told me that the conductor of the cars was on board, that he had spoken to him, and he had promised to take care of us. I was very much surprised at receiving so much kindness. I don't

[201] Reference to Matthew 4:17. It is a comment on Mary Willis's righteousness.

know whether the pleasing face of my little girl had won his heart, or whether the stewardess inferred from Lawyer Hopper's manner that I was a fugitive, and had pleaded with him in my behalf.

When the boat arrived at Stonington, the conductor kept his promise, and showed us to seats in the first car, nearest the engine. He asked us to take seats next [to] the door, but as he passed through, we ventured to move on toward the other end of the car. No incivility was offered us, and we reached Boston in safety.

The day after my arrival was one of the happiest of my life. I felt as if I was beyond the reach of the bloodhounds; and, for the first time during many years, I had both my children together with me. They greatly enjoyed their reunion, and laughed and chatted merrily. I watched them with a swelling heart. Their every motion delighted me.

I could not feel safe in New York, and I accepted the offer of a friend, that we should share expenses and keep house together. I represented to Mrs. Hobbs that Ellen must have some schooling, and must remain with me for that purpose. She felt ashamed of being unable to read or spell at her age, so instead of sending her to school with Benny, I instructed her myself till she was fitted to enter an intermediate school. The winter passed pleasantly, while I was busy with my needle, and my children with their books.

XXXVII. A VISIT TO ENGLAND

In the spring, sad news came to me. Mrs. Bruce was dead.[202] Never again, in this world, should I see her gentle face, or hear her sympathizing voice. I had lost an excellent friend, and little Mary had lost a tender mother. Mr. Bruce wished the child to visit some of her mother's relatives in England, and he was desirous that I should take charge of her. The little motherless one was accustomed to me, and attached to me, and I thought she would be happier in my care than in that of a stranger. I could also earn more in this way than I could by my needle. So I put Benny to a trade, and left Ellen to remain in the house with my friend and go to school.[203]

We sailed from New York, and arrived in Liverpool after a pleasant voyage of twelve days. We proceeded directly to London, and took

[202]Mary Stace Willis died delivering a stillborn baby on March 25, 1845.

[203]In a letter to his sister on September 7, 1845, John Jacobs made a reference suggesting that Joseph was apprenticed to the printing office of a weekly newspaper, the *Saturday Rambler* (Jacobs, *Incidents*, ed. Yellin, 287n).

lodgings at the Adelaide Hotel. The supper seemed to me less luxurious than those I had seen in American hotels; but my situation was indescribably more pleasant. For the first time in my life I was in a place where I was treated according to my deportment, without reference to my complexion. I felt as if a great millstone had been lifted from my breast. Ensconced in a pleasant room, with my dear little charge, I laid my head on my pillow, for the first time, with the delightful consciousness of pure, unadulterated freedom.

As I had constant care of the child, I had little opportunity to see the wonders of that great city; but I watched the tide of life that flowed through the streets, and found it a strange contrast to the stagnation in our Southern towns. Mr. Bruce took his little daughter to spend some days with friends in Oxford Crescent, and of course it was necessary for me to accompany her. I had heard much of the systematic method of English education, and I was very desirous that my dear Mary should steer straight in the midst of so much propriety. I closely observed her little playmates and their nurses, being ready to take any lessons in the science of good management. The children were more rosy than American children, but I did not see that they differed materially in other respects. They were like all children—sometimes docile and sometimes wayward.

We next went to Steventon, in Berkshire. It was a small town, said to be the poorest in the county. I saw men working in the fields for six shillings, and seven shillings, a week, and women for sixpence, and sevenpence, a day, out of which they boarded themselves. Of course they lived in the most primitive manner; it could not be otherwise, where a woman's wages for an entire day were not sufficient to buy a pound of meat. They paid very low rents, and their clothes were made of the cheapest fabrics, though much better than could have been procured in the United States for the same money. I had heard much about the oppression of the poor in Europe. The people I saw around me were, many of them, among the poorest poor. But when I visited them in their little thatched cottages, I felt that the condition of even the meanest and most ignorant among them was vastly superior to the condition of the most favored slaves in America. They labored hard; but they were not ordered out to toil while the stars were in the sky, and driven and slashed by an overseer, through heat and cold, till the stars shone out again. Their homes were very humble; but they were protected by law. No insolent patrols could come, in the dead of night, and flog them at their pleasure. The father, when he closed his cottage door, felt safe with his family around him. No master or overseer could come and take from him his wife, or his daughter. They must separate to earn their living; but the parents knew where their children were going, and could communicate with them by letters. The relations of husband and wife, parent and child, were too sacred for the richest noble in the land to violate with impunity. Much was being done to enlighten these poor people. Schools were established among them, and benevolent societies were active in efforts to ameliorate their condition. There was no law forbidding them to learn to read and write; and if they helped each other in spelling out the Bible, they were in no danger of thirty-nine lashes, as was the case with myself and poor, pious, old uncle Fred. I repeat that the most ignorant and the most destitute of these peasants was a thousand fold better off than the most pampered American slave.

I do not deny that the poor are oppressed in Europe. I am not disposed to paint their condition so rose-colored as the Hon. Miss Murray paints the condition of the slaves in the United States.[204] A small portion of *my* experience would enable her to read her own pages with anointed eyes. If she were to lay aside her title, and, instead of visiting among the fashionable, become domesticated, as a poor governess, on some plantation in Louisiana or Alabama, she would see and hear things that would make her tell quite a different story.

My visit to England is a memorable event in my life, from the fact of my having there received strong religious impressions. The contemptuous manner in which the communion had been administered to colored people, in my native place; the church membership of Dr. Flint, and others like him; and the buying and selling of slaves, by professed ministers of the gospel, had given me a prejudice against the Episcopal church. The whole service seemed to me a mockery and a sham. But my home in Steventon was in the family of a clergyman, who was a true disciple of Jesus. The beauty of his daily life inspired me with faith in the genuineness of Christian professions. Grace entered my heart, and I knelt at the communion table, I trust, in true humility of soul.[205]

[204] Amelia Matilda Murray (1795–1884) wrote favorably about slavery in her 1856 travel book *Letters from the United States, Cuba and Canada* (Ibid.).

[205] According to Yellin, they stayed with Mary Willis's sister Anne and her husband, Reverend William Vincent (Yellin, *Harriet Jacobs*, 86). This acceptance of grace marked the end of Jacobs's struggles with doubt and constituted a turning point in her life, placing her tale rhetorically within the tradition of conversion narratives. Jacobs, however, used abolitionist rhetoric attacking religious hypocrisy to suggest that it was the Christianity of white America that needed conversion, not she. Compare with John S. Jacobs's attack on the hypocrisy of "the Church" and "the State" (*A True Tale of Slavery*, chap. VII; see Document 11).

I remained abroad ten months, which was much longer than I had anticipated. During all that time, I never saw the slightest symptom of prejudice against color. Indeed, I entirely forgot it, till the time came for us to return to America.

XXXVIII. RENEWED INVITATIONS TO GO SOUTH

We had a tedious winter passage, and from the distance spectres seemed to rise up on the shores of the United States. It is a sad feeling to be afraid of one's native country. We arrived in New York safely, and I hastened to Boston to look after my children. I found Ellen well, and improving at her school; but Benny was not there to welcome me. He had been left at a good place to learn a trade, and for several months every thing worked well. He was liked by the master, and was a favorite with his fellow-apprentices; but one day they accidentally discovered a fact they had never before suspected—that he was colored! This at once transformed him into a different being. Some of the apprentices were Americans, others American-born Irish; and it was offensive to their dignity to have a "nigger" among them, after they had been told that he was a "nigger." They began by treating him with silent scorn, and finding that he returned the same, they resorted to insults and abuse. He was too spirited a boy to stand that, and he went off. Being desirous to do something to support himself, and having no one to advise him, he shipped for a whaling voyage. When I received these tidings I shed many tears, and bitterly reproached myself for having left him so long. But I had done it for the best, and now all I could do was to pray to the heavenly Father to guide and protect him.

Not long after my return, I received the following letter from Miss Emily Flint, now Mrs. Dodge:—[206]

> In this you will recognize the hand of your friend and mistress. Having heard that you had gone with a family to Europe, I have waited to hear of your return to write to you. I should have answered the letter you wrote to me long since, but as I could not then act independently of my father, I knew there could be nothing done satisfactory to you. There were persons here who were willing to buy you and run the risk of getting you. To this I would not consent. I have always been attached to you, and would

[206]Mary Matilda Norcom married Daniel Messmore in 1846.

> not like to see you the slave of another, or have unkind treatment. I am married now, and can protect you. My husband expects to move to Virginia this spring, where we think of settling. I am very anxious that you should come and live with me. If you are not willing to come, you may purchase yourself; but I should prefer having you live with me. If you come, you may, if you like, spend a month with your grandmother and friends, then come to me in Norfolk, Virginia. Think this over, and write as soon as possible, and let me know the conclusion. Hoping that your children are well, I remain you[r] friend and mistress.

Of course I did not write to return thanks for this cordial invitation. I felt insulted to be thought stupid enough to be caught by such professions.

> "Come up into my parlor," said the spider to the fly;
> "'Tis the prettiest little parlor that ever you did spy."[207]

It was plain that Dr. Flint's family were apprised of my movements, since they knew of my voyage to Europe. I expected to have further trouble from them; but having eluded them thus far, I hoped to be as successful in future. The money I had earned, I was desirous to devote to the education of my children, and to secure a home for them. It seemed not only hard, but unjust, to pay for myself. I could not possibly regard myself as a piece of property. Moreover, I had worked many years without wages, and during that time had been obliged to depend on my grandmother for many comforts in food and clothing. My children certainly belonged to me; but though Dr. Flint had incurred no expense for their support, he had received a large sum of money for them. I knew the law would decide that I was his property, and would probably still give his daughter a claim to my children; but I regarded such laws as the regulations of robbers, who had no rights that I was bound to respect.

The Fugitive Slave Law had not then passed. The judges of Massachusetts had not then stooped under chains to enter her courts of justice, so called. I knew my old master was rather skittish of Massachusetts. I relied on her love of freedom, and felt safe on her soil. I am now aware that I honored the old Commonwealth beyond her deserts.

[207]Mary Howitt (1799–1888), "The Spider and the Fly" (1829).

XXXIX. THE CONFESSION

For two years my daughter and I supported ourselves comfortably in Boston.[208] At the end of that time, my brother William offered to send Ellen to a boarding school. It required a great effort for me to consent to part with her, for I had few near ties, and it was her presence that made my two little rooms seem home-like. But my judgment prevailed over my selfish feelings. I made preparations for her departure. During the two years we had lived together I had often resolved to tell her something about her father; but I had never been able to muster sufficient courage. I had a shrinking dread of diminishing my child's love. I knew she must have curiosity on the subject, but she had never asked a question. She was always very careful not to say any thing to remind me of my troubles. Now that she was going from me, I thought if I should die before she returned, she might hear my story from some one who did not understand the palliating circumstances; and that if she were entirely ignorant on the subject, her sensitive nature might receive a rude shock.

When we retired for the night, she said, "Mother, it is very hard to leave you alone. I am almost sorry I am going, though I do want to improve myself. But you will write to me often; won't you, mother?"

I did not throw my arms round her. I did not answer her. But in a calm, solemn way, for it cost me great effort, I said, "Listen to me, Ellen; I have something to tell you!" I recounted my early sufferings in slavery, and told her how nearly they had crushed me. I began to tell her how they had driven me into a great sin, when she clasped me in her arms, and exclaimed, "O, don't, mother! Please don't tell me any more."

I said, "But, my child, I want you to know about your father."

"I know all about it, mother," she replied; "I am nothing to my father, and he is nothing to me. All my love is for you. I was with him five months in Washington, and he never cared for me. He never spoke to me as he did to his little Fanny.[209] I knew all the time he was my father, for Fanny's nurse told me so; but she said I must never tell any body, and I never did. I used to wish he would take me in his arms and kiss me,

[208]They lived at 87 Charter Street with Jacobs sewing to support them while Louisa attended school. As mentioned earlier in the narrative, Joseph had quit his apprenticeship and signed on with a whaling voyage. John Jacobs (now using the middle initial "S.") was also in Boston, becoming deeply involved in the antislavery movement as a speaker and writer in the Garrisonian mold with calls for immediate abolition. According to Yellin, Harriet eschewed activism at this time to avoid drawing attention to herself as a fugitive (Yellin, *Harriet Jacobs*, 87–89).

[209]Laura, Sawyer's daughter, born in the winter of 1839.

as he did Fanny; or that he would sometimes smile at me, as he did at her. I thought if he was my own father, he ought to love me. I was a little girl then, and didn't know any better. But now I never think any thing about my father. All my love is for you." She hugged me closer as she spoke, and I thanked God that the knowledge I had so much dreaded to impart had not diminished the affection of my child. I had not the slightest idea she knew that portion of my history. If I had, I should have spoken to her long before; for my pent-up feelings had often longed to pour themselves out to some one I could trust. But I loved the dear girl better for the delicacy she had manifested towards her unfortunate mother.

The next morning, she and her uncle started on their journey to the village in New York, where she was to be placed at school.[210] It seemed as if all the sunshine had gone away. My little room was dreadfully lonely. I was thankful when a message came from a lady, accustomed to employ me, requesting me to come and sew in her family for several weeks. On my return, I found a letter from brother William. He thought of opening an anti-slavery reading room in Rochester, and combining with it the sale of some books and stationery; and he wanted me to unite with him.[211] We tried it, but it was not successful. We found warm anti-slavery friends there, but the feeling was not general enough to support such an establishment. I passed nearly a year in the family of Isaac and Amy Post, practical believers in the Christian doctrine of human brotherhood.[212] They measured a man's worth by his character, not by his complexion. The memory of those beloved and honored friends will remain with me to my latest hour.

XL. THE FUGITIVE SLAVE LAW

My brother, being disappointed in his project, concluded to go to California; and it was agreed that Benjamin should go with him. Ellen liked her school, and was a great favorite there. They did not know her

[210]The Reverend Hiram H. Kellogg's Young Ladies' Domestic Seminary in tiny Clinton, New York, founded with the support of wealthy antislavery donors, admitted black and white students.

[211]The reading room opened in March 1849, one month after John Jacobs and Frederick Douglass gave a joint lecture tour. It was located above the offices of Frederick Douglass's *North Star* (Yellin, *Harriet Jacobs*, 98–99).

[212]Amy Post (1802–1889) and Isaac Post (1798–1872) were pacifists, radical feminists, and Garrisonian abolitionists. For more on their circle, see Nancy A. Hewitt, *Women's Activism and Social Change: Rochester, New York, 1822–1872* (Ithaca, N.Y.: Cornell University Press, 1984).

history, and she did not tell it, because she had no desire to make capital out of their sympathy. But when it was accidentally discovered that her mother was a fugitive slave, every method was used to increase her advantages and diminish her expenses.

I was alone again. It was necessary for me to be earning money, and I preferred that it should be among those who knew me. On my return from Rochester, I called at the house of Mr. Bruce, to see Mary, the darling little babe that had thawed my heart, when it was freezing into a cheerless distrust of all my fellow-beings. She was growing a tall girl now, but I loved her always. Mr. Bruce had married again, and it was proposed that I should become nurse to a new infant. I had but one hesitation, and that was my feeling of insecurity in New York, now greatly increased by the passage of the Fugitive Slave Law. However, I resolved to try the experiment. I was again fortunate in my employer. The new Mrs. Bruce was an American, brought up under aristocratic influences, and still living in the midst of them; but if she had any prejudice against color, I was never made aware of it; and as for the system of slavery, she had a most hearty dislike of it.[213] No sophistry of Southerners could blind her to its enormity. She was a person of excellent principles and a noble heart. To me, from that hour to the present, she has been a true and sympathizing friend. Blessings be with her and hers!

About the time that I reentered the Bruce family, an event occurred of disastrous import to the colored people. The slave Hamlin, the first fugitive that came under the new law, was given up by the bloodhounds of the north to the bloodhounds of the south.[214] It was the beginning of a reign of terror to the colored population. The great city rushed on in its whirl of excitement, taking no note of the "short and simple annals of the poor."[215] But while fashionables were listening to the thrilling voice of Jenny Lind in Metropolitan Hall, the thrilling voices of poor hunted colored people went up, in an agony of supplication, to the Lord, from

[213]In October 1846, Nathaniel Willis married Cornelia Grinnell (1825–1904) of New Bedford, Massachusetts. (New Bedford was a prosperous port city and the first stop in New England for many fugitive slaves, including Harriet's brother and Frederick Douglass.) In September 1850, the Willises had two young children, Grinnell, who was two and a half, and five-month-old Lila.

[214]James Hamlet was the first fugitive slave seized in New York under the provisions of the Fugitive Slave Act. Speaking at Zion Chapel on October 1, 1850—one month after the ratification of the act—John Jacobs called for "my colored bretheren" to arm themselves against "our tyrants" (*National Anti-Slavery Standard*, October 10, 1850, quoted in Yellin, *Harriet Jacobs*, 108). The meeting raised $800 to buy Hamlet's freedom.

[215]The quotation is from "Elegy Written in a Country Churchyard" (1751) by Thomas Gray (1716–1771). This elegy for the commoner was a favorite of nineteenth-century Americans of humble birth, including Abraham Lincoln.

Zion's church.[216] Many families, who had lived in the city for twenty years, fled from it now. Many a poor washerwoman, who, by hard labor, had made herself a comfortable home, was obliged to sacrifice her furniture, bid a hurried farewell to friends, and seek her fortune among strangers in Canada. Many a wife discovered a secret she had never known before—that her husband was a fugitive, and must leave her to insure his own safety. Worse still, many a husband discovered that his wife had fled from slavery years ago, and as "the child follows the condition of its mother," the children of his love were liable to be seized and carried into slavery. Every where, in those humble homes, there was consternation and anguish. But what cared the legislators of the "dominant race" for the blood they were crushing out of trampled hearts?

When my brother William spent his last evening with me, before he went to California, we talked nearly all the time of the distress brought on our oppressed people by the passage of this iniquitous law; and never had I seen him manifest such bitterness of spirit, such stern hostility to our oppressors. He was himself free from the operation of the law; for he did not run from any Slaveholding State, being brought into the Free States by his master. But I was subject to it; and so were hundreds of intelligent and industrious people all around us. I seldom ventured into the streets; and when it was necessary to do an errand for Mrs. Bruce, or any of the family, I went as much as possible through back streets and by-ways. What a disgrace to a city calling itself free, that inhabitants, guiltless of offence, and seeking to perform their duties conscientiously, should be condemned to live in such incessant fear, and have nowhere to turn for protection! This state of things, of course, gave rise to many impromptu vigilance committees. Every colored person, and every friend of their persecuted race, kept their eyes wide open. Every evening I examined the newspapers carefully, to see what Southerners had put up at the hotels. I did this for my own sake, thinking my young mistress and her husband might be among the list; I wished also to give information to others, if necessary; for if many were "running to and fro," I resolved that "knowledge should be increased."[217]

This brings up one of my Southern reminiscences, which I will here briefly relate. I was somewhat acquainted with a slave named Luke, who belonged to a wealthy man in our vicinity. His master died, leaving a son

[216]"Jenny Lind (1820–1887), "the Swedish Nightingale," was touring the United States. Metropolitan Hall, on lower Broadway, was built specifically for her 1850 American debut.

[217]Reference to Daniel 12:4.

and daughter heirs to his large fortune. In the division of the slaves, Luke was included in the son's portion. This young man became a prey to the vices growing out of the "patriarchal institution," and when he went to the north, to complete his education, he carried his vices with him. He was brought home, deprived of the use of his limbs, by excessive dissipation. Luke was appointed to wait upon his bed-ridden master, whose despotic habits were greatly increased by exasperation at his own helplessness. He kept a cowhide beside him, and, for the most trivial occurrence, he would order his attendant to bare his back, and kneel beside the couch, while he whipped him till his strength was exhausted. Some days he was not allowed to wear any thing but his shirt, in order to be in readiness to be flogged. A day seldom passed without his receiving more or less blows. If the slightest resistance was offered, the town constable was sent for to execute the punishment, and Luke learned from experience how much more the constable's strong arm was to be dreaded than the comparatively feeble one of his master. The arm of his tyrant grew weaker, and was finally palsied; and then the constable's services were in constant requisition. The fact that he was entirely dependent on Luke's care, and was obliged to be tended like an infant, instead of inspiring any gratitude or compassion towards his poor slave, seemed only to increase his irritability and cruelty. As he lay there on his bed, a mere degraded wreck of manhood, he took into his head the strangest freaks of despotism; and if Luke hesitated to submit to his orders, the constable was immediately sent for. Some of these freaks were of a nature too filthy to be repeated.[218] When I fled from the house of bondage, I left poor Luke still chained to the bedside of this cruel and disgusting wretch.

One day, when I had been requested to do an errand for Mrs. Bruce, I was hurrying through back streets, as usual, when I saw a young man approaching, whose face was familiar to me. As he came nearer, I recognized Luke. I always rejoiced to see or hear of any one who had escaped from the black pit; but, remembering this poor fellow's extreme hardships, I was peculiarly glad to see him on Northern soil, though I no longer called it *free* soil. I well remembered what a desolate feeling it was to be alone among strangers, and I went up to him and greeted him cordially. At first, he did not know me; but when I mentioned my name,

[218]Given the similarity of language between this passage and her descriptions of Norcom's abuse, this seems to be a reference to homosexual relations, an argument made by P. Gabrielle Foreman, "Earwitness: Female Abolitionism, Sexuality, and *Incidents in the Life of a Slave Girl*," in *Harriet Jacobs and* Incidents in the Life of a Slave Girl*: New Critical Essays*, ed. Deborah M. Garfield and Rafia Zafar (New York: Cambridge University Press, 1996), 100–130.

he remembered all about me. I told him of the Fugitive Slave Law, and asked him if he did not know that New York was a city of kidnappers.

He replied, "De risk ain't so bad for me, as 'tis fur you. 'Cause I runned away from de speculator, and you runned away from de massa. Dem speculators vont spen dar money to come here fur a runaway, if dey ain't sartin sure to put dar hans right on him. An I tell you I's tuk good car 'bout dat. I had too hard times down dar, to let 'em ketch dis nigger."

He then told me of the advice he had received, and the plans he had laid. I asked if he had money enough to take him to Canada. "'Pend upon it, I hab," he replied. "I tuk car fur dat. I'd bin workin all my days fur dem cussed whites, an got no pay but kicks and cuffs. So I tought dis nigger had a right to money nuff to bring him to de Free States. Massa Henry he lib till ebery body vish him dead; an ven he did die, I knowed de debbil would hab him, an vouldn't vant him to bring his money 'long too. So I tuk some of his bills, and put 'em in de pocket of his ole trousers. An ven he was buried, dis nigger ask fur dem ole trousers, an dey gub 'em to me." With a low, chuckling laugh, he added, "You see I didn't *steal* it; dey *gub* it to me. I tell you, I had mighty hard time to keep de speculator from findin it; but he didn't git it."

This is a fair specimen of how the moral sense is educated by slavery. When a man has his wages stolen from him, year after year, and the laws sanction and enforce the theft, how can he be expected to have more regard to honesty than has the man who robs him? I have become somewhat enlightened, but I confess that I agree with poor, ignorant, much-abused Luke, in thinking he had a *right* to that money, as a portion of his unpaid wages. He went to Canada forthwith, and I have not since heard from him.

All that winter I lived in a state of anxiety. When I took the children out to breathe the air, I closely observed the countenances of all I met. I dreaded the approach of summer, when snakes and slaveholders make their appearance. I was, in fact, a slave in New York, as subject to slave laws as I had been in a Slave State. Strange incongruity in a State called free!

Spring returned, and I received warning from the south that Dr. Flint knew of my return to my old place, and was making preparations to have me caught. I learned afterwards that my dress, and that of Mrs. Bruce's children, had been described to him by some of the Northern tools, which slaveholders employ for their base purposes, and then indulge in sneers at their cupidity and mean servility.

I immediately informed Mrs. Bruce of my danger, and she took prompt measures for my safety. My place as nurse could not be supplied immediately, and this generous, sympathizing lady proposed that I should carry her baby away. It was a comfort to me to have the child with me; for the heart is reluctant to be torn away from every object it loves. But how few mothers would have consented to have one of their own babes become a fugitive, for the sake of a poor, hunted nurse, on whom the legislators of the country had let loose the bloodhounds! When I spoke of the sacrifice she was making, in depriving herself of her dear baby, she replied, "It is better for you to have baby with you, Linda; for if they get on your track, they will be obliged to bring the child to me; and then, if there is a possibility of saving you, you shall be saved."

This lady had a very wealthy relative, a benevolent gentleman in many respects, but aristocratic and pro-slavery. He remonstrated with her for harboring a fugitive slave; told her she was violating the laws of her country; and asked her if she was aware of the penalty. She replied, "I am very well aware of it. It is imprisonment and one thousand dollars fine. Shame on my country that it *is* so! I am ready to incur the penalty. I will go to the state's prison, rather than have any poor victim torn from *my* house, to be carried back to slavery."

The noble heart! The brave heart! The tears are in my eyes while I write of her. May the God of the helpless reward her for her sympathy with my persecuted people!

I was sent into New England, where I was sheltered by the wife of a senator, whom I shall always hold in grateful remembrance. This honorable gentleman would not have voted for the Fugitive Slave Law, as did the senator in "Uncle Tom's Cabin"; on the contrary, he was strongly opposed to it; but he was enough under its influence to be afraid of having me remain in his house many hours.[219] So I was sent into the country, where I remained a month with the baby. When it was supposed that Dr. Flint's emissaries had lost track of me, and given up the pursuit for the present, I returned to New York.

[219]This refers to Cornelia Willis's parents, although her father, Joseph Grinnell, was not a senator but a member of the House of Representatives from 1843 to 1851. Like many Northerners, he abstained from voting on the fugitive slave bill in order to enable the Compromise of 1850 to pass (Jacobs, *Incidents*, ed. Yellin, 190n). The reference is to Harriet Beecher Stowe (1811–1896), *Uncle Tom's Cabin; or, Life among the Lowly* (1852), chap. IX. See Document 5 for Jacobs's letter to Amy Post discussing her disappointment with Stowe.

XLI. FREE AT LAST[220]

Mrs. Bruce, and every member of her family, were exceedingly kind to me. I was thankful for the blessings of my lot, yet I could not always wear a cheerful countenance. I was doing harm to no one; on the contrary, I was doing all the good I could in my small way; yet I could never go out to breathe God's free air without trepidation at my heart. This seemed hard; and I could not think it was a right state of things in any civilized country.

From time to time I received news from my good old grandmother. She could not write; but she employed others to write for her. The following is an extract from one of her last letters:—

> Dear Daughter: I cannot hope to see you again on earth; but I pray to God to unite us above, where pain will no more rack this feeble body of mine; where sorrow and parting from my children will be no more.[221] God has promised these things if we are faithful unto the end. My age and feeble health deprive me of going to church now; but God is with me here at home. Thank your brother for his kindness. Give much love to him, and tell him to remember the Creator in the days of his youth, and strive to meet me in the Father's kingdom.[222] Love to Ellen and Benjamin. Don't neglect him. Tell him for me, to be a good boy. Strive, my child, to train them for God's children. May he protect and provide for you, is the prayer of your loving old mother.

These letters both cheered and saddened me. I was always glad to have tidings from the kind, faithful old friend of my unhappy youth; but her messages of love made my heart yearn to see her before she died, and I mourned over the fact that it was impossible. Some months after I returned from my flight to New England, I received a letter from her, in which she wrote, "Dr. Flint is dead.[223] He has left a distressed family. Poor old man! I hope he made his peace with God."

[220]Line from an anonymous Negro spiritual. Frederick Douglass commented on the meaning of slave songs in his *Narrative of the Life of Frederick Douglass* (1845, chap. II). The meaning of African American songs is also explored in W. E. B. Du Bois (1868–1963), *The Souls of Black Folk* (1903), and Lawrence W. Levine, *Black Culture and Black Consciousness: Afro-American Folk Thought from Slavery to Freedom* (New York: Oxford University Press, 1977).

[221]Reference to Revelations 21:4.

[222]Reference to Ecclesiastes 12:1.

[223]Norcom died on November 9, 1850.

I remembered how he had defrauded my grandmother of the hard earnings she had loaned; how he had tried to cheat her out of the freedom her mistress had promised her, and how he had persecuted her children; and I thought to myself that she was a better Christian than I was, if she could entirely forgive him. I cannot say, with truth, that the news of my old master's death softened my feelings towards him. There are wrongs which even the grave does not bury. The man was odious to me while he lived, and his memory is odious now.

His departure from this world did not diminish my danger. He had threatened my grandmother that his heirs should hold me in slavery after he was gone; that I never should be free so long as a child of his survived. As for Mrs. Flint, I had seen her in deeper afflictions than I supposed the loss of her husband would be, for she had buried several children; yet I never saw any signs of softening in her heart. The doctor had died in embarrassed circumstances, and had little to will to his heirs, except such property as he was unable to grasp. I was well aware what I had to expect from the family of Flints; and my fears were confirmed by a letter from the south, warning me to be on my guard, because Mrs. Flint openly declared that her daughter could not afford to lose so valuable a slave as I was.

I kept close watch of the newspapers for arrivals; but one Saturday night, being much occupied, I forgot to examine the Evening Express as usual. I went down into the parlor for it, early in the morning, and found the boy about to kindle a fire with it. I took it from him and examined the list of arrivals. Reader, if you have never been a slave, you cannot imagine the acute sensation of suffering at my heart, when I read the names of Mr. and Mrs. Dodge, at a hotel in Courtland Street.[224] It was a third-rate hotel, and that circumstance convinced me of the truth of what I had heard, that they were short of funds and had need of my value, as *they* valued me; and that was by dollars and cents. I hastened with the paper to Mrs. Bruce. Her heart and hand were always open to every one in distress, and she always warmly sympathized with mine. It was impossible to tell how near the enemy was. He might have passed and repassed the house while we were sleeping. He might at that moment be waiting to pounce upon me if I ventured out of doors. I had never seen the husband of my young mistress, and therefore I could not distinguish him from any

[224]The listing of the Messmores' arrival at Taylor's Hotel appeared in the "Arrivals at City Hotels" column of the *New York Evening Express*, February 28, 1852. These listings were part of the newspapers' local society coverage (Yellin, *Harriet Jacobs*, 114). See also Jacobs, *A True Tale of Slavery*, chap. VI (Document 11).

other stranger. A carriage was hastily ordered; and, closely veiled, I followed Mrs. Bruce, taking the baby again with me into exile. After various turnings and crossings, and returnings, the carriage stopped at the house of one of Mrs. Bruce's friends, where I was kindly received. Mrs. Bruce returned immediately, to instruct the domestics what to say if any one came to inquire for me.

It was lucky for me that the evening paper was not burned up before I had a chance to examine the list of arrivals. It was not long after Mrs. Bruce's return to her house, before several people came to inquire for me. One inquired for me, another asked for my daughter Ellen, and another said he had a letter from my grandmother, which he was requested to deliver in person.

They were told, "She *has* lived here, but she has left."

"How long ago?"

"I don't know, sir."

"Do you know where she went?"

"I do not, sir." And the door was closed.

This Mr. Dodge, who claimed me as his property, was originally a Yankee pedler in the south; then he became a merchant, and finally a slaveholder. He managed to get introduced into what was called the first society, and married Miss Emily Flint. A quarrel arose between him and her brother, and the brother cowhided him. This led to a family feud, and he proposed to remove to Virginia. Dr. Flint left him no property, and his own means had become circumscribed, while a wife and children depended upon him for support. Under these circumstances, it was very natural that he should make an effort to put me into his pocket.

I had a colored friend, a man from my native place, in whom I had the most implicit confidence. I sent for him, and told him that Mr. and Mrs. Dodge had arrived in New York. I proposed that he should call upon them to make inquiries about his friends at the south, with whom Dr. Flint's family were well acquainted. He thought there was no impropriety in his doing so, and he consented. He went to the hotel, and knocked at the door of Mr. Dodge's room, which was opened by the gentleman himself, who gruffly inquired, "What brought you here? How came you to know I was in the city?"

"Your arrival was published in the evening papers, sir; and I called to ask Mrs. Dodge about my friends at home. I didn't suppose it would give any offence."

"Where's that negro girl, that belongs to my wife?"

"What girl, sir?"

"You know well enough. I mean Linda, that ran away from Dr. Flint's plantation, some years ago. I dare say you've seen her, and know where she is."

"Yes, sir, I've seen her, and know where she is. She is out of your reach, sir."

"Tell me where she is, or bring her to me, and I will give her a chance to buy her freedom."

"I don't think it would be of any use, sir. I have heard her say she would go to the ends of the earth, rather than pay any man or woman for her freedom, because she thinks she has a right to it. Besides, she couldn't do it, if she would, for she has spent her earnings to educate her children."

This made Mr. Dodge very angry, and some high words passed between them. My friend was afraid to come where I was; but in the course of the day I received a note from him. I supposed they had not come from the south, in the winter, for a pleasure excursion; and now the nature of their business was very plain.

Mrs. Bruce came to me and entreated me to leave the city the next morning. She said her house was watched, and it was possible that some clew to me might be obtained. I refused to take her advice. She pleaded with an earnest tenderness, that ought to have moved me; but I was in a bitter, disheartened mood. I was weary of flying from pillar to post. I had been chased during half my life, and it seemed as if the chase was never to end. There I sat, in that great city, guiltless of crime, yet not daring to worship God in any of the churches. I heard the bells ringing for afternoon service, and, with contemptuous sarcasm, I said, "Will the preachers take for their text, 'Proclaim liberty to the captive, and the opening of prison doors to them that are bound'? or will they preach from the text, 'Do unto others as ye would they should do unto you'?"[225] Oppressed Poles and Hungarians could find a safe refuge in that city; John Mitchell was free to proclaim in the City Hall his desire for "a plantation well stocked with slaves";[226] but there I sat, an oppressed American, not daring to show my face. God forgive the black and bitter thoughts I indulged on that Sabbath day! The Scripture says, "Oppression makes even a wise man mad"; and I was not wise.[227]

[225]References to Isaiah 61:1 and Matthew 7:12.

[226]John Mitchel (1815–1875), a proslavery Irish nationalist and founder of the short-lived *Citizen*, stirred up discussion in Garrison's *Liberator* with this pronouncement: "We, for our part, wish we had a good plantation, well-stocked with healthy negroes, in Alabama" (Jacobs, *Incidents*, ed. Yellin, 291n).

[227]Reference to Ecclesiastes 7:17.

I had been told that Mr. Dodge said his wife had never signed away her right to my children, and if he could not get me, he would take them.[228] This it was, more than any thing else, that roused such a tempest in my soul. Benjamin was with his uncle William in California, but my innocent young daughter had come to spend a vacation with me. I thought of what I had suffered in slavery at her age, and my heart was like a tiger's when a hunter tries to seize her young.

Dear Mrs. Bruce! I seem to see the expression of her face, as she turned away discouraged by my obstinate mood. Finding her expostulations unavailing, she sent Ellen to entreat me. When ten o'clock in the evening arrived and Ellen had not returned, this watchful and unwearied friend became anxious. She came to us in a carriage, bringing a well-filled trunk for my journey—trusting that by this time I would listen to reason. I yielded to her, as I ought to have done before.

The next day, baby and I set out in a heavy snow storm, bound for New England again. I received letters from the City of Iniquity, addressed to me under an assumed name. In a few days one came from Mrs. Bruce, informing me that my new master was still searching for me, and that she intended to put an end to this persecution by buying my freedom. I felt grateful for the kindness that prompted this offer, but the idea was not so pleasant to me as might have been expected. The more my mind had become enlightened, the more difficult it was for me to consider myself an article of property; and to pay money to those who had so grievously oppressed me seemed like taking from my sufferings the glory of triumph.[229] I wrote to Mrs. Bruce, thanking her, but saying that being sold from one owner to another seemed too much like slavery; that such a great obligation could not be easily cancelled; and that I preferred to go to my brother in California.

Without my knowledge, Mrs. Bruce employed a gentleman in New York to enter into negotiations with Mr. Dodge. He proposed to pay three hundred dollars down, if Mr. Dodge would sell me, and enter into obligations to relinquish all claim to me or my children forever after.[230] He who called himself my master said he scorned so small an

[228]Jacobs did not know that Norcom had legalized his sale of her children in 1837 with a bill of substitution assigning two other slave children to his daughter's estate (Jacobs, *Incidents*, ed. Yellin, 291n). This meant that Harriet's children were no longer Norcom's daughter's property, despite her husband's claim.

[229]Possible allusion to Job 19:9.

[230]Cornelia Willis had contacted the Reverend John B. Pinney of the New York Colonization Society, who effected the purchase. She described the transaction in a letter to Elizabeth Davis Bliss Bancroft (on May 3, 1852) (Jacobs, *Incidents*, ed. Yellin, 291).

offer for such a valuable servant. The gentleman replied, "You can do as you choose, sir. If you reject this offer you will never get any thing; for the woman has friends who will convey her and her children out of the country."

Mr. Dodge concluded that "half a loaf was better than no bread," and he agreed to the proffered terms. By the next mail I received this brief letter from Mrs. Bruce: "I am rejoiced to tell you that the money for your freedom has been paid to Mr. Dodge. Come home to-morrow. I long to see you and my sweet babe."

My brain reeled as I read these lines. A gentleman near me said, "It's true; I have seen the bill of sale." "The bill of sale!" Those words struck me like a blow. So I was *sold* at last! A human being *sold* in the free city of New York! The bill of sale is on record, and future generations will learn from it that women were articles of traffic in New York, late in the nineteenth century of the Christian religion. It may hereafter prove a useful document to antiquaries, who are seeking to measure the progress of civilization in the United States. I well know the value of that bit of paper; but much as I love freedom, I do not like to look upon it. I am deeply grateful to the generous friend who procured it, but I despise the miscreant who demanded payment for what never rightfully belonged to him or his.[231]

I had objected to having my freedom bought, yet I must confess that when it was done I felt as if a heavy load had been lifted from my weary shoulders. When I rode home in the cars I was no longer afraid to unveil my face and look at people as they passed. I should have been glad to have met Daniel Dodge himself; to have had him see me and know me, that he might have mourned over the untoward circumstances which compelled him to sell me for three hundred dollars.

When I reached home, the arms of my benefactress were thrown round me, and our tears mingled. As soon as she could speak, she said, "O Linda, I'm *so* glad it's all over! You wrote to me as if you thought you were going to be transferred from one owner to another. But I did not buy you for your services. I should have done just the same, if you had been going to sail for California to-morrow. I should, at least, have the satisfaction of knowing that you left me a free woman."

[231] It is worthwhile to compare Jacobs's reaction to her purchase with that of Frederick Douglass, whose abolitionist friends arranged for his purchase without his knowledge. Douglass regarded the payment as being like a ransom or "money extorted by a robber" (Frederick Douglass, *My Bondage and My Freedom* [1855; repr., New York: Library of America, 1994], 376–77).

My heart was exceedingly full. I remembered how my poor father had tried to buy me, when I was a small child, and how he had been disappointed. I hoped his spirit was rejoicing over me now. I remembered how my good old grandmother had laid up her earnings to purchase me in later years, and how often her plans had been frustrated. How that faithful, loving old heart would leap for joy, if she could look on me and my children now that we were free! My relatives had been foiled in all their efforts, but God had raised me up a friend among strangers, who had bestowed on me the precious, long-desired boon.[232] Friend! It is a common word, often lightly used. Like other good and beautiful things, it may be tarnished by careless handling; but when I speak of Mrs. Bruce as my friend, the word is sacred.

My grandmother lived to rejoice in my freedom; but not long after, a letter came with a black seal. She had gone "where the wicked cease from troubling, and the weary are at rest."[233]

Time passed on, and a paper came to me from the south, containing an obituary notice of my uncle Phillip.[234] It was the only case I ever knew of such an honor conferred upon a colored person. It was written by one of his friends, and contained these words: "Now that death has laid him low, they call him a good man and a useful citizen; but what are eulogies to the black man, when the world has faded from his vision? It does not require man's praise to obtain rest in God's kingdom." So they called a colored man a *citizen*! Strange words to be uttered in that region![235]

[232]This echoes a passage from a Quaker autobiography of Jane Hoskens (1694–176?), *A Short Memoir of the Life of the Faithful Servant of Christ* (Philadelphia: Friends' Library, 1837). Given her friendship with the Quaker Posts, it is possible that Jacobs would have read this work.

[233]Jacobs's third use of this quotation, Job 3:17.

[234]"Time passed on" covers six years of Jacobs's life, bringing her up to the time of her writing. Her uncle Mark Ramsey died in the fall of 1858. Jacobs received the news in a letter from Josiah Collins, her uncle Joseph's former master, while she was in England seeking a publisher for her book (Yellin, *Harriet Jacobs*, 139).

[235]As Yellin notes, the North Carolina Supreme Court had ruled in 1844 that free blacks were "not to be considered as citizens" (Jacobs, *Incidents*, ed. Yellin, 292). However, Jacobs may have had in mind a more recent court ruling, that issued by the U.S. Supreme Court in March 1857 in the case of Dred Scott's suit for freedom. Laying out a broad opinion that resonated well beyond the particulars of the case, the Southern-dominated Court ruled that not only was Dred Scott still a slave but also that no black person could be a U.S. citizen with rights anyone was bound to respect, meaning that Scott had no right to bring his lawsuit in the first place. For a thorough accounting of this long, complex, and pivotal case, see Don E. Fehrenbacher, *The Dred Scott Case: Its Significance in American Law and Politics* (New York: Oxford University Press, 1978).

Reader, my story ends with freedom; not in the usual way, with marriage.[236] I and my children are now free! We are as free from the power of slaveholders as are the white people of the north; and though that, according to my ideas, is not saying a great deal, it is a vast improvement in my condition. The dream of my life is not yet realized. I do not sit with my children in a home of my own. I still long for a hearthstone of my own, however humble. I wish it for my children's sake far more than for my own. But God so orders circumstances as to keep me with my friend Mrs. Bruce. Love, duty, gratitude, also bind me to her side. It is a privilege to serve her who pities my oppressed people, and who has bestowed the inestimable boon of freedom on me and my children.

It has been painful to me, in many ways, to recall the dreary years I passed in bondage. I would gladly forget them if I could. Yet the retrospection is not altogether without solace; for with those gloomy recollections come tender memories of my good old grandmother, like light, fleecy clouds floating over a dark and troubled sea.[237]

APPENDIX

The following statement is from Amy Post, a member of the Society of Friends in the State of New York, well known and highly respected by friends of the poor and the oppressed. As has been already stated, in the preceding pages, the author of this volume spent some time under her hospitable roof. L.M.C.

> The author of this book is my highly-esteemed friend. If its readers knew her as I know her, they could not fail to be deeply interested in her story. She was a beloved inmate of our family nearly the whole of the year 1849. She was introduced to us by her affectionate and

[236]Possibly a reference to "Reader, I married him," the opening line of the concluding chapter of Charlotte Brontë's *Jane Eyre* (1847), reiterating Jacobs's theme of the exclusion of black women from the culture's genteel narratives.

[237]A letter Lydia Maria Child wrote to Jacobs in 1860, before the narrative's publication, reveals that Jacobs originally had concluded her narrative with a chapter on the radical abolitionist John Brown (1800–1859) but that Child had suggested she replace this with the death of her grandmother (see Document 8). This shifts the focus of the conclusion from revolution to domesticity, from patriarchal to maternal, from ongoing defiance to troubled resolution. For more on this topic, see Jennifer Fleischner, *Mastering Slavery: Memory, Family, and Identity in Women's Slave Narratives* (New York: New York University Press, 1996), chap. 3, and Bruce Mills, "Lydia Maria Child and the Endings to Harriet Jacobs's *Incidents in the Life of a Slave Girl*," *American Literature* 64, no. 2 (June 1992): 255–72.

conscientious brother, who had previously related to us some of the almost incredible events in his sister's life. I immediately became much interested in Linda; for her appearance was prepossessing, and her deportment indicated remarkable delicacy of feeling and purity of thought.

As we became acquainted, she related to me, from time to time some of the incidents in her bitter experiences as a slave-woman. Though impelled by a natural craving for human sympathy, she passed through a baptism of suffering, even in recounting her trials to me, in private confidential conversations. The burden of these memories lay heavily upon her spirit—naturally virtuous and refined. I repeatedly urged her to consent to the publication of her narrative; for I felt that it would arouse people to a more earnest work for the disinthralment of millions still remaining in that soul-crushing condition, which was so unendurable to her. But her sensitive spirit shrank from publicity. She said, "You know a woman can whisper her cruel wrongs in the ear of a dear friend much easier than she can record them for the world to read." Even in talking with me, she wept so much, and seemed to suffer such mental agony, that I felt her story was too sacred to be drawn from her by inquisitive questions, and I left her free to tell as much, or as little, as she chose. Still, I urged upon her the duty of publishing her experience, for the sake of the good it might do; and, at last, she undertook the task.

Having been a slave so large a portion of her life, she is unlearned; she is obliged to earn her living by her own labor, and she has worked untiringly to procure education for her children; several times she has been obliged to leave her employments, in order to fly from the man-hunters and woman-hunters of our land; but she pressed through all these obstacles and overcame them. After the labors of the day were over, she traced secretly and wearily, by the midnight lamp, a truthful record of her eventful life.

This Empire State is a shabby place of refuge for the oppressed; but here, through anxiety, turmoil, and despair, the freedom of Linda and her children was finally secured, by the exertions of a generous friend. She was grateful for the boon; but the idea of having been *bought* was always galling to a spirit that could never acknowledge itself to be a chattel. She wrote to us thus, soon after the event: "I thank you for your kind expressions in regard to my freedom; but the freedom I had before the money was paid was dearer to me. God gave me *that* freedom; but man put God's image in the scales with the paltry sum of three hundred dollars. I served for my liberty as faithfully as Jacob served for Rachel.[238] At the end, he had large possessions; but I was robbed of my victory; I was obliged to resign my crown, to rid myself of a tyrant."

Her story, as written by herself, cannot fail to interest the reader. It is a sad illustration of the condition of this country, which boasts of its civilization, while it sanctions laws and customs which make the experiences of the present more strange than any fictions of the past. Amy Post.

Rochester, N.Y., Oct. 30th, 1859.[239]

The following testimonial is from a man who is now a highly respectable colored citizen of Boston. L.M.C.

This narrative contains some incidents so extraordinary, that, doubtless, many persons, under whose eyes it may chance to fall, will be ready to believe that it is colored highly, to serve a special purpose. But, however it may be regarded by the incredulous, I know that it is full of living truths. I have been well acquainted with the author from my boyhood. The circumstances recounted in her history are perfectly familiar to me. I knew of her treatment from her master; of the imprisonment of her children; of their sale and redemption; of her seven years' concealment; and of her subsequent escape to the North. I am now a resident of Boston, and am a living witness to the truth of this interesting narrative. George W. Lowther.[240]

[238]Reference to Genesis 29:20–28.

[239]In a letter to Post on June 21, 1857 (Document 7), Jacobs outlined what she thought Post should write in her endorsement, which in some ways reiterated Child's introduction. Jacobs requested that Post go beyond the common guarantees of her existence and her literacy. Following Jacobs's suggestions, Post begins here with her intimate friendship with Jacobs, and then turns to Jacobs's reluctance to expose her history of sexual abuse. Post's point that Jacobs is "naturally virtuous and refined" is an important antiracist defense. But Post goes beyond this to assert that Jacobs has been chosen, as if by God, by virtue of her story of suffering: Her story of desecration is "sacred."

[240]George W. Lowther (1822–1898) was a free black neighbor of Jacobs's grandmother in Edenton. In 1838, he moved to Boston, where he earned his living as a hairdresser and became a member of the circle of black activist William C. Nell (1816–1874), who was also a friend of Jacobs and her brother. After the Civil War, Lowther became active in the Republican party, and in 1878 and 1879, he served in the Massachusetts House of Representatives. According to Yellin, he renewed his friendship with Jacobs in the 1850s (Jacobs, *Incidents*, ed. Yellin, 292n).

PART THREE

Related Documents

1

Title Page of the First Edition of Incidents in the Life of a Slave Girl

1861

The title page for the first edition of Incidents *identifies the well-known abolitionist Lydia Maria Child as the narrative's editor, but does not identify Harriet Jacobs as its author. This is consistent with Jacobs's use of a pseudonym throughout the narrative to protect family and friends who were still enslaved. Adding "Written by Herself" or ". . . Himself" was typically used in the titles of slave narratives to guarantee that these were first-person, eyewitness accounts. At the same time, identifying a white editor, in this case Lydia Maria Child, was the guarantee of authenticity.*

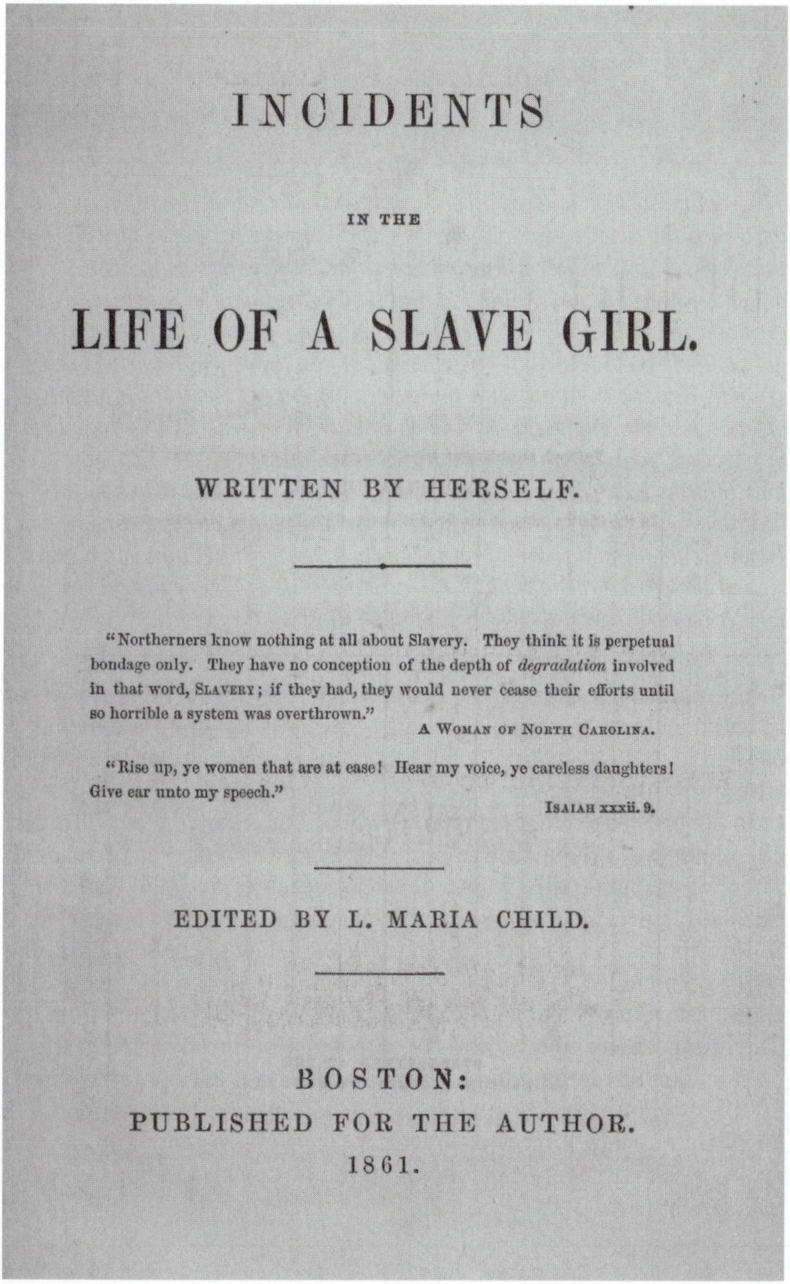

INCIDENTS

IN THE

LIFE OF A SLAVE GIRL.

WRITTEN BY HERSELF.

"Northerners know nothing at all about Slavery. They think it is perpetual bondage only. They have no conception of the depth of *degradation* involved in that word, SLAVERY; if they had, they would never cease their efforts until so horrible a system was overthrown."

A WOMAN OF NORTH CAROLINA.

"Rise up, ye women that are at ease! Hear my voice, ye careless daughters! Give ear unto my speech."

ISAIAH xxxii. 9.

EDITED BY L. MARIA CHILD.

BOSTON:
PUBLISHED FOR THE AUTHOR.
1861.

2

Will of Margaret Horniblow

April 8, 1825

The reading of this will, of Jacobs's mistress, Margaret Horniblow, destroyed the twelve-year-old Jacobs's and her family's hopes that she might be left free by her ailing mistress. Jacobs saw this as the end of her relatively happy childhood and the beginning of her tortured girlhood in the household of Dr. James Norcom. In the draft of her will dated April 1825, Horniblow willed all of her "Earthly property" to her mother, Elizabeth, along with her slaves, whom she includes in her list of "articles." Among these are Jacobs herself; her uncle, Mark Ramsay; her brother, John, and an unidentified slave named Nancy. Barely four months later, on the day she died, a codicil was added to her will that doomed Jacobs to enslavement in the household of Dr. Norcom, Horniblow's physician and brother-in-law. Notice that Horniblow never signed the codicil, even though it was witnessed by Henry Flury and Dr. Norcom.

In the name of God, Amen; I Margaret Horniblow of the town of Edenton and State of North Carolina being sound in mind and memory, but feeble in body and in declining health do make and ordain the following my last will and testament.

In the first place I desire that my body be buried in a decent Christian like manner at the discretion of my Executor to be hereafter named; Then, after paying all my just debts I give unto my beloved Mother Elizabeth Horniblow all the Earthly property I possess of every Kind & description whatsoever consisting of the following articles, viz; one negro man named Mark one negro Girl named Nancy one negro Girl named Harriett one negro boy named John, the debut due me from the Said Elizabeth Horniblow, the balance that may be due me from my friend Doctor James Norcom after a fair and just settlement of our accounts, my bed, bedstead, and furniture, and all my clothes—apparel & furniture of every kind whatsoever; . . . as well as every thing which may here be discovered belonging to me or to which I may be in any manner entitled.

Jean Fagan Yellin, ed., *The Harriet Jacobs Family Papers*, Vol. I (Chapel Hill: University of North Carolina Press, 2008).

And I hereby nominate and appoint my friend Doct. James Norcom Executor of this my last will and testament. In testimony of which I have hereunto Set my hand and Seal the eighth Day of April 1825

Margaret Horniblow [seal]
Witness Jno M. Jones[1]
Henry Flury....[*illegible*][2]

Codicil; It is my will & desire that the fore going devise be so-far altered, that my negro girl Harriet be given to my niece Mary Matilda Norcom Daughter of Dr. James Norcom; and I further give & bequeathe to my said niece my Bureau & work table & their contents –

The above Codisil was acknoleged before us the 3 day of July the year above write

Henry Flury
Jno Norcom

[1]John M. Jones was an Edenton merchant.
[2]Henry Flury was a member of the North Carolina House of Commons.

3

AMERICAN BEACON

Advertisement for the Capture of Harriet Jacobs

July 4, 1835

In addition to the posted broadside that Jacobs quotes in her narrative (page 115), Dr. James Norcom ran this ad for her capture in the American Beacon *(Norfolk, Virginia) on Tuesdays, Thursdays, and Saturdays for two weeks beginning June 30, 1835. Notice how the ad differs from the poster. This may be because the ad was written for readers farther north, who would be seeing Jacobs "abroad" wearing clothes for travel, and who would not know Norcom's reputation or the reasons Jacobs had run away.*

$100 REWARD

Will be given for the apprehension and delivery of my Servant Girl HARRIET. She is a light mulatto, 21 years of age, about 5 feet 4 inches high, of a thick and corpulent habit, having on her head a thick covering of black hair that curls naturally, but which can be easily combed straight. She speaks easily and fluently, and has an agreeable carriage and address. Being a good seamstress, she has been accustomed to dress well, has a variety of very fine clothes, made in the prevailing fashion, and will probably appear, if abroad, tricked out in gay and fashionable finery. As this girl absconded from the plantation of my son without any known cause or provocation, it is probable she designs to transport herself to the North.

The above reward, with all reasonable charges, will be given for apprehending her, or securing her in any prison or jail within the U. States.

All persons are hereby forewarned against harboring or entertaining her, or being in any way instrumental in her escape, under the most rigorous penalties of the law.

JAMES NORCOM

Edenton, N.C. June 30

4

HARRIET JACOBS

Letter to Amy Post

1852?

Jacobs wrote this response to her white abolitionist friend Amy Post's proposal that Jacobs write her autobiography. In it, Jacobs struggles with her feelings about telling her story of sexual exploitation. She feared that a public recital would leave her open to charges of moral degradation, yet she also felt that keeping her experiences secret, when revealing

Harriet Jacobs to Amy Post, 1852?, Isaac and Amy Post Family Papers, Department of Rare Books and Special Collections, University of Rochester Library, Rochester, N.Y.

them might help others, would be selfish. This letter is also noteworthy for Jacobs's admission that she avoided "the Antislavery people" when she arrived in the North precisely because she felt that she could not be open about her experiences without risking her respectability. Notice that although the letter begins with her ambivalence about authorship, it ends with an outline of her book and her ambitions for coauthorship with Harriet Beecher Stowe. Post, a Quaker abolitionist and women's rights advocate, lived in Rochester, New York. She befriended Jacobs when Jacobs moved there in 1849 to be near her brother, John.

Cornwall Orrang Co

My Dear Friend

Yours of the 24 was received on the 27th and my pen will fail to describe my greatful feelings on reading it although you could never be forgotten yet you do not know how much itt cheers my sad heart and how much I appreciate a word of sympathy and friendship from those I love for you little know how much I have had to pass through since we last meet but it is a blessing that we can say a word in this way to each other many far more deserving than myself has been debared from this privilege . . .

Your proposal to me has been thought over and over again but not with out some most painful rememberances dear Amy if it was the life of a Heroine with no degradation associated with it far better to have been one of the starving poor of Ireland whose bones had to bleach on the highways than to have been a slave with the curse of slavery stamped upon yourself and Children your purity of heart and kindly sympathies won me at one time to speak of my children it is the only words that has passed my lips since I left my Mothers door I had determined to let others think as . . . they pleased but my lips should be sealed and no one had a right to question me for this reason when I first came North I avoided the Antislavery people as much as possible because I felt that I could not be honest and tell the whole truth often have I gone to my poor Brother with my grieved and mortified spirits he would mingle his tears with mine while he would advise me to do what was right my conscience approved it but my stubborn pride would not yeild I have tried for the last two years to conquer it and I feel that God has helped me or I never would consent to give my past life to any one for I would not do it with out giving the whole truth if it could help save another from my fate it would be selfish and unchristian in me to keep it back situated as

I am I do not see any way that I could put it forward Mrs Willis thinks it would do much good in Mrs Stowe hand but I could not ask her to take any step Mr W is too proslavery he would tell me that it was very wrong and that I was trying to do harm or perhaps he was sorry for me to undertake it while I was in his family Mrs Willis thinks if is not done in my day it will a good legacy for my children to do it after my death but now is the time when there is so much excitement everywhere Mrs Hallowell said in her letter that you thought of going to New York in the course of a few weeks if you will let me know when I will meet you there I can give you my Ideas much better than write them

If the Antislavery society could prapare this I would be willing to exert myself in any way that they thought best for the welfare of the cause they do not know me they have heard of me as John Jacobs sister

my dear friend would you be willing to make this proposal I would rather have you do it than any one else you could do it better I should be happier in remembering it was you if Mrs Stowe would under take it I should like to be with her a Month I should want the History of my childhood and the first five years in one volume and the next three and my home in the northern states in the secont besids I could give her some fine sketches for her pen on slavery give my love to your dear Husband and sons kiss Willie for me love to all God bless Yours

Harriet

5

HARRIET JACOBS

Letter to Amy Post

April 4, 1853

In this letter, Jacobs candidly expresses her anger about Harriet Beecher Stowe's patronizing response to her suggestion that Stowe take Jacobs's daughter, Louisa, with her to England. More striking, however, is

Harriet Jacobs to Amy Post, April 4, 1853, Isaac and Amy Post Family Papers, Department of Rare Books and Special Collections, University of Rochester Library, Rochester, N.Y.

Jacobs's forceful rejection of Stowe's proposal to incorporate her story into Stowe's next book, A Key to Uncle Tom's Cabin. *Note Jacobs's "spirit of rivalry" with Stowe and her confidence in the importance of her own story for the antislavery movement.*

April 4th

My Dear Friend

I steal this moment to scratch you a few lines I should have written you before but I have been waiting with the hope of having some thing to tell you from our friend Mrs Stowe but as it is I hardly know where to begin for my thoughts come rushing down with such a spirit of rivalry each wishing to be told you first so that they fill my heart and make my eyes dim therefore my silence must express to you what my poor pen is not capable of doing but you know dear Amy that I have a heart towards you filled with love and gratitude for all the interest you have so kindly shown in my behalf I wish that I could sit by you and talk instead of writing but that pleasure is denied and I am thankful for this Mrs Stowe recieved your letter and Mrs Willis['s] she said it would be much care to her to take Louisa as she went by invitation it would not be right and she was afraid that if her situation as a Slave should be known it would subject her to much petting and patronizing which would be more pleasing to a young Girl than useful and the English was very apt to do it and sh[e] was very opposed to it with this class of people I will leave the rest for you to solve but remem that I mene to pay Louisa expenses your letter she sent to Mrs Willis asking might she trouble her so far as to ask if this most extraordinary event was true in all its bearings and if she might use it in her key I had never opened my lips to Mrs Willis concerning my Children in the Charitableness of her own heart she sympathized with me and never asked their origin my suffering she knew it embarrassed me at first but I told her the truth but we both thought it was wrong in Mrs Stowe to have sent you[r] letter she might have written to enquire if she liked Mrs Willis wrote her a very kind letter [begging] that she would not use any of the facts in he[r] key saying that I wished it to be a history of my life entirely by itsslf which would do more good and it needed no romance but if she wanted some facts for her book that I would be most happy to give her some she never answered the letter she [Mrs. Willis] wrote again and I wrote twice with no better success it was not Ladylike to treat Mrs Willis so she would not have done it to any one I think she did not like my objectian I cant help it

6

HARRIET JACOBS

Letter to Amy Post

March 1854

Jacobs reveals in this letter the reasons she had difficulty finding time to write her book and why she felt she must write secretly at night. Also significant is her reference to the "Nebraska bill," which was being debated in Congress at the time. The central question of this bill was whether Kansas would be admitted to the Union as a slave or free state. The legislation that resulted, the Kansas–Nebraska Act, essentially repealed the Missouri Compromise of 1820, which had prohibited slavery from the territories north of latitude 36°30′.

Cornwall March

My Dear Friend

I recieved your kind and welcome letter and should have replied to it much earlier but various hindrances have prevented me and when I would have written I was in Bed with a sever attack of Rheumatism so that I could not raise my hands to my head I am still suffering with it in my shoulders and we have had much sickness in the family this winter I know my plea for want of time will find its way to your heart

my dear friend let me thank you for your kind and generous offer of the hospitality of your pleasant home which would afford me much pleasure to accept but as yet I cannot decide my friends Mr & Mrs Brockett is very anxious that I should go to their home and write they live very quietly and retired they were here and spent a day and night with me and saw from my daily duties that it was hard for me to find much time to write as yet I have not written a single page by daylight Mrs W don't know from my lips that I am writing for a Book and has never seen a line of what I have written I told her in the Autumn that I would give her Louisa services through the winter if she would allow me my winter evenings to myself but with the care of the little baby and the big Babies and at the houshold['s] calls I have but a little time to think or write but I have tried in my poor way to do my best and that is not much

Harriet Jacobs to Amy Post, March 1854, Isaac and Amy Post Family Papers, Department of Rare Books and Special Collections, University of Rochester Library, Rochester, N.Y.

And you my dear friend must not expect much where there has been so little given Yes dear Amy there has been more than a bountiful share of suffering given enough to crush the finer feelings of stouter hearts than this poor timid one of mine but I will try and not send you a portriature of feelings just now the poor Book is in its Chrysalis state and though I can never make it a butterfly I am satisfied to have it creep meekly among some of the humbler bugs I sometimes wish that I could fall into a Rip Van Winkle sleep and awake with the blest belief of that little Witch Topsy that I never was born but you will say it is too late in the day I have outgrown the belief oh yes and outlived it too but you know that my bump of hope is large how is my dear old friend Mr Post I have no doubt but that he is at his Post[1] perhaps heading a mighty Phalanx to put the Nebraska bill through well he shall have my vote 1856 when Arnold and Belshazzar rools down the avalanche[2] remember me with much kindness to all the family tell Willie[3] I want to see him very much when you write tell me if I know the friend that you spoke of in your letter as soon as my plans are more matured I will write you again it will be very difficult for to get some one in my place yet it will be left for me to do I know of but one person she is a Ladys nurse and her wages would be high but I think that [I] can get her she is a nice person I must stop this rambling letter let no one see it Lou[isa] sends much love to you I am sorry you dont know her better you would love her

God bless you write as soon as you can yours

H. Jacobs

[1]Isaac Post (1798–1872), Amy Post's husband. Along with his wife, Isaac Post was one of the founders of the Western New York Anti-Slavery Society.

[2]Possibly Benedict Arnold (1741–1801), Revolutionary War major general who switched loyalties from the Americans to the British. Balshazzar was king of Babylon when it fell. Jacobs seems to be suggesting that when activists like Post prevail, the profane and traitorous forces of proslavery will fall. The year 1856 would be the next presidential election.

[3]Willett Post, born 1847, Amy and Isaac Post's youngest child.

7

HARRIET JACOBS

Letter to Amy Post

June 21, 1857

This letter demonstrates the importance Jacobs gave to writing about her life "faithfully," despite the social impropriety of publicizing the kind of sexual exploitation she had suffered. She also emphasizes her identity as "a poor slave Mother" speaking on behalf of "thousands" of "Slave Mothers." Although she chose to use pseudonyms throughout her narrative, she did not intend to hide her real identity as the author of the book. Note that Jacobs relies on dashes to punctuate this letter, a common nineteenth-century device absent from her earlier letters. This shows her development as a writer.

June 21st

My Dear Friend

A heart full of thanks for your kind and welcome—letter which would have been answered immediately—but for want of time to think a moment. I would dearly love to talk with you as it would be more satisfactory—but as I cannot I will try to explain myself on paper as well as I can—

I have My dear friend—Striven faithfully to give a true and just account of my own life in slavry—God knows I have tried to do it in a Christian spirit—there are somethings that I might have made plainer I know—woman can whisper—her cruel wrongs into the ear of a very dear friend—much easier than she can record them for the world to read—I have left nothing out but what I thought—the world might believe that a Slave woman was too willing to pour out—that she might gain their sympathies I ask nothing—I have placed myself before you to be judged as a woman whether I deserve your pity or contempt. I have another object in view—it is to come to you just as I am a poor slave Mother—not to tell you what I have heard but what I have seen—and what I have suffered—and if there is any sympathy to give—let it be given to the thousands—of . . . Slave Mothers that are still in bondage—suffering far more than I have—let it plead for their helpless Children that they may enjoy the same liberties that my Children now enjoy—Say anything of me that you have had from a truthful source that you think best—ask me any question you like—in regard to the father of my Children I think I have stated all perhaps I did not tell you—that he was a member of Congress—at that time all of this I have writen—I think it would be best for you to begin with our acquaintance and the length of time that I was in your family you[r] advice about giving the history of my life in Slavry mention that I lived

---

Harriet Jacobs to Amy Post, June 21, 1857, Isaac and Amy Post Family Papers, Department of Rare Books and Special Collections, University of Rochester Library, Rochester, N.Y.

at service all the while that I was striving to git the Book out but do not say with whom I lived as I would not use the Willis name neither would I like to have people think that I was living an Idle life—and had got this book out merely to make money—my kind friend I do not restrict you in anything for you know far better than I do what to say I am only too happy to think that I am going to have it from you—

[Harriet]

8

LYDIA MARIA CHILD

Letter to Harriet Jacobs

August 13, 1860

This letter offers the only real glimpse we have into the changes Child made to Jacobs's manuscript. Notice the way Child underscores that the changes are minimal. Especially interesting is Child's suggestion that Jacobs include more details about the Nat Turner uprising, as well as the important change Child suggests for the ending of the manuscript.

Wayland, Aug. 13th 1860

Dear Mrs. Jacobs,

I have been busy with your M.S. ever since I saw you; and have only done one third of it. I have very little occasion to alter the language, which is wonderfully good, for one whose opportunities for education have been so limited. The events are interesting, and well told; the remarks are also good, and to the purpose. But I am copying a great deal of it, for the purpose of transposing sentences and pages, so as to bring the story into continuous order, and the remarks into appropriate places. I think you will see that this renders the story much more clear and entertaining.

I should not take so much pains, if I did not consider the book unusually interesting and likely to do much service to the Anti-Slavery cause. So you need not feel under great personal obligations. You know I would go through fire and water to help give a blow to Slavery. I suppose you

Lydia Maria Child to Harriet Jacobs, August 13, 1860, Isaac and Amy Post Family Papers, Department of Rare Books and Special Collections, University of Rochester Library, Rochester, N.Y.

will want to see the M.S. after I have exercised my bump of mental order upon it; and I will send it wherever you direct, a fortnight hence.

My object in writing at this time is to ask you to write what you can recollect of the outrages committed on the colored people, in Nat Turner's time. You say the reader would not believe what you saw "inflicted on men, women, and children, without the slightest ground of suspicion against them." What were those inflictions? Were any tortured to make them confess? and how? Were any killed? Please write down some of the most striking particulars, and let me have them to insert.

I think the last Chapter, about John Brown, had better be omitted. It does not naturally come into your story, and the M.S. is already too long. Nothing can be so appropriate to end with, as the death of your grand mother.

Mr. Child desires to be respectfully remembered to you.

Very cordially your friend,
Lydia Maria Child

9

WEEKLY ANGLO-AFRICAN

Review of Incidents in the Life of a Slave Girl

April 13, 1861

More than giving simple praise, this reviewer of Jacobs's autobiography implies that the author is a true American heroine. Notice the reviewer's emphasis on the narrator's purity, despite the sexual abuse she suffered, and the apocalyptic language the reviewer uses to prophesy the downfall of slavery.

In such volumes as this, the true romance of American life and history is to be found, Patient suffering, heroic daring, untiring zeal, perseverance seemingly unparalleled, and growth from surroundings of

Review of *Incidents in the Life of a Slave Girl, Written by Herself,* ed. L. Maria Child, *Weekly Anglo-African*, April 13, 1861, in New York City. Documenting the American South, Carolina Digital Library and Archives, University of North Carolina, http://docsouth.unc.edu/fpn/jacobs/support6.html

degradation and ignorance to education, refinement, and power; all find in these modest pages their simple, yet affecting narrative. It is the "oft told tale" of American slavery, in another and more revolting phase than that which is generally seen. More revolting because it is of the spirit and not the flesh. In this volume, a woman tells in words of fire, yet never overstepping the bounds of the truest purity, not, how she was scourged and maimed, but the far more terrible sufferings endured by and inflicted upon woman, by a system which legalizes concubinage, and offers a premium to licentiousness. No one can read these pages without a feeling of horror, and a stronger determination arising in them to tear down the cursed system which makes such records possible. Wrath, the fiery messenger which goes flaming from the roused soul and overthrows in its divine fury the accursed tyrannies of the earth will find in these pages new fuel for the fire, and new force for the storm which shall overthrow and sweep from existence American slavery.

The name of the editor of the volume, Mrs. Child, is a sufficient endorsement of its literary merit. It is due however to the author to state that but little change has been made [illegible (three or four words)]. Mrs. Child says:—"Such changes as I have made have been mainly for the purposes of condensation and orderly arrangement. I have not added anything to the incidents, or changed the import of her very pertinent remarks. With trifling exceptions, both the ideas and the language are her own. I pruned excresences [*sic*] a little, but otherwise I had no reason for changing her lively and dramatic way of telling her own story. The names of both persons and places are known to me; but for good reasons I suppress them."

10

"Am I Not a Woman and a Sister?"

1832

This image of the kneeling black slave was arguably the most recognized emblem of the Anglo-American abolitionist movement. In its original form, it was male—"Am I Not a Man and a Brother"; it was designed as a medallion in 1787 for the campaign against the British slave trade by the English potter Josiah Wedgewood. By the 1820s this female version was used in the cause to abolish British slavery in the West Indies, leading up to the passage of the Slavery Abolition Act of 1833. Later, American abolitionists popularized this emblem as part of their effort to depict the effects of slavery on women. From the start, the kneeling slave was interpreted as beseeching the master to recognize their common humanity. Yet others interpreted this image of the African in chains to be a show of faith, an appeal to a Christian god for succor and aid. Readers of Incidents in the Life of a Slave Girl *might see this image as a corollary to Jacobs's emotional appeal to her Northern reader—the white, middle-class woman—whose sympathies she wished to arouse for the "two millions of women at the South, still in bondage." Yet consider the ways Jacobs repudiates this identity of the abject, devout enslaved woman, both in her active resistance to her physical enslavement and in her own words as a writer.*

11

JOHN S. JACOBS

A True Tale of Slavery

1861

John S. Jacobs (1815–1873), Harriet Jacobs's brother, wrote this autobiographical narrative, which was serialized in February 1861, a month after Harriet's book was published, in the London journal Leisure Hour: A Family Journal of Instruction and Recreation. *John's focus on the degradation of black manhood under slavery provides a vastly different emphasis than his sister's discussion of the particular sufferings of the female slave. Notice how John avoids the details of his sister's sexual abuse when he writes about her experiences.*

CHAPTER I. SOME ACCOUNT OF MY EARLY LIFE[1]

I was born in Edenton, North Carolina, one of the oldest States in the Union, and had four different owners in eighteen years. My first owner was Miss Penelope H ——, the invalid daughter of an innkeeper. After her death I became the property of her mother. My only sister was given to a niece of hers, daughter of Dr. James R. N ——, also of Edenton.

My father and mother were slaves. I have a slight recollection of my mother, who died when I was young, though my father made impressions on my mind in childhood that can never be forgotten. I should do my dear old grandmother injustice did I not mention her too. There was a great difference between her meekness and my father's violent temper, although, in justice to him, I must say that slavery was the cause of it.

To be a man, and not to be a man—a father without authority—a husband and no protector—is the darkest of fates. Such was the condition of my father, and such is the condition of every slave throughout the United States: he owns nothing, he can claim nothing. His wife is not

[1]The writer of these autobiographical sketches has, since his escape from slavery, held positions of trust in free countries, and every statement may be relied on, although it is not thought advisable to publish names in full. [Original note—Ed.]

John S. Jacobs, *A True Tale of Slavery*, serialized in *Leisure Hour: A Family Journal of Instruction and Recreation*, February 7, 14, 21, and 28, 1861.

his: his children are not his; they can be taken from him, and sold at any minute, as far away from each other as the human flesh-monger may see fit to carry them. Slaves are recognised as property by the law, and can own nothing except by the consent of their masters. A slave's wife or daughter may be insulted before his eyes with impunity. He himself may be called on to torture them, and dare not refuse. To raise his hand in their defence is death by the law. He must bear all things and resist nothing. If he leaves his master's premises at any time without a written permit, he is liable to be flogged. Yet, it is said by slaveholders and their apologists, that we are happy and contented. I will admit that slaves are sometimes cheerful; they sing and dance, as it is politic for them to do. I myself had changed owners three times before I could see the policy of this appearance of contentment. My father taught me to hate slavery, but forgot to teach me how to conceal my hatred. I could frequently perceive the pent-up agony of his soul, although he tried hard to conceal it in his own breast. The knowledge that he was a slave himself, and that his children were also slaves, embittered his life, but made him love us the more.

Up to this time our services had not been required, and the old lady to whom I belonged had paid little or no attention to how our time was spent. Our father, when working in or near the town, made our home his home.

I should state here that my father was owned by a Mrs. K ——, a widow lady, who was, however, no relative of Mrs. H ——, to whom I belonged.

Dr. N ——, being related to the family of my owner, was permitted to take me from my father in my tenth year, and put me in his shop. He too well knew the value of knowledge, and the danger of communicating it to human "property," to allow it to be disseminated among his slaves; and he therefore instructed his sons, who had charge of me, to see that I did not learn to write. Soon after this, my sister was taken into his house, but no interdict against the acquisition of knowledge, such as he had imposed upon me, could avail in her case. Our father had endeavoured to bestow upon both of us some rays of intellectual light, which the tyrant could not rob us of.

In the meanwhile, my father's young mistress married a rich planter, named C ——, who lived in the neighbourhood of Edenton. Shortly afterwards the old lady died, and my father became Mr. James C ——'s property. Being, as he was then considered, the best house-carpenter in or near the town, he was not put to field-work, although the privilege of working out, and paying his owner monthly, which he once enjoyed, was now denied him. This added another link to his galling chain—sent another arrow to his bleeding heart. My father, who had an intensely acute feeling of the wrongs of slavery, sank into a state of mental dejection, which, combined with bodily illness, occasioned his death when I was eleven years of age. He left us the only legacy that a slave father can leave his child, his whips and chains. These he had taught us to hate, and we resolved to seek for liberty, though we travelled through the gates of death to find it.

CHAPTER II. A FURTHER ACCOUNT OF MY FAMILY, AND OF MY NEW MASTER

Time passed swiftly on, and in due season death smote down Mrs. H ——, my mistress. The hungry heirs ordered us slaves to mount the auction-block; and all of us, old and young, male and female, married and single, were sold to the highest bidder. Even my grandmother's grey hairs and many years' hard service in the public-house did not save her from the auctioneer's hammer. But, fortunately for her, she possessed a tried and trusty friend, in whose hands she placed the savings of thirty years, that he might purchase her and her son Mark. She had two other children, a son and a daughter, but they were owned by other parties.

They began to sell off the old slaves first, as rubbish. One very old man went for one dollar; the old cook sold for seventeen dollars. The prices varied from that to 1600 dollars, which was the price of a young man who was a carpenter. Dr. N —— bought me for a shop-boy. It would be in vain for me to attempt to give a description of my feelings while standing under the auctioneer's hammer: I can safely say that I shall not realize such feelings again.

The man whom my grandmother trusted to do her business for her acted very honourably. As soon as it could be done, after the sale, he procured her free papers and the bill of sale of her son, to show that he was her property by right of purchase. It may seem rather strange that my grandmother should hold her son a slave; but the law required it. She was obliged to give security that she would never be any expense to the town or state before she could come in possession of her freedom. Her property in him was sufficient to satisfy the law; he could be sold at any minute to pay her debts, though it was not likely this would ever be the case. They had a snug home of their own, but their troubles were not yet at an end.

My uncle Joseph, who was owned by Mr. J. C ——, ran away about this time, and got as far as New York, where he was seen by Mr. S ——

of Edenton, who had him taken and sent back to his master. He was heavily manacled, and lodged in gaol, where he remained most of the winter, and was then sold to go to New Orleans.

My uncle Mark, whom my grandmother had bought, was at that time steward on board of a packet or vessel of some kind, and some months after my uncle Joseph had been sold, my uncle Mark met him in New York. He had made his second escape. The vessel was about to sail, and they had but little time to spend with each other, though my uncle Joseph told him he had not come there to stop. His intention was to get beyond the reach of the stars and stripes of America. Unwilling to trust his liberty any longer in the hands of a professed Christian, he purposed seeking safety in another hemisphere.

But to return to my subject. I left my sister in the doctor's family. Some six or eight years have passed since I was sold, and she has become the mother of two children. After the birth of her second child, she was sent to live on his plantation, where she remained for two or three months, and then ran away. As soon as she was gone, my aunt, the two children, and myself, were sent to gaol. My aunt was married, but happily her children were beyond the power of slavery. God had taken them to his rest.

The old doctor no doubt thought that this would be the means of bringing my sister back; but you will by-and-by see that she did not leave with the intention of returning. She had not yet been called to make her back bare for the lash; but she had gone to live on the doctor's plantation, where she daily expected it. Her mental sufferings were more than she could longer bear. With her it was, in the language of one of our fathers, "liberty or death."[2]

The doctor offered 100 dollars reward for her, and threatened to punish to the extreme penalty of the law, any person or persons found harbouring, or assisting her in any way to make her escape. He then wrote a letter to a gentleman by the name of T——, living in New York, who had formerly lived in North Carolina. I am not prepared to say that Mr. T—— took an interest in this letter. I rather believe he did not. But the news was soon circulated among the slave-catchers of the north, and they were sticking their unwanted faces in every coloured man's door, on account of my sister. The doctor pretended to sell me and the two children to a negro trader. In two or three weeks he received a letter from New York, stating (erroneously, as it turned out) that my sister was taken, and safely lodged in gaol. This called the old man from home.

[2]Patrick Henry. See note 147 on page 117.

He had got to prove property and pay expenses. Now that the old doctor was gone, I had a good time. Mr. L——, the gaoler, was an old acquaintance of mine. Though he was a white man, and I a slave, we had spent many hours together in Mr. J——'s family. We had taken tea there.

To make my story short, and go back to the doctor—Mr. J—— had a very fine daughter, and we were very fond of each other. Mr. L—— had been a visitor of Mr. J——'s for many years. Now that he had me under lock and key, and knowing that it was not for any crime that I was there, he could not be otherwise than kind. He allowed me every indulgence. My friends, such as could come, could call and see me whenever they pleased, and stop as long as they liked; he would never turn the key on them. Sometimes he would give me the key on the inside. While the doctor had me here for safe keeping, I could have made my escape every day or night; but in the first place, if I had wanted to go, I would not have taken the advantage of Mr. L——'s kindness; in the second place, I saw no chance of bettering myself. I knew he would not get my sister, because she had not left town. My uncle-in-law, who was a seafaring man, had intended to take her to New York, but the doctor's threats frightened him so much, that he did not dare make the attempt.

While the old man was gone, I had a negro trader call with others to see me. His name was G——; he said he would buy me if the old doctor would sell me; I told him I thought he would—that he told me he intended to do so when he put me in gaol.

After some two weeks the doctor returned home without my sister. The woman that had been taken up and put in gaol was a free woman; but what could she do with the wretch who put her there? America is a free country, and a white man can do what he pleases with a coloured man or woman in most of the States. They may have a few friends now, who would not allow this if they knew it; but they are hated by the nation at large.

My aunt was taken out of gaol and sent home to the doctor's house; the children and myself were left in. The old man came to have a little talk with me about my sister.

"Well, John, I have not got Harriet, but I will have her yet. Don't you know where she is?"

"How can I know, sir? I have been in gaol ever since my sister left you. Mr. G—— was here while you were away, sir, and said that he wanted to buy me."

"Buy you! I don't want to sell you."

"You told me when you put me here that you did."

"Yes, but not if you will go back to the shop and behave yourself. Mr. G —— has not got money enough to buy you."

"I do not know how to behave differently from what I have done."

"Your behaviour will do; but I am afraid you are going to run away from me."

"I have not said anything about running away from you, sir."

"I know that; but your sister is gone, and you will be going next."

Up to this time I had heard nothing of my sister; but I felt sure that she was with her friends in Edenton.

CHAPTER III. MY UNCLE'S TROUBLES—MY FURTHER EXPERIENCE OF THE DOCTOR, AND OUR PARTING

While the events described in the foregoing chapter were transpiring, my uncle-in-law Stephen returned from sea. His master, Mr. B ——, was owner of the vessel in which he sailed; and, although he had had several chances to make his escape from slavery, yet he had returned on every voyage. The doctor, who owned my aunt, forbad his going to see her, although they had lived together for twenty years, and had never been known to quarrel. It was most cruel that they should be separated, not for their own, but for another's acts. The doctor was inexorable; they were strictly interdicted from seeing each other. The only tie that bound my uncle to slavery was his wife, to whom he was truly attached. When their sacred union—a union holy in the sight of God, however desecrated by wicked men—was broken, he would not longer submit to the yoke. He took advantage of his next voyage to release himself from it, and he returned no more. His wife was dead to him—ay, worse than dead. "That which God hath joined together, let no man put asunder," saith those Scriptures which the slaveholder professes to believe, but which he blasphemes day by day and hour by hour.

At the doctor's last visit to the jail, he described to me the wretchedness of the free people of colour in New York, and stated that they had not the comforts of his slaves, and how much better off we were than they. To this I said nothing. My mind was fully made up, that I must, in order to effect my escape, hide as much as possible my hatred to slavery, and affect a respect to my master, whoever he might be. The doctor and myself knew each other too well for me to hope to get away from him. I must change owners in order to do that. Secondly, I had made up my mind that, let the condition of the coloured people of New York be what it might, I would rather die a free man than live a slave. The doctor evidently did not want to sell me, neither did he want to run the risk of losing me. Not that he had any particular regard for me, but he could not replace me for the same money that a slave-trader would give for me.

Before he left the jail, he told me that he did not want to keep me in jail any longer, and would let me out at any time when I would get my uncle Mark to be security that I would not run away from him. When leaving, he told me to send for my uncle, and see if he would not do it for me. To all this I was dumb. I was in no particular hurry to get out of jail. I wanted a little time for serious reflection, and this was the only place where I could get an opportunity for it.

A few days passed, and he heard nothing from me. He saw my uncle, and told him that I wanted to see him at the jail. He accordingly came, and asked me if I wished him to become my security. I promptly told him no; that I wanted my liberty; that I would make good the first opportunity to secure it; that he might do as he pleased; but, God being my helper, I would die a free man. This satisfied my uncle at once, that he might as well take the money out of his pocket and pay for me as to become my security; and he thought, if I could get a chance to make my escape without bringing any expense on him, so much the better. Here we parted. The old doctor waited for an answer, but got none, which satisfied him that I no longer had a desire to make his shop my home.

There were two or three slaveholders in the town, that would give him more for me than he could get from a trader, but he would not sell me to any one in the town. Mr. S ——, who afterwards bought me, came to the jail, and asked me if I would live with him if he bought me. I told him that I would; but the question was not asked how long.

I had been here just two months when Mr. S —— got a negro trader to buy the two children for my grandmother and me for himself. The doctor at first tried to bind the trader not to sell me to any one in the State; but this he would not agree to, saying that he sold his slaves wherever he could get the most for them; he finally agreed to take me out of town in irons, but to sell me the first chance he could get. The old man did not think that he had bargained for me before I was sold. This important part of the business being settled, we were sold, the two children for 500 dollars, I believe, and I for 900 dollars. The blacksmith's tools, handcuffs, and chain were all in readiness at the jail. The chain was thirty or forty feet long, with handcuffs every two or three feet. The slaves were handcuffed right and left on each side of the chain. In the gang there was one who was free by birth. He was born not more than fifty miles from Edenton. He had been put in jail here for some trifling offence; not being able to pay the fine, he was sold for six months or a year to William R——, a planter, who was so cruel to him that he ran away from him. He was caught, and, after being flogged, was put in irons and set to work. He attempted to cut the irons off, and being caught in the act, was sent to jail, and finally sold to a trader. I saw the irons that he had been made to work in; they were fetters for the ankles, weighing from fifteen to twenty pounds in weight.

Now we were all snugly chained up, the children in the cart, and the women walking behind; friends weeping, and taking a farewell shake of the hand—wives of their husbands, and parents of their children. I went with the gang as far as Mr. J. B. S——'s, the man that had my uncle taken in New York. Here the cart was stopped and the blacksmith's tools taken out, and Mr. L—— began to hammer away at my irons. When they were off, he told me to take the children and go home to Mr. S——; the children went to my grandmother, and I to Mr. S——, who had purchased me for a body servant; but, knowing the temper of the doctor, who would be angry at being outwitted, he sent me to his plantation, where I stopped for three months. During that time I was often in town of an evening to see my grandmother; and on two occasions he tried to trap me. What he would have done to me I know not; but up to the day that I left North Carolina, I never dared to trust myself in his power. Again and again he searched my grandmother's house for my sister, and at length he put my uncle Mark in jail. After a few days he was taken before the magistrate. The doctor could prove nothing against him, and yet the magistrate made my uncle pay the jail fees. Had my grandmother been destitute of friends, as many of the coloured people in the Slave States are, doubtless the doctor would have tried to extort from my uncle my sister's hiding-place. It was for this purpose he wanted to get hold of me, for, with oaths of the most dreadful kind, he told me he would butcher me. I had seen too much of his cruelty to doubt his purpose.

CHAPTER IV. MY NEW MASTER'S PLANTATION—MY MEDICAL PRACTICE AMONG THE SLAVES—MY SISTER'S HIDING-PLACE

During the three months that I was on the plantation, my master changed overseers. The last one was a member of a Christian church. He was particularly fond of two things, namely, singing hymns and flogging slaves; but he had been told to spare me from the lash. I could see that it went very much against his wishes to do so. Soon after this overseer came on the plantation, my master took me into town to live with him. He had one brother and a sister, who were both subject to fits, returning about every four weeks. When his brother Dr. M. E. S —— was sick with them, I stopped by him for a few days, until the illness was over. His sister died soon after I went to live with him. My work had never been very hard, neither had I known, as many do, the want of food; and as for the lash, from a boy I had declared that I would never carry its stripes upon my back. It is true my condition was much bettered with my new master; but I was happier only as I could see my chance for escape clearer. At length I grew sick of myself in acting the deceitful part of a slave, and pretending love and friendship where I had none. Unpleasant as it was thus to act, yet, under the circumstances in which I was placed, I feel that I have done no wrong in so doing; I did everything that I could to please my master, who treated me with as much kindness as I could expect from any one to whom I was a slave.

Having been so long with Dr. N ——, my master thought me quite capable of visiting the sick slaves on the plantation. This part of my work caused the overseer much unpleasantness; he would sometimes want to give them oil, or something of the kind, saying they were not sick; at other times he would say they were well enough to go to work, and if they were too sick to work, they were too sick to eat. Knowing that he would not strike me for having my own way in what I was sent there for—to see if they were sick and give them what they needed—I took great pleasure in differing with him on all occasions when I thought my patient dangerously ill. My judgment in regard to such diseases as are most common on a plantation was considered very good for one of my age; so much so, that a young planter who was studying medicine at the time, offered my master one thousand five hundred dollars for me. The way I came to know this was thus: he asked me one day if I wanted to be sold. This woke up a little of the old feeling, and I had almost forgotten myself for a minute. "No, sir," I said, "I am not anxious to be sold, but I know I have got to serve some one." Here he made me a promise which I shall never forget, though it was not consoling to me. He said, "You shall not serve any one after me: I have been offered a very handsome price for you; but I don't want to sell you." True, I was glad to hear him say that I should serve no one after him; this required a little consideration; he was but a few years older than me, and to wait for him to die looked to me too much like giving a man who was in want of his daily bread a cheque on the bank to be paid when he is dead. To have prayed for his death would have been wrong; to have killed him would have been worse; so, finally, I concluded to let him live as long as the Lord was willing he should, and I would get off as soon as possible. My pride would not allow me to let a man feed and clothe me for nothing; I would work the ends of my fingers off first.

I have said nothing about Mr. S——'s plantation slaves; I have only spoken of his treatment to me. I am willing to acknowledge kindness, even in a slaveholder, wherever I have seen it; but had he treated all of his slaves as he treated me, the probability is that they would have been of as little value to him as I was. Some may try to make out of this a case of ingratitude; but I do not feel myself under the slightest obligation to any one who holds me against my will, though he starved himself to feast me. Doubtless he meant to do me a good turn; but he put it off too far. I appreciated his kindness, and endeavoured to be as useful as I could.

At this time my condition was so much better than my sister's, that I had almost ceased to speak of leaving in the presence of my grandmother; for there is an inexpressible feeling in the breast of a woman who has lost child after child, whether it has been taken by force or by the hand of death, that makes her cling with tighter grasp to the last one. No doubt many of my readers can picture to themselves the force of the prayers and tears of a pious mother under such trials. My uncle Joseph was gone, she knew not where, and my sister was so closely pursued that they were obliged to hide her in the house between the roof and the ceiling. They are now beyond the reach of the slave power, or I would not dare to tell how this was done.

My grandmother's house had seven rooms—two upper rooms, and five on the lower floor: on the west side there was a piazza. On the east side there were two rooms, with a lobby leading to the centre of the house. The room on the left on entering the lobby was used as a store-room; the ceiling of this room was of boards, the roof was shingled; the space between the roof and ceiling was from three and a half to four feet in height, running off to a point. My uncle made a cupboard in one corner of this room, with the top attached to the ceiling. The part of the board that covered the top of the cupboard was cut and made into a trap-door; the whole of it was so small and neatly done that no one would have believed it to be what it was—the entrance to her hiding-place. Everything that she received was put in that little cupboard. One of the upper rooms was lathed and plastered; a hole was broken in the wall, through which she could speak to my uncle or grandmother; and, to prevent her losing the use of her limbs, the windows were sometimes closed that she might come down and walk about the room. When she was sick, I visited her, and gave her such medicines as she needed. After my uncle-in-law left, Uncle Mark knew of no one in whom to confide; he was suspected by the doctor, and narrowly watched wherever he went; and although he could hear nothing of her, he somehow seemed to think that she had not made her escape. During the short time that my sister was on the plantation, she saw one of the women so cruelly whipped that she died in a few days: it was done by James N ——, the doctor's son. These are called isolated cases; but we shall never know the wrongs that have been perpetrated in the slave states of America, until the oppressor and the oppressed shall stand before the Judge of all the world. The doctor's wife was as anxious as himself to get my sister again, and made promises of handsome presents to the slaves if they would try to find out where she was, but to no effect. She remained in that strange place of concealment six years and eleven months before she could get away!

CHAPTER V. MY MASTER GOES TO WASHINGTON AS MEMBER OF CONGRESS—HE IS ENGAGED TO BE MARRIED—WEDDING TRIP TO CHICAGO—CANADA—NEW YORK—MY ESCAPE FROM SLAVERY

The latter end of the third year after I was sold, my master was elected Member of Congress. I was ordered to get ready for Washington. We were not many days on the way to this place, which I so much wanted to see. It is a very lively place during the Session, and much enjoyed by the slaves, their privileges being greatly extended. They get up balls and parties, and seem to be as happy as their masters. I have had the pleasure of meeting some of these slaves in the Northern States, with whom I have danced, whose happiness, like mine, ended with the ball.

I could tell many things I observed of the life of members of Congress when at Washington, but I refrain from mentioning more than one or two customs of social life.

I will say it is twelve o'clock. The ladies have taken breakfast. A visitor comes and rings the door-bell, and you, on answering it, tell her that the mistress is not in; the reply most invariably is, "Go and tell her who it is, and she will be in." Just as well say, "Go and tell her she has lied, not knowing who has called to see her." The same is the case of the gentlemen. Here is a bill before the House, the merits and demerits of which they have spent weeks in discussing; it is now to be voted on at such an hour. The sergeant-at-arms is sent out in search of the absent members; some of them are having a little game of cards—could not think of waiting until after four o'clock;[3] the pay is just the same for playing cards as though they were making laws, only you must lie a little when the sergeant-at-arms calls, and say that you are not in. I could not bear this system of lying. I avoided answering these calls whenever I could.

After my master had been there a short time, he went to board with Mrs. P——, who had two young nieces here, to one of whom he was soon engaged to be married. As good luck would have it, this young lady had a sister living in Chicago, and no place would suit her like that to get married in. I admired her taste much. I wanted to go there too. My master could not do otherwise than give his consent to go there with her. The next question to be settled was about taking me with him into a free state. Near the time for him to leave, he told me that he intended to marry. I was pleased at this, and anxious to know who the fortunate lady might be. He did not hesitate to tell me what he intended to do, stating at the same time that he would take me with him if I would not leave him. "Sir," said I, "I never thought that you suspected me of wanting to leave you."

"I do not suspect you, John. Some of the members of the House have tried to make me believe that you would run away if I took you with me. Well, get my things all ready; we are to leave on the first day of next week; I will try you, any how."

Everything was ready, and the hoped-for time came. He took his intended, and off we started for the West. When we were taking the boat at Baltimore for Philadelphia, he came up to me and said, "Call me Mr. Sawyer; and if anybody asks you who you are, and where you are going, tell them that you are a free man, and hired by me."

We stopped two or three days at the Niagara Falls; from thence we went to Buffalo, and took the boat for Chicago; Mr. Sawyer had been here but a few days before he was taken sick. In five weeks from the time of his arrival here, he was married and ready to leave for home. On our return, we went into Canada. Here I wanted to leave him, but there was my sister and a friend of mine at home in slavery; I had succeeded in getting papers that might have been of great value to my friend. I had tried, but could not get anything to answer my purpose. I tried to get a

[3]By then, the government offices were closed. These Congressmen are playing cards during work.

seaman's protection from the English Customhouse, but could not without swearing to a lie, which I did not feel disposed to do.

We left here for New York, where we stopped three or four days. I went to see some of my old friends from home, who I knew were living there. I told them that I wanted their advice. They knew me, they knew my master, and they knew my friends also. "Now tell me my duty," said I. The answer was a very natural one, "Look out for yourself first." I weighed the matter in my mind, and found the balance in favour of stopping. If I returned along with my master, I could do my sister no good, and could see no further chance of my own escape. I then set myself to work to get my clothes out of the Astor House Hotel, where we were stopping; I brought them out in small parcels, as if to be washed. This job being done, the next thing was to get my trunk to put them in. I went to Mr. Johnson's shop, which was in sight of the Astor House Hotel, and told him that I wanted to get my trunk repaired. The next morning I took my trunk in my hand with me: when I went down, whom should I see at the foot of the steps but Mr. Sawyer? I walked up to him, and showed him a rip in the top of the trunk, opening it at the same time that he might see that I was not running off. He told me that I could change it, or get a new one if I liked. I thanked him, and told him we were very near home now, and with a little repair the old one would do. At this we parted. I got a friend to call and get my trunk, and pack up my things for me, that I might be able to get them at any minute. Mr. Sawyer told me to get everything of his in, and be ready to leave for home the next day. I went to all the places where I had carried anything of his, and where they were not done, I got their cards and left word for them to be ready by the next morning. What I had got were packed in his trunk; what I had not been able to get, there were the cards for them in his room. They dine at the Astor at three o'clock; they leave the room at four o'clock; at half-past four o'clock I was to be on board the boat for Providence. Being unable to write myself at that time, and unwilling to leave him in suspense, I got a friend to write as follows:—

> Sir—I have left you, not to return; when I have got settled, I will give you further satisfaction. No longer yours,
>
> John S. Jacobs.

This note was to be put into the post-office in time for him to get it the next morning. I waited on him and his wife at dinner. As the town clock struck four, I left the room. I then went through to New Bedford, where I stopped for a few months.

Thank God! I am now out of their reach; the old doctor is dead; I can forgive him for what he did do, and would have done if he could. The lawyer I have quite a friendly feeling for, and would be pleased to meet him as a countryman and a brother, but not as a master.

CHAPTER VI. SENSATIONS OF FREEDOM—SELF-EDUCATION—A WHALING VOYAGE—I MEET MY SISTER, AND HEAR FROM HER ABOUT MY FRIENDS AT EDENTON—THE FUGITIVE SLAVE BILL

On arriving at New Bedford, I was introduced to Mr. William P——, a very fatherly old man, who had been a slave in Alexandria. For the first week or so I could not realize the great transformation from a chattel slave to a man; it seemed to me like a dream; but I soon began to feel my responsibility, and the necessity of mental improvement. The first thing, therefore, that I strove to do was to raise myself above the level of the beast, where slavery had left me, and fit myself for the society of man. I first tried this in New Bedford by working in the day and going to school at night. Sometimes my business would be such that I could not attend evening schools; so I thought the better plan would be to get such books as I should want, and go a voyage to sea. I accordingly shipped on board the "Frances Henrietta," of New Bedford. This was a whaling voyage; but I will not trouble you with any fishing stories. I will make it short. After being absent three years and a half, we returned home with a full ship, 1700 barrels of sperm oil and 1400 of whale oil.

I had made the best possible use of my leisure hours on board, and kept the object that drove me from my friends and my home before me when on shore. I had promised myself, if what money I had coming to me would be an inducement to any one to bring my sister off from the south, that I would have her; but there was better news than that, in the bosom of an old friend, waiting to be delivered. The ship dropped her anchor, and the shore boats came off with friends of different persons on board, among whom was R. P——. He had scarcely spoken to me before he began to tell me about my sister; her coming to New Bedford in search of me, and her going back to New York, where, he told me, I should find her. This news was to me quite unexpected. I said, if my sister was free from her oppressor, I was a happy man. I hurried on shore, drew some money of the owners, and made my way to New York. I found my sister living with a family as nurse at the Astor House. At first she did not look natural to me; but how should she look natural, after having been shut out from the light of heaven for six years and eleven months! I did not wish to know what her sufferings were, while living in her place of concealment. The change that it had made in her was enough to make one's soul cry out against this curse of curses, that has so long trampled humanity in the dust.

After she had recovered a little from the surprise of seeing me, I began to speak of home. "Oh, brother," she said, "grandmother was so disappointed in your stopping behind. Mr. S —— had written for them to make ready his house for his reception on such a day; grandmother got the news of it, and invited some of your old friends to come and spend the evening with you. Supper was all ready, and our ears were all intent to catch the first blast of the stage horn, when Uncle Mark left the room to go and meet you. The coach drove up to the tavern door, and the passengers had all got out, when Dr. W —— asked Mr. S —— what had become of you. He said the abolitionists had got you away from him in New York. When Uncle Mark returned, grandmother looked for awhile, and then asked, "Where is my child?' 'He is gone, mother; he left Mr. S —— in New York.'

"When she heard that you were gone, she wept like a child. Aunt Sue Bent was there, and on seeing grandmother's tears, said to her: 'Molly, my child, this is no time for crying. Dry up those tears, fall upon your knees, and thank God that one more has made his escape from the house of bondage. I came here to see him, but I am glad he is not here. God bless the boy, and keep him from all harm.'

"This (continued my sister) increased my anxiety, and caused me to adopt new plans for my escape. I wrote a letter to the doctor, asking him if he would sell me to my grandmother. It was sent to New York, and there mailed for Edenton. The letter was received by the doctor, and answered by his son Caspar.[4] He could now no longer doubt that I was gone, and resorted to a cunningly-devised artifice to bring me back. Part of his son's letter ran as follows—'Harriet, we are all glad to hear from you; and let me assure you, if our family ever did entertain anything different from the most friendly feelings for you, they exist no longer. We want to see you once more, with your old friends around you, made happy in your own home. We cannot sell you to your grandmother; the community would object to your returning to live in a state of freedom. Harriet, doubtless before this you have heard of the death

[4]Caspar Wistar Norcom (1818–1872). A doctor, Caspar Norcom committed suicide in California, where he had set up a practice.

of your aunt Betty. In her life she taught us how to live, and in her death she taught us how to die.'

"From that letter, my uncle saw that escape was my only hope, and that there was no time like the present for action. While everybody believed that I was in New York was the best time to get there. He accordingly made arrangements with the captain of a vessel running between New York and Edenton, for my passage to the former port.

"I had been here but a short time, when some of my friends sent for me to acquaint me of my danger. Mrs. T —— gave me a letter that Mr. T —— had received from Dr. N ——. In that letter he said he wanted to catch me, to make an example of, for the good of the institution of slavery. But, brother, I have now fallen into new hands. Mary Matilda N —— is married to a northern man. He, too, is trying to find out where I am stopping in New York. I know not where to go, nor what to do."

I could see my sister's danger, and well imagine her feelings. We selected Boston, Massachusetts, for our home, and remained there quietly for a few years. Massachusetts had so far precluded the slaveholders from her borders, as to make the hunted fugitive feel himself somewhat secure under the shadow of her laws. Her great men had not sold themselves to the slave power, and her little men had not learnt that they were slaves until after the passing of the Fugitive Slave Bill. From that hour I resolved to seek a home in some foreign clime.

Mrs. ——, on hearing my intention to leave the north, sent for me. I called on her and was shown to her room by my sister, when the following conversation took place.

"John, I understand you intend to leave for some years."

"I do, madam."

"Then my business with you is with respect to your sister. She has spent many years in our family, and we are still desirous to have her remain with us. John, I know that the law is an absolute one, and that the prosecutors are deaf to the claims of justice and humanity; but I have resolved that Harriet shall not be taken out of my house. This I will promise you as a lady."

A few months after the passing of the Fugitive Slave Bill, my sister was looking over the list of arrivals in one of the daily papers, when she saw the names of Mr. and Mrs. M —— of Edenton. She immediately made it known to Mrs. ——, who sent her out of the house with out a moment's delay. As the little girl that she had charge of at the time would not be separated from her, they were both sent off together. In due time Mr. M —— came rapping at the door, not as an honest man, but as a slave-catcher. The door being opened, he said to the woman, "Go and tell Harriet that I have got a letter for her; it is from her grandmother, and I have promised to deliver it to her myself." The message was taken to Mrs. ——, who informed him that my sister had left town, and that he could not see her. M —— saw that all of his plans were frustrated, and sold my sister for 300 dollars. She was paid for by her mistress and her friends, and is now living in safety.

CHAPTER VII. CRUEL TREATMENT OF SLAVES—THE FUGITIVE SLAVE LAW—SLAVERY OPPOSED TO NATURAL RIGHTS AND TO CHRISTIANITY

In concluding this short statement of my experience of slavery, I beg the reader to remember that I am not writing of what I have heard, but of what I have seen, and of what I defy the world to prove false. There lived about two miles up a river emptying itself into the Albemarle Sound, a planter, whose name was Carabas.[5] His plantation was called Pembroke. At his death his slaves were sold. I mention this because slaves seldom or ever have more than one name; their surname is most generally that of their first master. The person I am now about to allude to was known by the name of George Carabas. After the death of his own master, he was owned by Mr. Popelston: after that by young John Horton, who sold him to a negro trader.

George was chained in the gang with other slaves, and dragged from his wife and his friends. After a few days' travel on the road, by some means or other he made his escape, and returned back to that spot where he knew he could find one heart to feel for him, and in whom he could confide; but he had not been there long before the bloodthirsty negro-hunters got on his trail, one beautiful Sunday morning, about midsummer, while the church-bells were ringing. Four of the pursuers overtook poor George, and shot him dead.

"If he is outlawed," they doubtless argued, "we only need show his head, and the reward is ours; but if he is not outlawed, what then? Why, they may try to make us pay for him; but we will not be fools enough to say that we shot him, unless we are to be paid for shooting him." His body is put into a canoe, his head thrown in, which lies on his breast. These four southern gentlemen now return to the town, leaving the canoe to inquire how the advertisement reads. On finding that the reward was to be given to any one who would apprehend and

[5]Stephen Cabarrus, brother of Auguste (see note 97, page 78), died in 1807.

confine him in any jail in the State, they saw that they could not publicly boast of their fiendish work.

Now, the question is, what had this man done that he should be so inhumanly butchered and beheaded? The crime that he had committed, and the only crime, was to leave the unnatural trader in slaves and the souls of men, to return to his natural and affectionate wife. Nothing is done to the murderers. They only made a blunder. Slaves are outlawed and shot with impunity, and the tyrant who shoots them is paid for it; but in this case George was not outlawed, so their trouble was all for nothing, and the glory only known to themselves.

Tom Hoskins was a slave belonging to James N ——, the son of Dr. N ——. This slave was found just out of the town, in the scrub. He was shot in the back, and must have been killed instantly. There was no pay for this —— only a feast of blood. Tom's crime was running away from one whom I know to be an unmerciful tyrant. Another was shot, but not killed. There were three brothers, William, James, and Josiah N ——. I know not which of the three this slave belonged to. They had been out that day with their bloodhounds hunting slaves. They shot Sirus a little before dark. By some means or other he made his escape from them, and reached Dr. S ——'s shop soon after dark. He was taken in, and as many of the shots taken out of him as they could get at, and his wounds dressed. This being done, Dr. S —— sent a despatch to Mr. C ——, to let him know that the slave that they had shot had come in to him, and got his wounds dressed. As soon as they received this intelligence, they mounted their horses, and rode off in fiendish glee for town. They came up to the shop, hooting and yelling as if all Bedlam was coming. When they had reached the door, the first cry from them was, "Bring him out—finish him." The doctor came out and said to them, "Gentlemen, the negro has given himself up to me, and I will be responsible for his safe delivery to you as soon as he is able to be moved from hence; but at present he is not." Seeing that the doctor would not let them have him, they returned home.

The C ——s were very rich; they owned a great many slaves, and shooting with them was common. They did not feel the loss of a slave or two; it was a common thing for them to offer fifty or a hundred dollars reward for a slave, dead or alive, so that there was satisfactory proof of his being killed.

Just at the back of the court-house and in front of the jail is a whipping post, where I have seen men and women stripped, and struck from fifteen to one hundred times and more. Some whose backs were cut to pieces were washed down with strong brine or brandy; this is done to increase pain. But the most cruel torture is backing; the hands are crossed and tied, then taken over the knee and pinned by running a stick between the arms and the legs, which tightens the skin and renders the slave as helpless as a child. The backing paddle is made of oak, about an inch and a quarter thick, and five by eight inches in the blade, with about twelve inches of a handle. The blade is full of small holes, which makes the punishment severer. I have seen the flesh like a steak. Slaves flogged in this way are unable to sit down for months.

I will give you but one case of flogging in detail; that will be of Agnes, the slave of Augustus M ——. She was hired to John B ——; she was some six months advanced in pregnancy at the time. Being in an unfit state for field labour, she could not do as much as other slaves. For this cause, B —— tied her up and commenced whipping her. With my own hands have I dressed her back, and I solemnly declare that she had not a piece of skin left on it as wide as my finger. She was a hired slave. Had B —— killed her at a single blow, her master could have punished B ——, if he could have got white witnesses to certify to that effect, which is not likely; but she might have died in an hour after being cut down, and there was no law to harm him. It would have been death caused by moderate correction, which North Carolina does not punish a slaveholder for.

I know that the picture I have drawn of slavery is a black one, and looks most unnatural; but here you have the State, the town, and the names of all the parties. One who has never felt the sting of slavery would naturally suppose that it was to the slaveholder's advantage to treat his slaves with kindness; but the more indulgent the master the more intelligent the slave; the more intelligent the slave, the nearer he approximates to a man; the nearer he approximates to a man, the more determined he is to be a free man; and to argue that the slaves are happy, or can be happy while in slavery, is to argue that they have been brutalized to that degree that they cannot be considered men. What better proof do you want in favour of universal freedom than can be given? You can find thousands of ignorant men who will lay down their lives for their liberty; can you find one intelligent man who would prefer slavery?

The last thing that remained to be done to complete this hell on earth was done in 1850, in passing the Fugitive Slave Law. There is not a State, a city, nor a town left as a refuge for the hunted slave; there is not a United States officer but what has sworn to act the part of the bloodhound in hunting me down, if I dare visit the land of Stars and Stripes, the home of the brave, and land of the free. Yet, according to the American declaration of independence, it is a self-evident truth that all men are created by their Maker free and equal, and endowed with certain inalienable rights—life, liberty, and the pursuit of happiness.[6] Where are the coloured man's rights to-day in America? They once had rights allowed them. Yes, in the days that tried men's souls[7] they had a right to bleed and die for the country; but their deeds are forgotten, their swords and bayonets have been beaten into chains and fetters to bind the limbs of their children. The first man that was seen to fall in the revolutionary struggle for liberty, was a coloured man; and I have seen one of his brethren, who had fled from his whips and chains, within sight of that monument erected to liberty, dragged from it into slavery, not by the slave-owners of the south, for they knew not of his being there, but by northern men.

I cannot agree with that statesman who said, "What the law makes property, is property."[8] What is law, but the will of the people—a mirror to reflect a nation's character? Robbery is robbery; it matters not whether it is done by one man or a million, whether they were organized or disorganized; the principle is the same. No law, unless there be one that can change my nature, can make property of me. Freedom is as natural for man as the air he breathes, and he who robs him of his freedom is also guilty of murder; for he has robbed him of his natural existence. On this subject the Church and the State are alike. One will tell a lie, and the other will swear to it. The State says, "That which the law makes property is property." The Church says that "organic sin is no sin at all"; both parties having reference to slavery. With a few exceptions, their politics and religion are alike oppressive, and rotten, and false. None but political tyrants would ever establish slavery, and none but religious hypocrites would ever support it. What says Matthew, 15th chapter, 8th and 9th verses: "This people draweth nigh unto me with their mouth, and honoureth me with their lips; but their heart is far from me. But in vain they worship me, teaching for doctrines the commandments of men."

[6]Reference to the beginning lines of the Declaration of Independence (1776).

[7]Reference to Thomas Paine's "These are the times that try men's souls," from *The Crisis* (1776–1777).

[8]Earliest use of statement appears in an 1831 issue of *Blackwood's Edinburgh Magazine*, an influential conservative bimonthly journal. This postulate was adopted by proslavery ideologues to justify holding slaves as property and became a common point of debate between antislavery and proslavery forces.

What is to be hoped of a people like this? They are full of lies and hypocrisy. Give me liberty amidst savages, rather than slavery with such professed Christians. No man should hold unlimited power over his fellow-man. From the repeated abuses of this power, he becomes the most brutal of the human species; and the more he himself has been abused, the more eager he is to abuse others. But slavery is unnatural, and it requires unnatural means to support it. Everything droops that feels its sting. Hope grows dimmer and dimmer, until life becomes bitter and burdensome. At last death frees the slave from his chains, but his wrongs are forgotten. He was oppressed, robbed, and murdered. Better would it be for the slaves, if they must submit to slavery, if the immortal part of them were blotted out. But, since God has breathed undying life into the soul of man, rather let us blot that out of existence which stands between man and his rights, God and his laws, the world and its progress. The Christian religion, that binds heart to heart and hand to hand, and makes each and every man a brother, is at war with it; and shall we, whose very souls it has wrung out, be longer at peace. If possible, let us make those whom we have left behind feel that the ground they till is cursed with slavery, the air they breathe poisoned with its venom breath, and that which made life dear to them lost and gone.

In conclusion, let me say that the experience of the past, the present feeling, and above all this, the promise of God, assure me that the oppressor's rod shall be broken. But how it is to be done has been the question among our friends for years. After the prayers of twenty-five years, the slaves' chains are tighter than they were before, their escape more dangerous, and their cup of misery filled nearer its brim. Since I cannot forget that I was a slave, I will not forget those that are slaves. What I would have done for my liberty I am willing to do for theirs, whenever I can see them ready to fill a freeman's grave, rather than wear a tyrant's chain. The day must come; it will come. Human nature will be human nature; crush it as you may, it changes not; but woe to that country where the sun of liberty has to rise up out of a sea of blood. When I have thought of all that would pain the eye, sicken the heart, and make us turn our backs to the scene and weep, I then think of the oppressed struggling with their oppressors, and have a scene more horrible still. But I must drop this subject; I do not like to think of the past, nor look to the future, of wrongs like these.

12

HARRIET JACOBS

Life among the Contrabands

1862

This article shows Jacobs in a new phase of activism following the publication of her narrative. At the request of William Lloyd Garrison, editor of the leading abolitionist newspaper, the Liberator, *Jacobs wrote this article about her experiences helping the slave refugees, called contrabands, who flocked to the Washington, D.C., area during the Civil War. Between April 1862 and the spring of 1863, some 5,600 refugees—men, women, and children—fled north. Jacobs was one of many African Americans, a large number of them women, who volunteered their time and helped raise money to benefit the contrabands, who lived in deplorable conditions in camps in and around the capital. ("Duff Green's [or Green] Row," which she mentions in the article, was on East Capitol Street, where the Folger Shakespeare Library stands today.) Look for Jacobs's argument about the obligations of the antislavery movement to freed men, women, and children and the centrality of education for former slaves.*

Dear Mr. Garrison:

I thank you for the request of a line on the condition of the contrabands, and what I have seen while among them. When we parted at that pleasant gathering of the Progressive Friends at Longwood, you to return to the Old Bay State, to battle for freedom and justice to the slave, I to go to the District of Columbia, where the shackles had just fallen, I hoped that the glorious echo from the blow had aroused the spirit of freedom, if a spark slumbered in its bosom. Having purchased my ticket through to Washington at the Philadelphia station, I reached the capital without molestation. Next morning, I went to Duff Green's Row, Government head-quarters for the contrabands here. I found men, women and children all huddled together, without any distinction or regard to age or sex. Some of them were in the most pitiable condition. Many were sick with measles, diptheria [*sic*], scarlet and typhoid

---

Harriet Jacobs, "Life among the Contrabands," *Liberator*, September 5, 1862, 3.

fever. Some had a few filthy rags to lie on; others had nothing but the bare floor for a couch. There seemed to be no established rules among them; they were coming in at all hours, often through the night, in large numbers, and the Superintendent had enough to occupy his time in taking the names of those who came in, and of those who were sent out. His office was thronged through the day by persons who came to hire these poor creatures, who they say will not work and take care of themselves. Single women hire at four dollars a month; a woman with one child, two and a half or three dollars a month. Men's wages are ten dollars per month. Many of them, accustomed as they have been to field labor, and to living almost entirely out of doors, suffer much from the confinement in this crowded building. The little children pine like prison birds for their native element. It is almost impossible to keep the building in a healthy condition. Each day brings its fresh additions of the hungry, naked and sick. In the early part of June, there were, some days, as many as ten deaths reported at this place in twenty-four hours. At this time, there was no matron in the house, and nothing at hand to administer to the comfort of the sick and dying. I felt that their sufferings must be unknown to the people. I did not meet kindly, sympathizing people, trying to soothe the last agonies of death. Those tearful eyes often looked up to me with the language, "Is this freedom?"

A new Superintendent was engaged, Mr. Nichol, who seemed to understand what these people most needed. He laid down rules, went to work in earnest pulling down partitions to enlarge the rooms, that he might establish two hospitals, one for the men and another for the women. This accomplished, cots and mattresses were needed. There is a small society in Washington—the Freedman's Association—who are doing all they can; but remember, Washington is not New England. I often met Rev. W. H. Channing,[1] whose hands and heart are earnestly in the cause of the enslaved of his country. This gentleman was always ready to act in their behalf. Through these friends, an order was obtained from Gen. Wadsworth[2] for cots for the contraband hospitals.

At this time, I met in Duff Green Row, Miss Hannah Stevenson,[3] of Boston, and Miss Kendall. The names of these ladies need no comment. They were the first white females whom I had seen among these poor creatures, except those who had come in to hire them. These noble

[1]William Henry Channing (1810–1884), Unitarian minister in Cincinnati and Liverpool, England. Cousin to abolitionist and Unitarian minister William Ellery Channing.

[2]James S. Wadsworth (1807–1864).

[3]Hannah Stevenson (1807–1887), abolitionist. Volunteered as a nurse in Washington, D.C., from 1860–1863 during the Civil War.

ladies had come to work, and their names will be lisped in prayer by many a dying slave. Hoping to help a little in the good work they had begun, I wrote to a lady in New York, a true and tried friend of the slave, who from the first moment had responded to every call of humanity. This letter was to ask for such articles as would make comfortable the sick and dying in the hospital. On the Saturday following, the cots were put up. A few hours after, an immense box was received from New York. Before the sun went down, those ladies who have labored so hard for the comfort of these people had the satisfaction of seeing every man, woman and child with clean garments, lying in a clean bed. What a contrast! They seemed different beings. Every countenance beamed with gratitude and satisfied rest. To me, it was a picture of holy peace within. The next day was the first Christian Sabbath they had ever known. One mother passed away as the setting sun threw its last rays across her dying bed, and as I looked upon her, I could not but say—"One day of freedom, and gone to her God." Before the dawn, others were laid beside her. It was a comfort to know that some effort had been made to soothe their dying pillows. Still, there were other places in which I felt, if possible, more interest, where the poor creatures seemed so far removed from the immediate sympathy of those who would help them. These were the contrabands in Alexandria [Virginia]. This place is strongly secesh;[4] the inhabitants are kept quiet only at the point of Northern bayonets. In this place, the contrabands are distributed more over the city. In visiting those places, I had the assistance of two kind friends, women. True at heart, they felt the wrongs and degradation of their race. These ladies were always ready to aid me, as far as lay in their power. To Mrs. Brown, of 3d street, Washington, and Mrs. Dagans, of Alexandria, the contrabands owe much gratitude for the kindly aid they gave me in serving them. In this place, the men live in an old foundry, which does not afford protection from the weather. The sick lay on boards on the ground floor; some, through the kindness of the soldiers, have an old blanket. I did not hear a complaint among them. They said it was much better than it had been. All expressed a willingness to work, and were anxious to know what was to be done with them after the work was done. All of them said they had not received pay for their work, and some wanted to know if I thought it would be paid to their masters. One old man said, "I don't kere if dey don't pay, so dey give me freedom. I bin working for ole maas all de time; he nebber gib me five cent. I like de Unions fuss rate. If de Yankee Unions didn't come

[4]Secessionist.

long, I'd be working tu de old place now." All said they had plenty to eat, but no clothing, and no money to buy any.

Another place, the old school-house in Alexandria, is the Government head-quarters for the women. This I thought the most wretched of all the places. Any one who can find an apology for slavery should visit this place, and learn its curse. Here you see them from infancy up to a hundred years old. What but the love of freedom could bring these old people hither? One old man, who told me he was a hundred, said he had come to be free with his children. The journey proved too much for him. Each visit, I found him sitting in the same spot, under a shady tree, suffering from rheumatism. Unpacking a barrel, I found a large coat, which I thought would be so nice for the old man, that I carried it to him. I found him sitting in the same spot, with his head on his bosom. I stooped down to speak to him. Raising his head, I found him dying. I called his wife. The old woman, who seems in her second childhood, looked on as quietly as though we were placing him for a night's rest. In this house are scores of women and children, with nothing to do, and nothing to do with. Their husbands are at work for the Government. Here they have food and shelter, but they cannot get work. The slaves who come into Washington from Maryland are sent here to protect them from the Fugitive Slave Law. These people are indebted to Mr. Rufus Leighton,[5] formerly of Boston, for many comforts. But for their Northern friends, God pity them in their wretched and destitute condition! The superintendent, Mr. Clarke, a Pennsylvanian, seems to feel much interest in them, and is certainly very kind. They told me they had confidence in him as a friend. That is much for a slave to say.

From this place, I went to Birch's slave-pen in Alexandria.[6] This place forms a singular contrast with what it was two years ago. The habitable part of the building is filled with contrabands; the old jail is filled with secesh prisoners—all within speaking distance of each other. Many a compliment is passed between them on the change in their positions. There is another house on Cameron street, which is filled with very destitute people. To these places I distributed large supplies of clothing, given me by the ladies of New York, New Bedford, and Boston. They have made many a desolate heart glad. They have clothed the naked, fed the hungry. To them, God's promise is sufficient.

[5]Rufus Leighton edited the sermons and writings of abolitionist Unitarian minister Theodore Parker. In Washington during the Civil War, he promoted the education and welfare of former slaves.

[6]Slave dealers Price, Birch & Co. had their pens for holding slaves in Alexandria, Virginia.

Let me tell you of another place, to which I always planned my last visit for the day. There was something about this house to make you forget that you came to it with a heavy heart. The little children you meet at this door bring up pleasant memories when you leave it; from the older ones you carry pleasant recollections. These were what the people call the more favored slaves, and would boast of having lived in the first families in Virginia. They certainly had reaped some advantage from the contact. It seemed a miracle that they had all fallen together. They were intelligent, and some of the young women and children beautiful. One young girl, whose beauty I cannot describe, although its magnetism often drew me to her side, I loved to talk with, and look upon her sweet face, covered with blushes; besides, I wanted to learn her true position, but her gentle shyness I had to respect. One day, while trying to draw her out, a fine-looking woman, with all the pride of a mother, stepped forward, and said—"Madam, this young woman is my son's wife." It was a relief. I thanked God that this young creature had an arm to lean upon for protection. Here I looked upon slavery, and felt the curse of their heritage was what is considered the best blood of Virginia. On one of my visits here, I met a mother who had just arrived from Virginia, bringing with her four daughters. Of course, they belonged to one of the first families. This man's strong attachment to this woman and her children caused her, with her children, to be locked up one month. She made her escape one day while her master had gone to learn the news from the Union army. She fled to the Northern army for freedom and protection. These people had earned for themselves many little comforts. Their houses had an inviting aspect. The clean floors, the clean white spreads on their cots, and the general tidiness throughout the building, convinced me they had done as well as any other race could have done, under the same circumstances.

Let me tell you of another place—Arlington Heights. Every lady has heard of Gen. [Robert E.] Lee's beautiful residence, which has been so faithfully guarded by our Northern army. It looks as though the master had given his orders every morning. Not a tree around that house has fallen. About the forts and camps they have been compelled to use the axe. At the quarters, there are many contrabands. The men are employed, and most of the women. Here they have plenty of exercise in the open air, and seem very happy. Many of the regiments are stationed here. It is a delightful place for both the soldier and the contraband. Looking around this place, and remembering what I had heard of the character of the man who owned it before it passed into the hands of its present owner, I was much inclined to say, Although the wicked prosper for a season, the way of the transgressor is hard.[7]

When in Washington for the day, my morning visit would be up at Duff Green's Row. My first business would be to look into a small room on the ground floor. This room was covered with lime. Here I would learn how many deaths had occurred in the last twenty-four hours. Men, women and children lie here together, without a shadow of those rites which we give to our poorest dead. There they lie, in the filthy rags they wore from the plantation. Nobody seems to give it a thought. It is an every-day occurrence, and the scenes have become familiar. One morning, as I looked in, I saw lying there five children. By the side of them lay a young man. He escaped, was taken back to Virginia, whipped nearly to death, escaped again the next night, dragged his body to Washington, and died, literally cut to pieces. Around his feet I saw a rope; I could not see that put into the grave with him. Other cases similar to this came to my knowledge, but this I saw.

Amid all this sadness, we sometimes would hear a shout of joy. Some mother had come in, and found her long-lost child; some husband his wife. Brothers and sisters meet. Some, without knowing it, had lived years within twenty miles of each other.

A word about the schools. It is pleasant to see that eager group of old and young, striving to learn their A, B, C, and Scripture sentences. Their great desire is to learn to read. While in the school-room, I could not but feel how much these young women and children needed female teachers who could do something more than teach them their A, B, C. They need to be taught the right habits of living and the true principles of life.

My last visit intended for Alexandria was on Saturday. I spent the day with them, and received showers of thanks for myself and the good ladies who had sent me; for I had been careful to impress upon them that these kind friends sent me, and that all that was given by me was from them. Just as I was on the point of leaving, I found a young woman, with an infant, who had just been brought in. She lay in a dying condition, with nothing but a piece of an old soldier coat under her head. Must I leave her in this condition? I could not beg in Alexandria. It was time for the last boat to leave for Washington, and I promised to return in the morning. The Superintendent said he would meet me at the landing. Early next morning, Mrs. Brown and myself went on a begging expedition, and some old quilts were given us. Mr. Clarke met us, and

[7]Reference to Proverbs 13:15.

offered the use of his large Government wagon, with the horses and driver, for the day, and said he would accompany us, if agreeable. I was delighted, and felt I should spend a happy Sabbath in exploring Dixie, while the large bundles that I carried with me would help make others happy. After attending to the sick mother and child, we started for Fairfax Seminary. They send many of the convalescent soldiers to this place. The houses are large, and the location is healthy. Many of the contrabands are here. Their condition is much better than that of those kept in the city. They soon gathered around Mr. Clarke, and begged him to come back and be their boss. He said, "Boys, I want you all to go to Hayti." They said, "You gwine wid us, Mr. Clarke?" "No, I must stay here, and take care of the rest of the boys." "Den if you aint gwine, de Lord knows I aint a gwine." Some of them will tell Uncle Abe the same thing. Mr. Clarke said they would do anything for him—seldom gave him any trouble. They spoke kindly of Mr. Thomas, who is constantly employed in supplying their wants, as far as he can. To the very old people at this place, I gave some clothing, returned to Alexandria, and bade all good bye. Begging me to come back, they promised to do all they could to help themselves. One old woman said—"Honey tink, when all get still, I kin go an fine de old place? Tink de Union 'stroy it? You can't get nothin on dis place. Down on de ole place, you can raise ebery ting. I ain't seen bacca since I bin here. Neber git a libin here, where de peoples eben buy pasly." This poor old woman thought it was nice to live where tobacco grew, but it was dreadful to be compelled to buy a bunch of parsley. Here they have preaching once every Sabbath. They must have a season to sing and pray, and we need true faith in Christ to go among them and do our duty. How beautiful it is to find it among themselves! Do not say the slaves take no interest in each other. Like other people, some of them are designedly selfish, some are ignorantly selfish. With the light and instruction you give them, you will see this selfishness disappear. Trust them, make them free, and give them the responsibility of caring for themselves, and they will soon learn to help each other. Some of them have been so degraded by slavery that they do not know the usages of civilized life: they know little else than the handle of the hoe, the plough, the cotton pad, and the overseer's lash. Have patience with them. You have helped to make them what they are; teach them civilization. You owe it to them, and you will find them as apt to learn as any other people that come to you stupid from oppression. The negroes' strong attachment no one doubts; the only difficulty is, they have cherished it too strongly. Let me tell you of an instance among the contrabands. One day, while in the hospital, a woman came in to ask that she might take a little orphan child. The mother had just died, leaving two children, the eldest three years old. This woman had five children in the house with her. In a few days, the number would be six. I said to this mother, "What can you do with this child, shut up here with your own? They are as many as you can attend to." She looked up with tears in her eyes, and said—"The child's mother was a stranger; none of her friends cum wid her from de ole place. I took one boy down on de plantation; he is a big boy now, working mong de Unions. De Lord help me to bring up dat boy, and he will help me to take care dis child. My husband work for de Unions when dey pay him. I can make home for all. Dis child shall hab part ob de crust." How few white mothers, living in luxury, with six children, could find room in her heart for a seventh, and that child a stranger!

In this house there are scores of children, too young to help themselves, from eight years old down to the little one-day freeman, born at railroad speed, while the young mother was flying from Virginia to save her babe from breathing its tainted air.

I left the contrabands feeling that the people were becoming more interested in their behalf, and much had been done to make their condition more comfortable. On my way home, I stopped a few days in Philadelphia. I called on a lady who had sent a large supply to the hospital, and told her of the many little orphans who needed a home. This lady advised me to call and see the Lady Managers of an institution for orphan children supported by those ladies. I did so, and they agreed to take the little orphans. They employed a gentleman to investigate the matter, and it was found impossible to bring them through Baltimore. This gentleman went to the captains of the propellers in Philadelphia, and asked if those orphan children could have a passage on their boats. Oh no, it could not be; it would make an unpleasant feeling among the people! Some of those orphans have died since I left, but the number is constantly increasing. Many mothers, on leaving the plantations, pick up the little orphans, and bring them with their own children; but they cannot provide for them; they come very destitute themselves.

To the ladies who have so nobly interested themselves in behalf of my much oppressed race, I feel the deepest debt of gratitude. Let me beg the reader's attention to these orphans. They are the innocent and helpless of God's poor. If you cannot take one, you can do much by contributing your mite to the institution that will open its doors to receive them.

Linda.

13

HARRIET JACOBS

Letter to Ednah Dow Cheney

April 25, 1867

After the war, Jacobs returned to Edenton, North Carolina, where she had been enslaved before running away twenty-five years earlier. Other freed slaves, Frederick Douglass among them, made similar journeys home after the war ended and slavery was abolished. Jacobs shares her strong feelings about returning to her "old home" and describes the condition of freed slaves in the area in this letter to Ednah Dow Cheney, a member of the New England Freedmen's Aid Society.

Edenton April 25th

Dear Mrs Cheeny [Cheney]

I felt I would like to write you a line from my old home. I am sitting under the old roof. twelve feet from the spot where I suffered all the crushing weight of slavery. thank God, the bitter cup is drained of its last dreg. There is no more need of hiding places to conceal slave Mothers. yet it was little to purchase the blessings of freedom. I could have worn this poor life out there to save my Children from the misery and degradation of Slavery.

I had long thought I had no attachment to my old home. As I often sit here and think of those I loved of their hard struggle in life—their unfaltering love and devotion toward myself and Children. I love to sit here and think of them. they have made the few sunny spots in that dark life sacred to me.

I cannot tell you how I feel in this place. the change is so great I can hardly take it all in I was born here. and amid all these new born blessings. the old dark cloud comes over me. and I find it hard to have faith in rebels.

The past winter was very severe for this region of Country it caused much suffering—and the freedmen with but few exceptions were cheated out of their crop of cotton. their contract masters ship[p]ed it

---

Harriet Jacobs to Ednah Dow Cheney, April 25, 1867, New England Hospital Papers, Sophia Smith Collection, Smith College.

for them. and when they ask for a settlement. they are answered I am daily expecting the returns. these men have gone to work cheerfully. planted another crop without the returns to live on until their present crop is made. Many of the large plantations of the once wealthy Planter [are] worked under the control of colored men. the Owners let their Plantations to the freed men in prefference to the poor whites—they believe the Negro determined to make money. and they will get the largest portion of it. last years experience I think will be a proffitable lesson many will learn to act for themselves Negro suffrage is making a stir in this place. the rebels are striving to make these people feel they are their true friends. and they must not be led astray by the Yankees. the freedmen ask if Abraham Lincoln led them astray. that his friends is their friends his enemies their enemies.

I have spent much of my time on the Plantations distributing seed and trying to teach the women to make Yankee gardens. they plant everything to mature in the summer. like their corn and cotton fields. I have hunted up all the old people. done what I could for them. I love to work for these old people. many of them I have known from Childhood there is one School in Edenton well attended. on some of the Plantations there is from 15 to 25 Children that cannot attend School. the distance is so far. some of the freedmen are very anxious to establish Plantation schools. as soon as the more advanced Schools. can send out teachers. many of the freedmen are willing and will sustain their teachers. at present there is a great revival in the Colored Churches the whites say the niggers sung and prayed until they got their freedom. and they are not satisfied. now they are singing and praying for judgment. the white members of the Baptist Church invited the colored members to their Church. to help them sing and pray. I assure you they have done it with a will. I never saw such a state of excitment. the Churches have been open night and day. these people have time to think of their souls. now they are not compeled to think for the Negro.

My love to Miss Daisy.[1] I send her some Jassamine blossoms tell her they bear the fragrance of freedom.

Yours Truly

H. Jacobs

[1]Margaret Swan Cheney (b. 1855), Cheney's daughter.

A Harriet Jacobs Chronology (1813–1897)

The authors of slave narratives, fugitive or freed slaves, could not always say when they were born. No slave ever had a birth certificate, and slave births were rarely, if ever, recorded in the mistress's commonplace book (usually an inventory of plantation supplies and recipes) or the owner's family Bible. It is not clear whether Harriet Jacobs knew the year she was born. She marked the passage of time when she was a slave by the seasons or the passing of years, and as a result she could tell how old she was when something happened. However she did not—likely because she could not—specify the dates of early events. The narrative's numerous references to current events help date the occurrence of pre-escape events in her own life. But this chronology relies heavily on the devoted efforts of scholar Jean Fagan Yellin, who searched for clues to Jacobs's life within slavery in the letters of her master's household, plantation diaries, deeds, wills, property and tax records, census records, sales receipts, and ads selling slaves or seeking the recapture of runaways. Jacobs's postslavery life unfolds in her personal and published correspondence, her articles, and in her narrative.

1813 Harriet Jacobs is born in Edenton, Chowan County, North Carolina, to Delilah Horniblow and Elijah Knox. Surname "Jacobs" comes from Elijah's biological father.

1815 Harriet's brother, John Jacobs, is born.

1819 Harriet's mother, Delilah, dies; Harriet goes to the home of her mistress, Margaret Horniblow.

1825 *July* Margaret Horniblow dies; Harriet becomes the property of Horniblow's three-year-old niece, Mary Matilda Norcom, daughter of Dr. James Norcom.

1826 Harriet's father, Elijah, dies; Harriet experiences a crisis of faith.

1827 Norcom begins sexually pursuing Harriet; her uncle Joseph escapes slavery.

1828 *January* Norcom buys John Jacobs.

Spring Harriet's grandmother Molly Horniblow buys her own and her son Mark's freedom and moves into a home on West King Street, which she purchases for one dollar in 1830. Harriet falls in love with a free black man and begins an affair with white attorney Samuel Tredwell Sawyer. (He is the father of her two children.)

1829 Harriet's son, Joseph, is born.

1832/ 1833 Harriet's daughter, Louisa Matilda, is born.

1834/ 1835 Harriet is sent to Auburn plantation with Louisa; Joseph stays with Norcom.

1835 *June* Harriet runs away from the plantation.

June–July Norcom runs an ad in a Norfolk, Virginia, newspaper offering $100 for Harriet.

August Harriet goes into hiding in Molly's house.

1837 At Harriet's urging, Sawyer buys her brother and her children from Norcom.

1838 *August–September* While in New York City with Sawyer, John escapes. He eventually goes to Boston and New Bedford, Massachusetts, where he signs on with a whaling voyage.

1840 Sawyer sends Louisa to Brooklyn, New York, to live with his cousins.

1842 *June* Harriet escapes to New York City via Philadelphia and is reunited with Louisa; she finds work as a nurse in the home of Nathaniel Parker Willis and Mary Stace Willis.

1843 Harriet is reunited with John in New York; she arranges to have her son, Joseph, brought to Boston, where John is living.

1844 Harriet and Louisa flee New York to elude Norcom; they join John and Joseph in Boston. John becomes active in the antislavery movement and begins calling himself John S. Jacobs.

1845 *March* Mary Willis dies. Later that year, leaving her children in Boston, Harriet travels to England with Nathaniel Willis and his daughter; she experiences a religious conversion that erases earlier doubts about her faith.

1846 Harriet returns to Boston, where she rejoins Louisa; Joseph has shipped out on a whaling voyage.

1848 John sends Louisa to boarding school in Clinton, New York; before she leaves, Harriet "confesses" the identity of Louisa's father.

1849 Harriet moves to Rochester and works in the Anti-Slavery Office and Reading Room.

1850 Harriet moves back in with the Willis family; Nathaniel Willis is now married to Cornelia Grinnell Willis. John and Joseph go to California following passage of the Fugitive Slave Act. Upon hearing that Norcom is trying to capture her, Harriet goes into hiding with Cornelia Willis's parents in New Bedford.

November Norcom dies.

1852 *Spring* Without Harriet's knowledge, Cornelia Willis purchases her from Norcom's daughter and son-in-law. Harriet begins discussions with Willis and her white feminist, antislavery friend Amy Post about writing her life story; she asks Post to contact Harriet Beecher Stowe about writing the narrative for her.

1853 Harriet's grandmother Molly dies. Harriet publishes three letters from "A Fugitive Slave" in the *New York Tribune*. She rejects Stowe's offer to include her story in Stowe's new work, *A Key to Uncle Tom's Cabin*, and begins writing her narrative at night while living with the Willises in their new home, Idlewild, in Cornwall on Hudson, New York.

1854 Black activist William C. Nell visits Harriet at Idlewild and encourages her to complete her book, offering help promoting it. Harriet becomes more active in antislavery activities in Boston and New York.

1857 Harriet completes her manuscript.

1858 Carrying letters of introduction from Boston abolitionists, Harriet travels to England to try to find a publisher for her book; she returns home unsuccessful.

1860 A Boston publisher agrees to publish her manuscript if Lydia Maria Child will write an introduction.

Summer Through Nell, Harriet meets Child and asks for her help.

August–September Child makes editorial suggestions, writes an introduction, and negotiates a contract with different Boston publishers, Thayer and Eldridge. Joseph dies in California.

1861 *January* *Incidents in the Life of a Slave Girl, Written by Herself* is published. Harriet travels to Philadelphia to promote her book among antislavery activists; the book receives positive reviews in the *Liberator* and other antislavery and African American journals.

February John S. Jacobs's *A True Tale of Slavery* is serialized in the London journal *Leisure Hour.*

April Civil War begins.

Late Fall–Early Winter Harriet sends her book to British abolitionist Frederick Chesson and asks him to find a publisher for a British edition.

1862 *January* London publisher William Tweedie publishes Harriet's book under the title *The Deeper Wrong; or, Incidents in the Life of a Slave Girl, Written by Herself*; the book is well received by the London press. Harriet goes to Washington, D.C., and Alexandria, Virginia, to begin relief work with contrabands.

June William Lloyd Garrison invites Harriet to write an article about her work.

September "Life among the Contrabands" is published in the *Liberator* under Harriet's own name; she is identified as "the author of LINDA," a reference to the original title of *Incidents*.

1863–1864 Harriet continues her relief work; she travels in the North to raise money and supplies for refugees.

1864 *January* With Louisa, Harriet opens the Jacobs School, a free school for black children, in Alexandria, Virginia.

1865 *May* Harriet and Louisa travel to Richmond, Virginia, after the Civil War ends.

November With Louisa, Harriet travels to Savannah, Georgia, as a representative of the New England Freedmen's Aid Society in response to a request by the Georgia superintendent of education to send teachers for free black schools. Louisa opens a school in the city poorhouse and travels to plantations.

1866 Harriet publishes a series of articles in the New York newspapers the *Freedman*, the *Independent*, and the *Freedmen's Record* about the plight of former slaves in Georgia; she also raises funds for them.

February–April Louisa lectures for the American Equal Rights Association in upstate New York.

1867 *April* Harriet briefly visits Edenton, North Carolina. She travels with Louisa in December to London, where John is living with his British-born wife and two sons. When they return to America in August 1868, they settle in Cambridge, Massachusetts, where Jacobs opens a boardinghouse that caters to whites, including Harvard faculty.

1873 John moves to Cambridge but soon becomes ill and dies.

1877 Harriet and Louisa move to Washington, D.C., hoping that Louisa will be hired as a teacher. When that fails, Harriet opens a boardinghouse popular among white politicians and their wives.

1885 Harriet brings dinner to the impoverished widow and children of James Norcom Jr., son of her former master; it was from his plantation that she once escaped.

1886 Harriet opens a new boardinghouse in Washington for black elites.

1888 In failing health, Harriet closes her boardinghouse.

1894 Harriet is diagnosed with breast cancer and receives aid from Cornelia Willis.

1897 *March* Harriet dies in Washington. Six days later, she is buried in Mount Auburn Cemetery in Cambridge. Louisa continues the work she conducted with her mother and dies in 1917.

Questions for Consideration

1. What arguments does Jacobs make in the preface to *Incidents in the Life of a Slave Girl*? What arguments does the editor, Lydia Maria Child, make in her introduction to the narrative? In what ways do their arguments reinforce or contradict each other?
2. As a historical source, what does Jacobs's narrative tell us about the physical, psychological, and cultural experiences of slaves?
3. Jacobs argues that slavery was worse for girls and women than for boys and men. What evidence does she give to support this argument? Do you agree or disagree with her?
4. Examine some of the following themes in Jacobs's narrative: motherhood, sisterhood, sexuality, law, religion, power, secrecy, home. How does her narrative illuminate these issues for readers in her own time? How about for readers today?
5. Analyze Jacobs's relationship with each of the following people: her father, her grandmother, her brother, Dr. James Norcom, Samuel Tredwell Sawyer, Mary Stace Willis, and Cornelia Grinnell Willis. How did these relationships affect Jacobs's life and work?
6. How does Jacobs portray Mrs. Norcom? What strategy does this portrayal serve in her account?
7. What does Jacobs's narrative suggest about the effects of slavery on black and white Americans in both the North and the South?
8. Why does Jacobs address her reader directly? What values does she assume her reader to have? To what extent did Jacobs share these assumed values? To what extent did she reject them?
9. In what ways was Jacobs's family a source of support, strength, and conflict for her?
10. What is the significance of the full title of Jacobs's narrative?
11. What are some of the ways in which Jacobs is and is not free at the end of her narrative?
12. Compare John S. Jacobs's *A True Tale of Slavery* with *Incidents*. In what ways do the themes of *A True Tale* differ from those of *Incidents*?

How does John S. Jacobs's treatment of his sister's story differ from Harriet's?

13. What do Jacobs's letters tell us about her development as a writer? What do they reveal about her sense of herself as an author and activist?
14. Consider Jacobs's experiences with violence in her own life and the brutal dismantling of her community following Nat Turner's rebellion. How likely is it that Jacobs supported violent resistance to slavery?
15. How does Margaret Horniblow's will exemplify the commodification of enslaved people? What can we learn about the relationships between masters or mistresses and enslaved people from documents like Horniblow's will?
16. What were some of the struggles Jacobs had with her Christian faith? How were these doubts and tensions created or exacerbated by her experience as a slave?

Selected Bibliography

AUTOBIOGRAPHY

Andrews, William L., ed. *The North Carolina Roots of African-American Literature*. Chapel Hill: University of North Carolina Press, 2006.

Jacobs, Harriet. *Incidents in the Life of a Slave Girl, Written by Herself.* Boston, 1861.

Jacobs, John S. "A True Tale of Slavery" in *Leisure Hour: A Family Journal of Instruction and Recreation*, February 7, 14, 21, and 28, 1861.

Yellin, Jean Fagin, ed. *The Harriet Jacobs Family Papers*. Chapel Hill: University of North Carolina Press, 2008.

BIOGRAPHY

Yellin, Jean Fagan. *Harriet Jacobs: A Life*. New York: Basic Civitas Books, 2004.

CRITICAL STUDIES

Andrews, William L. *To Tell a Free Story: The First Century of Afro-American Autobiography, 1760–1865*. Urbana: University of Illinois Press, 1986.

Carby, Hazel V. *Reconstructing Womanhood: The Emergence of the Afro-American Woman Novelist*. New York: Oxford University Press, 1987.

Davis, Charles T., and Henry L. Gates Jr., eds. *The Slave's Narrative*. New York: Oxford University Press, 1985.

Davis, David Brion. *Inhuman Bondage: The Rise and Fall of Slavery in the New World*. New York: Oxford University Press, 2006.

Fleischner, Jennifer. *Mastering Slavery: Memory, Family, and Identity in Women's Slave Narratives*. New York: New York University Press, 1996.

Garfield, Deborah M., and Rafia Zafar, eds. *Harriet Jacobs and "Incidents in the Life of a Slave Girl": New Critical Essays*. New York: Cambridge University Press, 1996.

Gates, Henry L., Jr., and K. A. Appiah, eds. *Harriet Jacobs: Critical Perspectives Past and Present*. New York: Amistad, 1997.

Gwin, Minrose C. *Black and White Women of the Old South: The Peculiar Sisterhood in American Literature*. Knoxville: University of Tennessee Press, 1985.

Nelson, Dana D. *The Word in Black and White: Reading "Race" in American Literature, 1638–1867.* New York: Oxford University Press, 1992.

Sanchez-Eppler, Karen A. *Touching Liberty: Abolition, Feminism, and the Politics of the Body.* Berkeley: University of California Press, 1993.

Smith, Frances Foster. *Written by Herself: Literary Production by African American Women, 1746–1892.* Bloomington: Indiana University Press, 1993.

Smith, Valerie. *Self-Discovery and Authority in Afro-American Narrative.* Cambridge, Mass.: Harvard University Press, 1987.

Sollors, Werner. *Neither Black nor White yet Both.* New York: Oxford University Press, 1997.

Stepto, Robert. *From Behind the Veil: A Study in Afro-American Narrative.* Urbana: University of Illinois Press, 1979.

Sterling, Dorothy, ed. *We Are Your Sisters: Black Women in the Nineteenth Century.* New York: W. W. Norton, 1984.

HISTORICAL STUDIES

Berry, Daina Ramey. *The Price for Their Pound of Flesh: The Value of the Enslaved, from Womb to Grave, in the Building of a Nation.* Boston: Beacon Press, 2017.

Berlin, Ira. *Many Thousands Gone: The First Two Centuries of Slavery in North America.* Cambridge, Mass.: Harvard University Press, 1998.

Berlin, Ira, Barbara Fields, Steven F. Miller, Joseph P. Reidy, and Leslie S. Rowland, eds. *Free at Last: A Documentary History of Slavery, Freedom, and the Civil War.* New York: New Press, 1992.

Blassingame, John W. *The Slave Community: Plantation Life in the Antebellum South.* New York: Oxford University Press, 1972.

Boylan, Anne M. *The Origins of Women's Activism.* Chapel Hill: University of North Carolina Press, 2002.

Edwards, Laura F. *Gendered Strife and Confusion: The Political Culture of Reconstruction.* Urbana: University of Illinois Press, 1997.

Faulkner, Carol. *Women's Radical Reconstruction: The Freedmen's Aid Movement.* Philadelphia: University of Pennsylvania Press, 2003.

Fox-Genovese, Elizabeth. *Within the Plantation Household: Black and White Women in the Old South.* Chapel Hill: University of North Carolina Press, 1988.

Franklin, John Hope. *The Free Negro in North Carolina.* New York: W. W. Norton, 1999.

Franklin, John Hope, Jr., and Alfred A. Moss. *From Slavery to Freedom.* 8th ed. New York: Knopf, 2000.

Genovese, Eugene D. *Roll, Jordan, Roll: The World the Slaves Made.* New York: Random House, 1974.

Gutman, Herbert G. *The Black Family in Slavery and Freedom, 1750–1925.* New York: Random House, 1976.

Hewitt, Nancy A. *Women's Activism and Social Change: Rochester, New York, 1822–1872*. Ithaca, N.Y.: Cornell University Press, 1984.

Hine, Darlene Clark, et al., eds. *Black Women in America: An Historical Encyclopedia*. Brooklyn, N.Y.: Carlson, 1993.

Johnson, Walter. *Soul by Soul: Life Inside the Antebellum Slave Market*. Cambridge, Mass.: Harvard University Press, 1999.

Kantrowitz, Stephen. *More Than Freedom: Fighting for Black Citizenship in a White Republic, 1829–1889*. New York: Penguin, 2012.

Kaye, Anthony E. *Joining Places: Slave Neighborhoods in the Old South*. Chapel Hill: University of North Carolina Press, 2007.

Levine, Lawrence W. *Black Culture and Black Consciousness: African American Folk Thought from Slavery to Freedom*. New York: Oxford University Press, 1977.

McPherson, James. *The Struggle for Equality*. Princeton, N.J.: Princeton University Press, 1964.

Pease, Jane H., and William H. Pease. *They Who Would Be Free: Blacks' Search for Freedom, 1830–1861*. New York: Atheneum, 1974.

Quarles, Benjamin. *Black Abolitionists. 1969*. Reprint. New York: Oxford University Press, 1991.

Sinha, Manisha. *The Slave's Cause: A History of Abolition*. New Haven, Conn.: Yale University Press, 2016.

White, Deborah Gray. *Ar'n't I a Woman? Female Slaves in the Plantation South*. New York: W. W. Norton, 1985.

Index